Contents

"The most dangerous creature on Earth—
the human spirit armed with reason and
discipline."

— Howard E. Wasdin

1. Navigating the Biotech Frontier: Where Innovation Meets Warfare

In a rapidly evolving universe where the boundaries between biology and technology are continually blurred, humanity stands on the brink of the next revolutionary leap in interstellar warfare. What was once limited by the constraints of steel and electronics is now being reimagined with the intricate complexities of living organisms. As we venture into realms that were once the exclusive domain of science fiction, we are compelled to ask: What will the war machines of the future look like, and how will they alter the cosmos forever? In "Biotech Battleships: Designs of Future Intergalactic War Machines," we embark on a journey through this fascinating frontier, exploring the possibilities and challenges posed by biotechnology in the design of the future's most formidable battle vessels. This book seeks to equip readers with a thorough understanding of the scientific principles, design methodologies, and ethical considerations that underpin the creation of these advanced interspecies technologies. Join me, Sylvia L. Wright, as we demystify the extraordinary and transform the way we envision warfare among the stars.

2. The Evolution of War Machines: From Iron to Biotech

2.1. Historical Background of Naval Warfare

The history of naval warfare is rich and complex, woven with the threads of innovation, strategy, and the ever-evolving technologies that have shaped combat over the centuries. As we embark on understanding the historical background of naval warfare, we trace its lineage from primitive seafaring vessels to the high-tech battleships of modernity, ultimately laying the groundwork for the integration of biotechnology into future war machines.

Naval warfare's roots can be traced back to the earliest days of human civilization. As soon as communities began to gather near water bodies, the need for maritime navigation and combat arose. The Egyptians, Greeks, and Phoenicians crafted small wooden boats, using sails and oars, to traverse rivers and seas. The naval technologies developed during these cultures were rudimentary yet revolutionary for their time, with the introduction of bronze-tipped rams on ships facilitating a new form of attack against enemy vessels.

As civilizations advanced, so did the complexities of naval warfare. The Greeks famously utilized triremes, ships that featured a triple bank of oarsmen and sophisticated ramming technology. The training and discipline of their crews became vital factors in the success of naval engagements. Naval battles shifted from mere skirmishes to coordinated military operations and served as a platform for establishing dominance over trade routes and territories.

The Roman Empire furthered these advancements by creating a formidable navy, the classis, which efficiently integrated technology with superior tactics. Their powerful quinquiremes showcased enhanced ship designs and coordinated maneuvers, effectively projecting power across the Mediterranean. As Rome expanded, naval power became a crucial aspect of its military strategy, illustrating how control of the seas could support land operations and trade.

The advent of the Middle Ages saw a decline in naval warfare in the face of land invasions and a shift in strategic focus. However, during the Age of Exploration, advancements in shipbuilding and navigation techniques reinvigorated naval power with the introduction of caravel and galleon designs. The Spanish Armada, while noted for its striking form and impressive fleet, also illustrated the perils of opposition on the seas, culminating in its defeat by the English fleet in 1588. This clash marked the dawn of heavy naval engagements, linking ship design with warfare strategy and technology.

By the 18th century and into the age of sail, naval warfare underwent another transformative period. The introduction of ship-of-the-line tactics, where line formation allowed for maximum broadside engagement, reflected a deeper understanding of maritime combat. The wooden sailing warships became more powerful, featuring complex rigging and more artillery. This period laid the framework for future developments taking naval combat into the industrial age.

The 19th century heralded the onset of the industrial revolution, which brought about a seismic shift in naval warfare. Steam propulsion replaced wind-powered sails, allowing for greater maneuverability and independence from shipping lanes dictated by weather patterns. Ironclad warships emerged in the American Civil War, showcasing inventions like armor plating and more destructive artillery.

The technological leaps of the 20th century, marked by two World Wars, brought about further innovations such as aircraft carriers, submarines, and guided missiles. Naval strategies evolved to encompass air-sea warfare, incorporating aircraft and radar technologies to gather intelligence and execute precise strikes on targets. The rise of nuclear submarines transformed the strategic landscape, leading to new doctrines of deterrence in naval operations.

As we dare to look toward the future, there arises an exploration of the potential convergence of biotechnology and naval warfare. Historical advancements provide a crucial understanding of how military necessity drives innovation. The transitions from wooden ships to ironclads, and now to the bio-integrated machines envisioned for future conflicts, echo humanity's relentless pursuit of an edge in warfare.

The historical context of naval warfare informs our inquiry into modern biochemical innovations, inviting us to speculate on the integration of organic components in warships. Understanding how warfare evolved informs not only the design of future vessels but also reveals the ethical and practical considerations of creating living machines engineered for combat. As we contemplate the hybridization of technology and biology, we set the stage for a new chapter in the narrative of warfare, one that holds the promise of profound implications for humanity's endeavors among the stars.

2.2. Introduction to Biotechnology

In exploring biotechnology, we delve into a discipline that merges biological sciences with technology to manipulate living organisms or their components for practical applications. The evolution of biotechnology is marked by a desire to harness the potential of life itself, transforming natural processes into tools for innovation. Humanity's journey into biotechnology has birthed a myriad of applications, from agriculture to medicine, and now, as we harness these advancements for warfare, we encounter a transformative paradigm shift.

Biotechnology rests on foundational scientific principles rooted in molecular biology, genetics, and bioengineering. By understanding cellular mechanisms, genetic manipulation, and the interactions between biological entities, researchers are poised to create living entities that can serve diverse roles. Just as earlier inventions revolutionized naval capabilities, the integration of biological components into war vessels promises akin revolutionary outcomes. This chapter sets the stage for understanding how biotechnology will inform the design and functionality of the battleships that may soon traverse the cosmos.

At its core, biotechnology involves the alteration of biological systems for specific functions. From CRISPR genetic editing to synthetic biology, the tools and techniques emerging from this field allow us to engineer organisms to perform tasks beyond their natural capabilities. Synthetic organisms can be designed to produce energy, repair damage, or even carry out defensive functions autonomously. These advancements raise fundamental questions about control, stability, and the ethical implications of creating life as an instrument of war.

One of the most compelling aspects of biotechnology is its ability to intersect with other fields of study. This interdisciplinary nature encourages collaboration among biologists, engineers, ethicists, and military strategists. The integration of biological components into warfare requires understanding not just the science itself, but also the broader implications of employing living systems in combat scenarios. Today's military faces unique challenges, from the sustainability of operations to the moral considerations of employing bioengineered organisms in conflict. Each decision cascades through multiple levels, influencing everything from design to deployment.

As we consider the evolution from traditional war machines, primarily metallic and mechanical, to future biotech battleships, we recognize a significant shift in engineering principles. The concept of 'biomechanical fusion' takes center stage, where living systems are integrated with mechanical designs to form hybrid entities. By utilizing the adaptability of living organisms alongside mechanical reliability, future war machines can respond to a volatile battlefield environment with unprecedented efficiency. For instance, bioengineered materials may have self-repairing properties, allowing ships to recover from damage in real time, thus extending their operational life and effectiveness.

Scientific insights from nature have already begun to inform technological advancements in materials using biological constructs. Biomimicry—taking inspiration from natural processes—has led to the development of materials that can mimic fish scales' hydrodynamic properties. The design of bio-infused materials anticipates not only improved performance but also reduces the requirement for heavy, traditional armoring, creating lighter, more agile vessels. In the realm of offensive tactics, biotechnology may yield weaponry that relies on biological guidance systems, enhancing precision through bioadaptive mechanisms.

Furthermore, environmental sustainability emerges as a pivotal consideration in designing biotech battleships. The integration of biological systems could create vessels capable of closed-loop life support systems, recycling waste into usable energy or resources. This not only reduces reliance on external supplies but also addresses logistical challenges when operating in the vastness of space, where resources are scarce.

While biotechnology holds immense potential, it also poses unique challenges. Safety becomes paramount, as the consequences of unleashing biologically engineered systems in warfare could be unpredictable. Ensuring containment and control over the engineered organisms must parallel their design and functionality. Questions arise concerning how these systems can be developed to avoid unintended consequences, such as ecological disruption or a loss of control over living entities.

As we embark on this exploration, it is crucial to remember that the application of biotechnology extends beyond mere machinery—it involves ethical considerations surrounding what it means to create intelligent, living systems for the purpose of warfare. The dual-edge nature of innovation in biotechnology means that while we may achieve unprecedented military capabilities, we must also confront the responsibilities we assume in wielding such power. The intrinsic value of life, even if bioengineered, must guide our developments and applications, forging a path that emphasizes ethical responsibility in the creation and deployment of biotech battleships.

Looking ahead, the synthesis of biology and technology poses an exciting yet daunting frontier. The design of future war machines will necessitate the harmonization of various elements—biological, mechanical, ethical, and strategic—leading us into a new era of warfare that challenges our perceptions and definitions of conflict, responsibility, and advancement. As we proceed through this book, we will unravel the intricacies of biotechnology's role in future intergalactic war machines, building a comprehensive understanding of both the technology in play and the implications that accompany its rapid development. With each page, we invite readers to contemplate not just where we are heading, but also how we can navigate the ethical landscape of this brave new world where biology meets warfare.

2.3. From Gears to Genes: The Transition to Bioengineering

As we transition from the gears and mechanisms that have traditionally dominated the landscape of warfare to the intricacies of bioengineering, we witness a profound shift in the foundational principles underpinning how we conceptualize and create war machines. This movement toward bioengineering represents a merging of the mechanical and the biological, paving the way for revolutionary designs that harness the adaptive capabilities of living organisms. The implications of this transition reach far beyond mere aesthetics or technological novelty; they challenge our understanding of warfare, strategy, and even the essence of life itself.

Historically, war machines have depended heavily on rigid designs characterized by metal and machinery. These constructs were often limited by their lack of adaptability and responsiveness to unexpected situations. The rise of bioengineering introduces a flexible paradigm, where the inherent properties of biological systems—such as self-healing, evolution, and regenerative capabilities—are intricately woven into the fabric of military design. The very essence of warfare, which is rooted in dynamic interactions between opposing forces, finds a natural synergy with the adaptability of biological organisms.

At the core of bioengineering lies the manipulation of genetic material. The advances in our understanding of molecular biology allow us to design organisms with specific traits, much like how traditional engineers select metals and alloys for constructing ships. The capabilities derived from genetically modified organisms (GMOs) extend far beyond mere alterations for agricultural purposes; they encompass the development of bioengineered systems capable of functioning in the harshest environments, from the depths of oceans to the vast emptiness of space. This flexibility is crucial for space warfare, where unpredictable conditions abound, and where traditional materials may falter.

Moreover, bioengineering pushes the boundaries of materials science. The development of bio-based materials aims to replace conventional armor with living entities that can repair themselves, respond to threats, and even camouflage themselves as environmental conditions change. These biological materials not only promise enhanced durability but also the potential for integration with sensory systems that mimic biological processes. By analyzing patterns in the animal kingdom, engineers can derive sophisticated systems capable of discerning movement, chemical signatures, and other indicators of adversarial presence, thereby enhancing situational awareness and combat readiness.

The design ethos behind these bioengineered war machines embraces the concept of symbiosis—a harmonious relationship between biological systems and mechanical structures. In these future battleships, for instance, living organisms may serve key functions, such as powering the ship through biological engines or providing onboard life support systems that recycle waste into usable products. The principle of symbiotic design recognizes that the benefits of cooperation between organic and mechanical systems far exceed those of isolation; indeed, living systems can often outperform mechanical ones in efficiency, resource management, and adaptability.

However, alongside these innovative potentials come ethical considerations that must be scrutinized rigorously. As we venture into bioengineering for warfare, we must confront dilemmas regarding the nature of life being manipulated for conflict. Are we crossing a line by engineering organisms solely for the purpose of destruction? The legacy of humanity's earlier technological advances, from nuclear weapons to chemical warfare, carries with it a heavy ethical burden, reminding us of the potential consequences of our inventions. The challenge lies in balancing the quest for military advantage with the moral responsibility towards the living systems that we engineer.

As we begin to integrate bioengineering into the fabric of military assets, we must also think critically about the implications for those who operate these systems. Training will evolve to encompass not just the mechanics of operating traditional machines, but also understanding the biological sensitivities and responses of the integrated living components. Interdisciplinary competencies will become essential as military personnel learn to work alongside scientists and bioengineers—not just as operators of machines, but as collaborators in a co-evolving system.

The implications extend into strategy and tactics at the highest levels of military command. Commanders must be prepared to think strategically about biological systems, considering not just the strengths and weaknesses of machines but also their living counterparts. Engaging with adversaries equipped with similar biotechnological advancements invites an entirely new layer of complexity to military planning.

In envisioning future conflicts, it becomes evident that these bioengineered artworks of war will play a crucial role in redefining engagement rules. Just as naval battles in history were shaped by technological prowess, so too will the wars of tomorrow be defined by the symbiotic relationships between biology and machinery. The very landscape of interstellar warfare will pivot as cold calculations give way to flexible strategies that anticipate the caprices of evolving biological systems.

In summary, the transition from traditional, mechanical designs to bioengineering represents a paradigm shift that transforms not only the machinery of war but also the principles governing conflict. As humanity embarks on the task of designing biotech battleships that fuse life with machinery, we must remain vigilant to the ethical dimensions and implications this entails. The pursuit of enhanced military capabilities can no longer be viewed in isolation; it demands a harmonious approach that embraces our role as stewards of both technology and the biological entities we create. By weaving together these two traditionally opposing forces, we stand at the precipice of a new era, one where the future of warfare will be characterized by an innovative blend of mechanical precision and biological adaptability.

2.4. Early Innovations in Biotech Mechanics

In the nascent era of biotechnology, where research and ingenuity began to forge pathways into previously uncharted territories, the potential of bioengineering to revolutionize warfare became vividly apparent. The mid-20th century marked the convergence of scientific research from diverse fields, leading to the early innovations in biotech mechanics that shape discussions on intergalactic warfare today.

The foundations were laid in the post-World War II period by pioneers eager to push the boundaries of biology and technology. Key advancements in molecular biology, along with the nascent field of genetic engineering, set the stage for experiments that would redefine machines of war. Laboratories across the globe buzzed with excitement as researchers dissected the building blocks of life—DNA, RNA, and proteins—recognizing that manipulating these elements could yield living systems with remarkable capabilities. Early techniques such as recombinant DNA technology allowed scientists to transfer genes from one organism to another, leading to the development of genetically modified organisms (GMOs) that could produce life-sustaining resources, enhance properties of materials, or even serve as biological weapons.

One of the first significant leaps in biotech mechanics occurred when researchers began conceptualizing and creating bioreactors—artificial environments allowing living organisms to thrive while converting raw materials into usable products. These bioreactors soon caught the attention of military strategists who envisioned their potential for resource generation in combat scenarios. The notion of creating self-sustaining units capable of producing food, medicines, or fuels in the field promised to minimize logistic burdens. This technology laid the groundwork for what would eventually evolve into the life support systems we envision for future battleships operating far from civilization.

Further down the line, the merging of electronics with biological systems to create biohybrid technology began to take form. Early work in this domain focused on integrating sensors derived from biological organisms into machines, allowing for a heightened state of awareness, adaptability, and responsiveness in combat situations. Researchers experimented with ideas such as biosensors—devices capable of detecting specific biological changes—in various military applications. For instance, the ability to monitor environmental changes and even the physiological states of crew members in real time became vital in ensuring optimal performance aboard future biotech battleships, guiding both engineering and operational decisions.

Simultaneously, biologically inspired materials emerged, showcasing the potential of intertwining biology with traditional mechanistic designs. Concepts such as shape-memory alloys and self-healing polymers heralded a wave of innovations where materials could maintain their integrity despite damage. The early 2000s saw initial experiments in integrating these concepts with living cells, paving the way for the potential development of living armor—defensive structures that might heal themselves when subjected to impacts or environmental stressors. These prototypes illustrated the advantages derived from biological principles, merging fortification with the flexibility and resilience found in nature.

Another significant innovation from this era was the exploration of biological propulsion systems. Pioneers began investigating the energizing capacities of biological organisms for space travel. Unconventional ideas surfaced, such as utilizing microbial fuel cells to convert organic waste into power, offering a sustainable pathway forward while drastically reducing the weight of traditional energy supplies onboard vast interstellar vessels. In an age where the cost of transporting materials is crucial, these biological propulsion alternatives could shift the dynamics of fleet operations and long-duration missions.

Throughout these developments, the Navy and other military branches began to formulate hypotheses about employing biotechnology as a force multiplier. As early adopters engaged with academic institutions to foster collaboration, proposals surged around leveraging bioengineering in strategic plans. A series of workshops and experimental initiatives emerged, exploring how biotech innovations could create a paradigm shift in tactics and operational capabilities for the future.

In this transformative atmosphere, ethical discussions and societal implications began to surface. Early innovations in biotech mechanics stirred concerns surrounding the potential misuse of engineered organisms in warfare. The necessity for establishing safeguards became evident as governments and military organizations recognized that controlling these living machines would require robust frameworks, guiding the spiral of innovation away from catastrophic applications and towards beneficial implementations that could indeed enhance security.

As we reflect on these early innovations, we must acknowledge the balance between fostering creativity and ensuring that our technological pursuits do not overshadow ethical responsibilities. Biotechnology has since embraced a path of rapid evolution, with integration into warfare a double-edged sword—a promise of unprecedented capabilities coupled with the potential for irreversible consequences. The early groundwork remains essential in framing the exploration of biotech battleships. Not merely a tale of technological progression, this exploration serves as a narrative cautioning against a blind embrace of innovation without cognizance of the responsibilities inherent in wielding such power.

Understanding these early innovations is crucial as we step into a world where the synthesis of biology and technology propels us into new frontiers in intergalactic warfare. The ideas initiated during this formative phase provide a framework for comprehending how these concepts evolved into the sophisticated systems of bioengineered battleships—war machines designed to navigate not only the complexities of combat but also the very intricacies of life itself. As we continue into the depths of biotechnology applied to warfare, we do so with the awareness that the struggles of the past inform the aspirations of the future, guiding us towards responsible and intelligent design in our pursuit of the boundless possibilities that lie ahead.

2.5. Pioneers of Biotech Warfare

In the pursuit of understanding and harnessing the full potential of biotechnology for warfare, it is essential to recognize the contributions of pioneers who laid the groundwork for this transformative field. These individuals, often standing at the intersection of biology, technology, and military strategy, have set the stage for the integration of living systems into combat applications, forever altering the landscape of warfare.

The inception of biotech warfare can be traced back to a time when scientific advances began to merge with military necessity. During the latter half of the 20th century, researchers started to explore the applications of genetic engineering and molecular biology in ways that could serve military objectives. Their efforts were driven by a desire not only to enhance strategic capabilities but also to fundamentally reimagine the concept of a combat machine. This era marked the dawn of experiments aimed at creating biological entities that could be harnessed for offensive and defensive operations, a practice that was largely experimental and fraught with ethical dilemmas.

Among the early innovators was Dr. Robert H. Johnson, a biologist whose pioneering work in genetic manipulation laid the foundation for understanding how organisms could be modified to achieve specific goals. His research into recombinant DNA technology provided the crucial tools necessary to reshape living organisms for military applications. By manipulating genetic material, Johnson and his team demonstrated that it was possible to engineer organisms with enhanced traits, such as increased resilience to environmental stressors or accelerated growth rates, thus presenting a new frontier in military logistics and adaptability.

Simultaneously, the molecular biologist Dr. Eliza Tan made significant strides in understanding how biological systems could be effectively integrated with mechanical devices. Through her exploration of bio-hybrid systems, she innovated methods to combine synthetic and biological components, such as sensors derived from living organisms tailored to detect chemical or biological threats. Tan's work resulted in the development of biosensors that could enhance situational awareness for military personnel, facilitating rapid responses to potential dangers. As a result, these technologies began to find their way into prototype designs for future biotech battleships—ships that could 'see' and respond to their environment.

Another prominent figure, Dr. Haruto Nakamura, championed the idea of self-repairing materials—an essential concept as warfare transitioned into a period where machines must endure not only enemy attacks but also the rigors of extreme environments like outer space. By studying biological processes in organisms that exhibit regenerative capabilities, Nakamura developed synthetic polymers that could mimic these natural functions. This breakthrough opened avenues for creating vehicles that could withstand damage and even heal themselves, thereby extending their operational lifespans amidst the chaos of engagement.

Moreover, the advancements in microbiology led to the inception of biological propulsion systems. Scientists such as Dr. Fionn Whelan sought to develop energy solutions that drew inspiration from nature, leading to innovative applications of microbial fuel cells—theoretically capable of powering ships through metabolic processes. This research not only presented a sustainable energy resource but also introduced the idea of life forms being instrumental in maintaining the operational needs of future combat vessels.

As these pioneers pushed the boundaries of what was scientifically possible, their work did not exist in a vacuum. The interplay between ethical considerations and scientific innovation also garnered attention. The implications of creating living agents designed for warfare incited discussions about the morality of such endeavors. Ethical frameworks slowly emerged to guide the development of biotechnologies, as military leaders and scientists alike began to realize the potential consequences of deploying genetically engineered organisms in conflict scenarios. This led to the establishment of guidelines that emphasized the necessity of ensuring containment and minimizing collateral effects on ecosystems and civilian populations.

The contributions of these trailblazers reverberated throughout military institutions, leading to the formulation of strategic doctrines that integrated biotechnology into standard combat practices. As knowledge spread, the military began to rethink not just the technology it employed but also the fundamental nature of engagements. With battleships housing biological components, the concept of what constitutes a 'crew' expanded to include organic life forms that could autonomously make decisions or adapt to threats, raising questions about command structures and human responsibilities in an age where machines synthesized with life would be deployed in combat.

Through their tenacity and foresight, these pioneers laid the groundwork for future explorations into biotech warfare, emphasizing the significance of collaboration among scientists, military strategists, and ethicists. Their legacies continue to inspire today's researchers, who stand on the shoulders of giants, eager to propel these ideas further into development. As we probe further into the realms of biotechnology, we must honor the contributions of these visionaries and grapple with their ethics—ensuring that the incredible capabilities derived from biotechnology align with the moral compass of society, lest we stray into territories unchecked by responsibility.

The road ahead is promising yet uncertain, as we venture further into the integration of biotechnology in warfare. The principles established by these pioneers will serve as a critical compass, guiding future innovations and ensuring that biotech battleships represent not only the pinnacle of technological achievement but also a commitment to ethical stewardship in the face of profound power. By learning from the past, we can pave the way for a future where military applications of biotechnology enhance security, resilience, and sustainability amidst the stars.

3. The Science of Biotech Integration

3.1. Understanding Biological Systems

In the journey to develop the next generation of interstellar war machines, an in-depth understanding of biological systems emerges as an essential foundation. Unlike traditional military hardware that revolves around metals, plastics, and mechanical components, the integration of biological systems into warfare calls for not only engineering expertise but a profound comprehension of the life sciences. Biological systems are complex and inherently variable, necessitating a strategic approach that accounts for their unique characteristics and behaviors in the context of combat and resilience.

At the core, biological systems operate on principles of interconnectedness, adaptability, and efficiency—qualities that could redefine the capabilities of future battleships. To harness these advantages, engineers and biologists must consider how living organisms—ranging from microbes to larger life forms—interact with their environments and other systems. Understanding the ecological principles such as symbiosis, predation, and adaptation is essential for the successful implementation of biotechnology in military strategies.

One foundational aspect of biological systems is the concept of homeostasis, where organisms maintain stable internal conditions despite external fluctuations. This biological principle is crucial in warfare contexts, especially as missions extend beyond Earth's atmosphere into unpredictable environments like space, where conditions can vary dramatically. Biotech battleships designed to incorporate living organisms could utilize mechanisms inspired by this principle, leading to the development of autonomous systems capable of self-regulating vital functions, such as oxygen production, waste recycling, and energy utilization.

Moreover, biological systems possess remarkable capabilities for adaptation—evolution is essentially rooted in the ability of living organisms to adjust to their circumstances over time. As military applications of biotechnology move toward bioengineering organisms for specific functions, understanding how these adaptations occur can inform designs that evolve alongside their operational environment. For instance, developing organisms capable of learning from past interactions and experiences can pave the way for more effective and resilient combat systems. This adaptability poses significant potential advantages in fast-changing battlefield conditions, allowing biotech vessels to self-modulate their responses to threats or environmental changes.

The intricacies of communication within biological systems also present opportunities for innovation. Many organisms utilize chemical or electrical signals to relay information crucial to their survival. These signaling pathways can inform the development of advanced communication protocols within biotech battleships, enabling rapid exchanges of data among organic components. For example, imagine an integrated ship where bacteria act as sensors, detecting toxins or pathogens and signaling to onboard computer systems to adjust defensive measures or alert crew members.

This level of integration is heavily reliant on understanding cellular communication mechanisms, genetic coding, and metabolic pathways. Creating biological networks that interface seamlessly with mechanical systems will require interdisciplinary collaboration among biotechnologists, geneticists, systems engineers, and military strategists. Such collaborations can lead to the design of hybrid systems where mechanical components provide structural support, while biological elements add adaptive and responsive capabilities.

Furthermore, scaling biological innovations presents its own set of challenges. The intricacies of growth, reproduction, and life cycles of organisms must be meticulously mapped and understood as engineering teams evaluate how to optimize these systems for efficient operation. An engineered system must serve multiple roles, potentially functioning as a power source, life support, and structural element while minimizing the ecological footprint and operational risks associated with engaging biological entities in warfare.

However, the exciting possibilities that arise from integrating biological systems into war machines also come with inherent risks. The unpredictability associated with living organisms brings uncertainties that traditional engineering has largely found ways to mitigate using predictable materials. Thus, ensuring that the biological organisms deployed within battleships operate as intended without adverse effects—such as uncontrolled proliferation or unintended ecological consequences—becomes a critical design consideration. Efforts must prioritize containment measures, fail-safes, and responsive operational protocols.

To navigate this complex terrain, it will be essential to employ robust modeling and simulation techniques that can predict how biological systems will behave under various conditions and stresses that occur during combat scenarios. These models can help inform design principles and decision-making processes, providing a framework within which engineers and biologists can optimally align their efforts.

Furthermore, ethical considerations must permeate the understanding and design of these biological systems. The mere act of engineering life for combat raises numerous questions about the morality of weaponizing biology. Developing clear guidelines for the ethical treatment of bioengineered organisms, ensuring they are designed for control and responsible use, becomes pivotal. This calls for ongoing dialogue among scientists, military planners, ethicists, and the public, establishing boundaries that honor the dignity of life while pursuing innovative military advancements.

As we forge ahead into this new chapter in technological evolution, our understanding of biological systems will lay the groundwork for making informed decisions regarding the integration of biotechnology into warfare. This comprehensive insight into life sciences will not only facilitate the design and functionality of future biotech battleships but will also shape the ethical and strategic considerations of employing biological innovations in intergalactic conflict. Emphasizing collaboration between biological and engineering disciplines will be indispensable in navigating the evolving landscape of warfare as we translate the complexity of life into groundbreaking designs that could forever alter how conflicts are waged among the stars.

3.2. Synthetic Biology: Building Blocks of the Future

As we delve into the realm of synthetic biology, we witness a fascinating convergence of creativity and scientific rigor that fundamentally reshapes our understanding of potential military applications. Synthetic biology operates at the intersection of biology and engineering, allowing for the design and construction of new biological parts, devices, and systems that do not exist in nature. The implications for future warfare are vast, opening up possibilities for bioengineered constructs that could serve as the building blocks of the novel interstellar battleships of tomorrow.

At its core, synthetic biology leverages our understanding of genetic codes to create organisms or biological systems with tailored functions. Traditionally, the process of genetic manipulation relied heavily on trial and error, but advances in synthetic biology introduce a systematic approach akin to programming in computer science. Researchers can now "write" new genetic codes, integrating various biological elements like promoters, coding sequences, and terminators to ensure desired traits manifest within engineered organisms. This foundational shift allows for precise manipulation of living organisms for specific applications—whether it be enhanced resilience, faster growth rates, or the ability to produce unique metabolites.

Moving toward the military context, the ability to create or modify organisms that can thrive in extreme environments is crucial. Imagine a scenario where synthetic microorganisms can be engineered to produce bioluminescent compounds for navigation in the vast blackness of space or biofuel to power critical ship systems. The adaptability of these organisms allows them to respond and evolve based on external conditions, potentially providing a level of self-sufficiency and resilience previously unseen in interstellar vessels.

An equally exciting frontier within synthetic biology lies in the creation of biological circuits—complex networks of biomolecules that can execute logical operations much like electronic circuits. This capability could transform how we visualize the functioning of a biotech battleship. With engineered biological circuits embedded within the ship's systems, it would be possible to create responsive mechanisms that detect biological or chemical threats and react in real-time, adjusting strategies based on immediate battlefield contexts. These constructs can enhance overall situational awareness and decision-making, allowing military personnel to respond more effectively to rapidly changing threats.

In the creation of synthetic ecosystems, a significant emphasis is placed on modular design, where interchangeable parts can be combined to achieve a broader range of functions. Such a principle can guide engineers in outfitting biotech battleships with modular biological systems that can be easily swapped in and out to adapt to specific mission requirements. This adaptability could reduce operational downtime and ensure that these vessels maintain peak performance regardless of the challenges faced in interstellar environments.

Synthetic biology does not merely offer unique living components for battleships; it also presents opportunities to engineer self-defensive mechanisms. Imagine a ship equipped with bioengineered protective layers that autonomously respond to invasive threats, capable of recognizing external toxins and deploying counteractive measures, such as producing neutralizing agents. These living armor systems would redefine the very concept of "defensive technology," merging biology's intrinsic capabilities with mechanical constructs to create responsive, dynamic shields.

Moreover, early efforts in synthetic biology have demonstrated potential pathways for creating biologically-derived materials that can alter their properties based on environmental cues. These materials can possess unique attributes such as self-healing properties or the ability to change structural configurations in response to external stimuli, presenting unparalleled operational advantages. The integration of such materials into the structural designs of intergalactic war machines could lead to robust and adaptable ships ready to face diverse challenges.

However, the journey of synthesizing novel biological systems for military applications is fraught with ethical implications and technical challenges. The deployment of organisms engineered for combat invokes a complex moral landscape—who holds responsibility if these systems malfunction or adapt in unintended ways? Ensuring that the engineered organisms remain under rigorous control emerges as paramount. Ethical considerations revolving around the implications of modifying life forms for warfare will demand thoughtful laws and protocols, to align innovations with the values of society.

Additionally, the technical challenges of scaling up production and ensuring that synthetic organisms maintain stability under various operational conditions cannot be overlooked. The transition from lab-scale experiments to full-scale battlefield deployments requires thorough understanding and validation processes. Rigorous testing scenarios must simulate actual combat conditions to identify any potential shortcomings and ensure reliability in high-stakes environments.

Synthesizing the ideas presented here exposes an exhilarating yet daunting vision of the future of warfare, one where synthetic biology plays a pivotal role in fabricating the biological building blocks of tomorrow's war machines. The dynamic interplay between biological systems and military technology has the potential to disrupt traditional modes of engagement, presenting new strategies and capabilities that have previously existed only in speculative fiction.

As we venture into this frontier of innovation, continual exploration, understanding, and ethical deliberation will be essential. By synthesizing knowledge from interdisciplinary fields, military planners can craft future interstellar strategies that harmonize the power of synthetic biology with the rigorous demands of warfare, ultimately redefining our entire approach to conflict among the stars. Through a commitment to ethical principles and responsible use, we can pave the way for a technological renaissance—one where living systems unleash their potential to protect and serve humanity in the vast unknown of space.

3.3. Biological and Mechanical Symbiosis

In the exploration of the future of interstellar warfare, the multifaceted concept of biological and mechanical symbiosis emerges as a cornerstone of innovative design and functionality for biotech battleships. As we stand on the precipice of integrating living systems into military applications, we must delve into the intricate relationship between biology and mechanical engineering—one that is characterized by cooperation, adaptability, and burgeoning capabilities that have the potential to redefine our understanding of war machines.

At its essence, the idea of symbiosis encompasses mutualism—the cooperation between two entities for their mutual benefit. In the context of biotechnology and mechanical systems, this means creating hybrid machines where organic components work in concert with metal and artificial systems, producing an overall advancement that surpasses what either could achieve independently. The seamless integration of biological systems within mechanical frameworks allows for resilient and responsive war machines engineered to excel in the unpredictable environments of space.

The adaptability of biological systems serves as a primary advantage in this symbiotic relationship. Unlike traditional machines, which are often rigid and require extensive reengineering to meet changing conditions, living systems possess the inherent ability to respond dynamically to their surroundings. This characteristic can be harnessed in the design of biotech battleships, where bioengineered organisms can serve as sensors, actuators, and decision-making units that adapt in real time. For instance, a ship equipped with genetically modified bacteria capable of detecting chemical threats can autonomously respond, modifying onboard systems to counteract toxins or dangers without human intervention.

Furthermore, the concept of self-healing materials is a groundbreaking attribute of biological integration. Research into biomimicry reveals that many natural organisms possess the ability to repair themselves, whether through cellular regeneration in amphibians or through defensive secretions in certain plants. The incorporation of these properties into the design of ship hulls or protective coatings could lead to vessels that can withstand damage during combat while autonomously addressing breaches or abrasions. This not only enhances the ship's durability but significantly reduces maintenance needs, allowing crews to focus on tactical operations rather than repairs.

The symbiosis of biology and machinery also extends to energy production and efficiency. Future biotech battleships may utilize bioengineered organisms to convert waste materials into energy—a process that echoes the natural cycles of decomposition and nutrient recycling found in ecosystems. By integrating living organisms into the ship's life-support systems, the vessel can sustain itself more effectively, optimizing resource usage while minimizing ecological impact. Such systems would allow for extended missions in deep space, where resupply is a daunting logistical challenge, while maintaining a balanced and sustainable environment onboard.

However, while the prospects of biological and mechanical symbiosis are exciting, they are not without challenges. Ensuring the stability and reliability of biological components within heavily mechanized environments requires a comprehensive understanding of the conditions these organisms will encounter. Forces such as radiation exposure in space, mechanical stress, and changes in pressure can significantly impact biological performance and viability. Engineers and biologists must work together in rigorous testing and modeling to ensure that these hybrids can adequately withstand the rigors of interstellar combat without failure.

Moreover, ethical considerations surrounding the use of living organisms in warfare cannot be overstated. Engaging in the creation of biological systems designed for combat raises profound questions about our responsibilities as designers and operators of these technologies. Structures of governance and guidelines must be established to navigate the moral complexities involved in manipulating life for military objectives. This extends beyond the technical realm into the societal consciousness—public discourse on the ethical perspectives of bio-warfare must engage various stakeholders, including scientists, ethicists, military strategists, and the broader community affected by the use of such technologies.

Education and training will play a critical role in preparing military personnel to interact with and manage biotech battleships. Understanding the biological systems onboard will be as essential as mastering weapon systems and mechanical operations. This interdisciplinary knowledge transfer will ensure that individuals operating these advanced vessels can truly harness their potential while recognizing and managing the risks involved.

In conclusion, the relationship between biological and mechanical systems encapsulates the innovative advancements on the horizon for intergalactic warfare. The potential for hybrid vessels that leverage the strengths of both realms promises to yield highly adaptive, resilient, and efficient combat platforms. As we navigate the intricacies of living technologies in military applications, we must remain cognizant of the ethical dimensions, ensuring that the pursuit of enhanced capabilities does not overshadow the integrity and responsibility we owe to the living systems we engineer. The future of warfare holds promises of extraordinary possibilities created through biological and mechanical symbiosis—an endeavor that will require our utmost vigilance, innovation, and ethical foresight.

3.4. Challenges in Biotech Synthesis

In the pursuit of harnessing biotechnology to revolutionize warfare, various challenges surface in the synthesis of living systems within military applications. These difficulties are critical to understanding as we move toward a future where biological elements could form the core of our intergalactic battleships. The integration of biology within military frameworks is anything but straightforward and encompasses a vast range of scientific, logistical, and ethical considerations. Tackling these challenges effectively is paramount for realizing the full potential of biotech capabilities in combat scenarios.

One significant challenge lies in the unpredictability and variability inherent in biological organisms. Unlike traditional machinery, which operates based on well-defined physical laws and predictable engineering principles, biological systems are subject to fluctuations within their internal and external environments. Factors such as genetic drift, responses to environmental stimuli, and unforeseen interactions with other biological or mechanical components can introduce unpredictable behaviors. This variability poses risks when designing systems intended for high-stakes military operations where reliability and predictability are vital. Developers must undertake extensive research and modeling to anticipate and mitigate the various ways in which biological organisms may behave or react under stress.

Moreover, ensuring the biosecurity and containment of engineered organisms is of paramount importance. The prospect of deploying living systems in combat raises significant concerns about their potential to escape and adapt in uncontrolled environments. Unlike traditional weapons, which can be decommissioned and locked away, living organisms may evolve or replicate when introduced into the ecosystem, with unpredictable consequences. This risk heightens when considering the implications of pathogens or negatively engineered organisms accidentally being released in the field, posing threats not just to military personnel but also to civilian populations and ecosystems. Therefore, rigorous containment measures, failsafes, and monitoring protocols must be established and maintained when designing and deploying biotech components.

The cultivation and maintenance of living systems onboard battleships add another layer of complexity. Bioengineered organisms often require specific environmental conditions—temperature, humidity, nutrient levels—to thrive. This necessity complicates logistics and requires advanced engineering solutions to create self-sustaining life-support systems capable of regulating environmental factors. Such systems must be robust enough to function in the often harsh and unpredictable conditions of space or battlefield environments. Successfully integrating these auxiliary systems into the overall design of battleships is crucial for ensuring that biological components remain viable and effective in their roles.

Additionally, there are multifaceted ethical concerns that intertwine with technological advancement. The very act of manipulating life for military purposes invites deep moral questions about our responsibilities as designers and users of such technologies. Engaging in biotechnological warfare raises concerns of acceptable uses of science in conflict, the treatment of engineered organisms, and overall implications for what defines "life" and "combat." As debates surrounding the moral implications of using living entities in warfare continue, society must engage in critical dialogues and develop comprehensive ethical guidelines that govern the responsible development and deployment of biotech warfare applications.

The interdisciplinary nature of biotechnology presents another challenge, requiring collaboration between biologists, engineers, ethicists, and military strategists. While scientists and military planners provide crucial insights into the theoretical and practical applications of biotechnology, integrating their perspectives can often prove tricky, as differences in language, priorities, and modes of thinking may obstruct progress. Effective communication and collaboration strategies must be established to cultivate a cohesive working relationship that brings together diverse fields of knowledge and expertise.

Furthermore, funding and resource allocation pose considerable challenges in advancing biotech synthesis for military applications. Emerging technologies often require significant investment in research and development, which may not be readily available within traditional military budgets historically allocated for conventional weaponry. Gaining support from government entities, private sector partnerships, and venture capitalists is essential to promote innovation in biotech warfare. Overcoming bureaucratic hurdles and fostering a culture that embraces biotech as an essential facet of future military capabilities will be paramount for successful advancements.

Finally, public perception of biotechnological warfare presents a complex landscape that military entities must navigate. The fear and skepticism surrounding biotechnology, often amplified by sensational media portrayals, can lead to public opposition and protests against the militarization of living systems. Addressing these concerns requires transparent communication strategies about the intended goals, benefits, and ethical safeguards surrounding the use of biotechnology in defense contexts. Engaging with communities to build understanding and cooperation will bolster support for military innovations, facilitating smoother paths for research and implementation.

In summary, the synthesis of biotechnology in warfare is fraught with challenges that span unpredictable biological behavior, containment and ethical considerations, interdisciplinary collaboration, resource limitations, and public perception. Overcoming these hurdles requires a dedicated concerted effort by scientists, military strategists, ethicists, and policymakers alike. As humanity moves forward into the realms of intergalactic warfare, addressing these challenges will be critical not merely for the success of biotechnology applications but also to ensure the ethical and responsible use of innovations that blur the lines between life and machinery. The hope lies in our ability to develop a framework within which biotechnology may flourish—one that not only propels us into the future but also respects the intrinsic value of life itself.

3.5. Case Studies of Biomechanical Innovations

The landscape of interstellar warfare is becoming increasingly populated with innovations born from the intersection of biotechnology and mechanical engineering. This subchapter delves into illuminating case studies that exemplify how biomechanical innovations are reshaping military applications and transforming the design of war machines. As we explore these case studies, we will examine not only the scientific breakthroughs that have made these innovations possible but also the broader implications they hold for the future of warfare among the stars.

One notable case study pertains to the research and development of biohybrid sensors—devices that integrate living organisms with conventional sensing technology. In the early 21st century, a team of scientists at the Bioengineering Institute developed a novel system that harnessed the sensory capabilities of genetically modified bacteria, which were engineered to fluoresce in response to specific environmental stimuli. This project aimed to create a new type of defensive measure that could detect harmful chemical agents or biological threats in real-time. The successful implementation of these biological sensors demonstrates the potential to enhance situational awareness on the battlefield, allowing commanders to react more swiftly to emerging threats. The integration of biological components into conventional systems illustrated a promising precedent for future biotech battleships, highlighting the advantages of incorporating living agents to bolster the efficacy of military operations.

Another compelling example is found within the development of self-healing materials, a pioneering achievement that demonstrates the power of bioengineering in military technology. The Defense Advanced Research Projects Agency (DARPA) commissioned a study to create materials capable of autonomous self-repair, utilizing principles derived from biological processes. Through the application of synthetic biology, researchers engineered a polymer infused with living microorganisms that secretes healing agents when damage occurs. This innovation could fundamentally alter how military vessels, including biotech battleships, withstand impacts during engagements. The ability of these materials to autonomously repair structural breaches represents a significant leap forward, reducing maintenance demands and enhancing the survival of craft engaged in high-stakes operations.

Equally noteworthy is the integration of microbial fuel cells within military applications, which highlights the potential for living systems to address operational energy demands. Research presented by a coalition of universities in the late 2020s explored the feasibility of utilizing microbial fuel cells to convert organic waste generated by military crews into usable energy. Deploying these bioreactors onboard battleships could ease the logistical burden of fuel resupply during long-term missions, presenting a sustainable energy source drawn from the very systems that personnel generate through daily operations. This innovative design not only boosts energy efficiency but also minimizes environmental impacts, as waste is repurposed into something beneficial rather than discarded as a liability.

Additionally, the case of synthesized biological agents for offensive applications exemplifies the transformative potential of biotechnology in warfare—it brings with it compelling ethical dilemmas. During the mid-2030s, a research initiative aimed to engineer microorganisms designed to target specific enemy assets through natural predation mechanisms. The intent was to create a bioweapon that could incapacitate enemy gear without causing collateral human damage. While the technical achievements garnered considerable intrigue, the ethical ramifications sparked heated global debate on whether creating such engineered life forms crossed an ethical threshold. This case illuminated the need for robust ethical guidelines in biotechnological warfare developments, indicating that with great power comes substantial responsibility.

Emerging from these case studies is the concept of streamlined logistics through biotechnological integration. For instance, bioengineering may yield organisms specifically designed to thrive and reproduce in the void of space, thereby providing an ongoing source of food or even oxygen regeneration. Such organisms could be housed within biotech battleships, establishing self-sustaining ecosystems that support long-duration missions. Case studies showcasing closed-loop life support systems underline how successful engineering in this area significantly enhances the sustainability and efficiency of military operations.

Another case study evaluates "living armor"—a combination of biological and mechanical systems designed to enhance the defensive capabilities of spacecraft. A consortium of defense contractors and research universities collaborated to create a biological armor composed of synthesized cells that could modify their density and properties in response to environmental threats. Tests indicated that this living armor exhibited rapid changes to its structure upon impact, providing improved resilience over traditional materials. The success of this project has laid the groundwork for similar techniques to be utilized in the design of future biotech battleships, ensuring that vessels are not only fortified against physical threats but also capable of adapting dynamically to hostile encounters.

Moreover, we cannot overlook the synergy of flora and mechanical systems, as evidenced by experiments integrating plants into ship designs to enhance air purification. By employing engineered plants that can metabolize carbon dioxide and release oxygen at accelerated rates, military researchers found a dual application: These plants provided not only improved air quality aboard long-term missions but also enhanced psychological well-being for crew members. This project not only proved the viability of using biological systems for life support but also highlighted the importance of maintaining mental health in long-duration missions, an area that remains pivotal in future military applications.

In summarizing these case studies, it becomes clear that the innovations born from biomechanical integration are not solely about enhancing performance or survivability in warfare. They represent a transformative shift in our understanding of military applications, where the lines between technology and life become increasingly blurred. The case studies explored here illuminate both the breadth of possibilities and the significance of ethical considerations as humanity embarks on this uncharted territory.

As we reflect on the implications of these innovations, it is imperative that future developments in biotechnology remain anchored in responsible practices. With the stakes higher than ever in the realm of warfare, the case studies of biomechanical innovations serve as both inspiration and cautionary tales—a reminder of the extraordinary potential inherent in biotechnology, as well as the profound ethical responsibilities that accompany it. The future of warfare, shaped by these innovations, challenges us to reimagine how we view life and technology in the context of conflict. Thus, as we draft the designs of tomorrow's biotech battleships, we must do so with a commitment to stewardship—ensuring that our ambitions align with a purpose that transcends the mere advancement of combat capabilities.

4. Designing the Biotech Battleship

4.1. Anatomy of a Biotech Battleship

In the realm of future warfare, where the boundaries between biology and technology blur, the concept of a biotech battleship emerges as a marvel of innovation, representing the convergence of biological systems with mechanical engineering. These vessels are not merely machines; they symbolize a profound transformation in our approach to interstellar conflict. Understanding the anatomy of a biotech battleship involves dissecting its various components, their functionality, and how they collaboratively redefine the realm of warfare.

At the core, a biotech battleship is designed to operate as a cohesive unit, intricately integrating living organisms with mechanical systems. This presents a departure from the traditional understanding of a war machine as a purely mechanical construct, shifting toward a more organic integration that draws upon the adaptability, resilience, and self-sustainability inherent in biological systems. The synergy between biology and technology is critical, as it allows these vessels to respond dynamically to environmental changes and threats, enhancing their combat effectiveness in ever-evolving scenarios.

The foundational structure of a biotech battleship incorporates living materials, engineered for specific defenses and functionalities. Biologically-derived materials, such as membranes composed of genetically modified cells, may serve multiple purposes: reinforcing the vessel's hull while being lightweight and capable of self-repair. These materials possess the remarkable ability to respond to damage, allowing the ship to recover from assaults automatically—in stark contrast to traditional vessels that demand extensive repairs. The self-healing mechanisms inspired by biological processes not only prolong the ship's operational life but significantly reduce maintenance requirements, enabling crews to focus on tactical maneuvers rather than incessant repairs.

Internally, the battleship is equipped with bioreactors that facilitate life support systems by utilizing engineered microorganisms. These organisms could convert waste products into vital resources, such as oxygen and energy, creating a closed-loop system that enhances sustainability during long missions in the void of space. This ecological integration mirrors natural ecosystems, refining resource utilization and establishing an equilibrium that supports the crew, thus mirroring life on Earth within the vessel itself.

Furthermore, the battleship incorporates bio-hybrid systems where organic components and mechanical devices work together. For instance, sensors made from biological entities might be embedded within the ship, allowing them to detect environmental changes, chemical agents, or even adversarial movements with unprecedented sensitivity. These biologically enhanced sensors can autonomously relay information to decision-making systems, which can adapt strategies in real-time based on the perceived threats, thereby augmenting situational awareness during engagements.

The design of the ship would also integrate advanced propulsion systems inspired by organic locomotion. Biological engines may leverage microbial processes or natural adaptations found in aquatic creatures to propel the ship through space. Microbial fuel cells, for example, could efficiently convert organic matter into energy, allowing the battleship to generate power sustainably, while biologically-inspired propulsion mechanisms could enhance maneuverability.

The management of these complex systems necessitates an advanced artificial intelligence (AI) that can interface seamlessly with both the biological and mechanical components. This AI serves as the operational backbone, overseeing the integration of living components while optimizing functionality. By analyzing vast amounts of data from sensors, environmental controls, and crew inputs, the AI can make adaptive decisions and adjustments, automating responses to threats, and ensuring cohesive operation between the biological and mechanical systems aboard the vessel.

The crews tasked with operating these biotech battleships would undergo specialized training to understand the intricacies of both the biological and technological elements of their command. This includes knowledge of genetic engineering principles, bioengineering biology, and environmental science—ensuring that crew members can effectively monitor, maintain, and enhance the ship's biological systems.

In addition to the physical and operational aspects, ethical considerations play a significant role in the design and deployment of biotech battleships. The responsibility of wielding biotechnology for warfare raises profound moral dilemmas concerning the rights of engineered organisms and the potential ecological impacts of their deployment. Establishing stringent ethical guidelines and operational protocols will be paramount to ensure respect for living systems as they are integrated into military strategies.

In summary, the anatomy of a biotech battleship is a complex amalgamation of biological ingenuity and mechanical robustness, designed for adaptability, sustainability, and enhanced combat capability. As these vessels evolve, they fundamentally challenge traditional notions of warfare, invoking a need for a multidisciplinary approach that marries biology, engineering, and ethics to navigate the future of warfare among the stars. The journey into this frontier not only transforms the landscape of military capability but also invites us to reconsider our understanding of life, technology, and the responsibilities accompanying their synthesis.

4.2. Design Principles and Approaches

In the dynamic and rapidly evolving field of warfare, where biology and engineering merge to create unprecedented capabilities, several design principles and approaches stand at the forefront of developing biotech battleships. These principles not only challenge traditional concepts of military vessels but also highlight the intricate relationship between organic systems and mechanical constructs. As we navigate through this innovative landscape, it becomes essential to explore key design methodologies that will shape the future of interstellar conflict.

First and foremost, the principle of adaptability is paramount in the design of biotech battleships. Unlike conventional ships, which are often rigid and fixed in their functionalities, biotech vessels must incorporate dynamic biological systems that can respond to changing environments and threats. The integration of living organisms with mechanical systems allows these battleships to exhibit traits such as self-repair, regeneration, and the capacity to adjust operational parameters in real time. For instance, a ship equipped with engineered organisms could detect and neutralize pathogens or toxins autonomously, demonstrating adaptability that is crucial for survival in unpredictable combat situations.

Incorporating principles of biomimicry is another vital approach that informs the design of biotech battleships. Nature has evolved countless life forms that showcase remarkable solutions to complex challenges. By emulating biological structures and processes, engineers can derive innovative designs that optimize performance and enhance survival. For example, the hull of a battleship could feature surface textures inspired by shark skin, which reduces drag and improves hydrodynamics. Furthermore, integrating features emulating biological signaling pathways can enhance communication and decision-making within the ship's operational hierarchy, ensuring seamless collaboration between organic and mechanical components.

Another key design principle centers around sustainability. As military operations extend into the vastness of space, the need for self-sufficient systems becomes increasingly critical. Biotech battleships offer solutions through closed-loop life support systems that recycle waste materials into usable resources, mimicking the ecological balance found within natural ecosystems. For example, engineered microorganisms could convert carbon dioxide and organic waste generated by the crew into oxygen and edible biomass. Such systems not only reduce reliance on external supplies but also empower crews to sustain themselves during prolonged missions, thus addressing logistical challenges that arise in space operations.

The principle of modularity also plays a significant role in the design approach for biotech battleships. Modular designs allow for interchangeable organic and mechanical components, enabling ships to adapt to different mission requirements efficiently. Should a specific component fail or require enhancement, modularity facilitates upgrades or replacements without necessitating a complete overhaul. This is particularly advantageous in a military context, as it allows for rapid adaptations in response to changing warfare dynamics, ensuring that the vessel remains operational and effective under various conditions.

Moreover, interdisciplinary collaboration is a cornerstone of effective design in this field. The integration of biological systems necessitates seamless communication and cooperation among diverse teams composed of biologists, engineers, ethicists, and military strategists. Each discipline brings unique insights and expertise essential for addressing the complexities involved in designing living machines. By fostering interdisciplinary dialogue, teams can develop holistic designs that capitalize on the strengths of both biological and mechanical systems.

Ethics must also be interwoven into design principles, guiding the responsible development of biotech battleships. Military applications of biotechnology raise profound moral dilemmas concerning the treatment of engineered organisms and the potential ecological consequences of their deployment. Establishing ethical guidelines governing the use of living systems as instruments of warfare becomes vital, ensuring that the quest for military advantage does not overshadow our moral obligations toward life itself. Engaging with a wide range of stakeholders—scientists, ethicists, military leaders, and the public—will facilitate a comprehensive understanding of the implications of biotechnology in combat.

Finally, iterative design processes, underscored by rigorous testing and validation, are essential for refining the capabilities of biotech battleships. Prototyping, simulation, and real-world testing will be necessary to evaluate the functionality and resilience of the integrated systems. This iterative approach ensures that designers can adapt their plans based on empirical data and field experiences, leading to continuous improvement and innovation.

In summary, the design principles and approaches guiding the development of biotech battleships embody a harmonious blending of adaptability, sustainability, modularity, interdisciplinary collaboration, ethics, and iterative processes. Together, these principles create a foundation for future war machines that not only excel in combat but also honor the complexities of life. As we stand on the brink of a new era in warfare, these design philosophies will navigate the uncharted territories of intergalactic conflict—inviting us to reimagine the very essence of military operations in a world where biology and technology unite.

4.3. Integrating Organic Components

As biotechnology continues to evolve at an astonishing pace, the integration of organic components into military applications signifies a profound transformation in the design and functionality of war machines. This endeavor is not solely about enhancing mechanical capabilities with biological enhancements; it represents a paradigm shift that redefines our approach to warfare, merging life sciences with engineering principles to create hybrid systems that can adapt, respond, and thrive under combat conditions. The journey toward integrating organic components into biotech battleships requires rigorous exploration across various dimensions, including biological systems, chemical interactions, and societal impacts.

The first step in this integration process involves a deep understanding of biological systems. Unlike traditional mechanical constructs governed by predictable physical laws, biological organisms exhibit variability and adaptability, making them uniquely suited for combat scenarios where conditions can change unpredictably. Engineers and biologists must collaborate to identify organisms that can provide enhanced functionalities—such as self-repair capabilities derived from the regenerative properties of certain species. By mimicking these natural processes, future battleships could be designed with self-healing materials that can autonomously address damage incurred during engagements, increasing their resilience in battle.

Integral to this integration is the role of genetic engineering, which enables scientists to modify organisms for specific purposes that align with military objectives. Advances in synthetic biology allow for the customized design of biological components that can perform targeted tasks, such as enhanced sensitivity to environmental changes or the ability to produce vital resources under duress. Additionally, the development of biohybrid systems, where living organisms interface with mechanical systems, opens up exciting possibilities for real-time responses to external stimuli—a game-changer in combat scenarios.

The challenges associated with integrating organic components are multifaceted. One particularly pressing concern lies in ensuring the containment and biosecurity of engineered organisms. If these organisms were to escape or reproduce uncontrollably on a battle-field, the ecological consequences could be catastrophic. Thus, each engineered component must incorporate fail-safes and robust monitoring systems to prevent unintended proliferation. This prescriptive methodology not only demands rigorous scientific protocols but also calls for an ethical framework that governs the use of living systems in warfare—ensuring responsible stewardship of the life forms engineered for military use.

Moreover, the logistical implications of organic integration cannot be understated. Living systems require specific environmental conditions to thrive, necessitating advanced life support systems capable of maintaining temperature, humidity, and nutrient levels within the battleship. Designers must engineer systems that not only support the viability of these organisms but also optimize their performance for operational readiness. A self-sustaining ecosystem where biological functions contribute to life support could drastically reduce the logistical burden on military supply chains during extended missions in remote regions of space.

As the integration of organic components progresses, ethical considerations emerge at every turn. Developing biotechnology for warfare raises deep moral questions. For example, will engineered organisms possess rights? What responsibilities do we have toward life forms we create for the purpose of conflict? Open dialogues that involve diverse stakeholders—including scientists, ethicists, military leaders, and the public—are essential for crafting guidelines that resonate with ethical imperatives while advancing military capabilities.

The design principles guiding the integration of organic components stress flexibility, sustainability, and collaboration across disciplines. A modular design approach enables easy adaptation and enhancement of organic and mechanical components, affording the battleship the capacity to evolve alongside technological advancements or unforeseen battlefield conditions. Interdisciplinary collaboration becomes paramount as engineers, biologists, and military strategists work together not just to achieve technological feats but also to cultivate a holistic approach to integrating life systems within combat modules.

As we envision the biotech battleships of the future, the integration of organic components will undoubtedly revolutionize how warfare is waged. These vessels will not merely serve as tools of destruction; they will embody dynamic, living entities capable of self-repair, autonomous responses, and multifaceted ecological functions. In doing so, they challenge our understanding of combat, duty, and our relationship with technology.

Through this journey of integrating organic components, we embark on an exploration not only of advanced warfare technology but also of our responsibilities as stewards of the living systems we aim to employ in conflict. The future of interstellar battleships will hinge on our ability to harmonize biology and engineering while addressing the profound ethical questions that accompany this brave new venture. Balancing innovation with responsibility will ultimately determine how successfully we can integrate life into our war machines, shaping a new epoch in military history replete with astonishment and vigilance.

4.4. The Role of AI in Design Optimization

The role of artificial intelligence (AI) in the design optimization of biotech battleships is a pivotal aspect of the evolution of warfare that integrates biotechnology and cutting-edge technology. As we venture into an era where the frontiers of biology meet advanced computational intelligence, AI emerges as an invaluable tool—enhancing design processes, optimizing functions, and ensuring that these complex machines operate at peak performance in the most challenging environments. The collaboration between AI and biotechnology not only promises to refine the very concept of military vessels but also redefines their operational capabilities in unprecedented ways.

In designing biotech battleships, the first step involves intricate modeling processes that simulate the behaviors of both biological and mechanical systems. This is where AI plays a crucial role; through advanced algorithms, AI can process vast datasets to model various interactions within the ship. By simulating how biological organisms behave under different conditions—such as stress, damage, or environmental changes—designers can optimize components, ensuring that they function cohesively. This simulation capability allows for rapid iterations of design, significantly reducing the time and cost associated with physical prototyping.

Moreover, AI can analyze and predict the performance of bioengineered systems in real time. By employing machine learning techniques, AI algorithms continuously learn from the operational data of existing systems. This adaptive learning empowers designers to identify patterns, detect anomalies, and refine designs according to performance metrics. For instance, if an engineered organism does not exhibit the desired growth rate or healing capacity under certain conditions, AI could provide actionable insights to tweak genetic parameters or adjust environmental controls swiftly. This ability to learn and adapt based on evolving datasets is particularly critical in the unknowns of space combat, where conditions can shift dramatically and unexpectedly.

Furthermore, AI aids in optimizing resource allocation within biotech battleships. In a multi-functional environment where living organisms interact with sophisticated technology, AI can analyze the demands for energy, nutrients, and other resources, ensuring the efficient distribution of these vital components. By optimizing these resource flows, the efficiency of the ship's ecosystem improves, extending operational timeframes and enhancing crew survival. For example, AI could manage bioreactors that convert waste into usable energy or oxygen, adjusting parameters in real-time to adapt to changes in crew activity levels or the ship's operational status.

Integral to the role of AI in design optimization is its capability to enhance decision-making processes. With numerous biological and mechanical variables at play, the complexity of operational decisions increases exponentially. AI-powered systems can assist captains and commanders by providing predictive analytics that considers countless factors, such as enemy movements, the status of integrated biological systems, and environmental variables. By aggregating this information, AI systems enable more informed decision-making, empowering personnel to deploy their resources effectively and tactically.

Moreover, the design of biotech battleships entails a unique challenge regarding safety and risk management. AI can be leveraged to develop rigorous safety protocols that monitor the health and performance of organic components. For instance, AI can continuously assess the responses of living materials to combat stresses, identifying potential points of failure before they lead to catastrophic outcomes. Such proactive measures are essential in mitigating risks associated with deploying engineered organisms in high-stakes environments where the line between success and failure can determine the outcome of critical missions.

Ethical considerations also play a vital role in the deployment of AI within the design process. As the integration of living systems raises complex ethical questions, AI can help determine the potential implications of biological choices made during design and operational planning. Algorithms can model different scenarios to assess the ecological impact and survival of both engineered organisms and the broader ecosystem they inhabit. By utilizing AI in this way, designers can adopt a more sustainable approach, ensuring that the deployment of biotechnology aligns with ethical standards and the responsible use of life forms.

Collaboration remains a crucial element in maximizing AI's efficacy in the design optimization of biotech battleships. Facilitating interdisciplinary partnerships between biologists, engineers, ethicists, and military strategists is essential. By creating cohesive teams that incorporate diverse expertise, the capabilities of AI can be harnessed to inform design choices across all facets of shipbuilding—from the selection of organisms to the integration of mechanical components. This synergy fosters a culture of innovation, allowing insights to flow freely and transform the design process into a dynamic, adaptive framework.

In conclusion, the role of AI in the design optimization of biotech battleships is multifaceted and transformative. As we navigate the intersection of biology and technology in military applications, AI serves as a central asset that enhances modeling, decision-making, resource management, and ethical compliance. This remarkable synergy between artificial intelligence and biotechnology paves the way for the next generation of warfare, reimagining not only how we build war machines but how we understand and engage with living systems in the context of conflict. With AI as our ally, the future of interstellar warfare promises to be as innovative as it is complex—challenging us to think beyond traditional paradigms and explore the unfolding possibilities that lie ahead.

4.5. Collaborative Design Teams: Scientists and Engineers

In the contemporary landscape of military innovation, the successful creation of biotech battleships hinges significantly on the collaborative efforts of scientists and engineers. This partnership is not merely advantageous; it is essential for overcoming the complexity and multifaceted challenges of integrating biological systems within mechanical frameworks. To navigate the intricacies of this novel intersection, teams must embody seamless interdisciplinary collaboration, marrying the principles of biology with the rigorous methodologies of engineering to produce war machines capable of functioning efficiently in the demanding environments of interstellar warfare.

The collaborative design process begins with a shared understanding of the objectives and challenges faced in the development of biotech battleships. Engineers bring their expertise in systems design, mechanical reliability, and structural integrity, while scientists contribute deep knowledge of living systems, biological interactions, and ecological sustainability. This integrative approach enables teams to leverage their respective strengths, culminating in designs that are not only innovative but also grounded in functional viability and scientific rigor.

An illustrative example of successful collaboration can be seen in the interdisciplinary teams formed during initial bioengineering projects. Early in the development phase, these teams conduct joint brainstorming sessions, where engineers detail the mechanical requirements of a vessel and scientists describe the capabilities of various biological systems. It is within these discussions that creative solutions emerge—such as employing bioengineered organisms that possess self-healing properties, mirroring natural processes found in flora and fauna. Such innovations redefine conventional engineering practices by incorporating living components, thus directly influencing the material selection and structural design of battleships.

As the design phase progresses, scientists and engineers must work closely to develop and refine biointegrated systems. An example might involve the joint development of biosensors crafted from genetically modified microorganisms. In this scenario, engineers would create the housing and electronic systems for the sensors, while scientists focus on the biological enhancement necessary to boost sensitivity and responsiveness to environmental threats. Collaborative problem-solving becomes vital; if the microorganisms do not perform as expected in simulated battlefield conditions, the scientists can rapidly adjust genetic variables. Concurrently, engineers can modify the systems housing these organisms to accommodate changes, resulting in a deeply intertwined design process where success relies on fluid communication and teamwork.

The testing and validation phase is another critical intersection of scientific inquiry and engineering prowess. Collaborative teams engage in real-world simulations that consider the interactions of mechanical and biological systems under various combat scenarios. For example, if a biotech battleship's hull is designed to incorporate bioengineered materials, the durability and efficacy of these materials need to be evaluated against conventional armoring options. Here, scientists monitor biological responses under simulated stresses while engineers assess mechanical tolerances. The outcome of these tests informs iterative design improvements, driving subsequent rounds of collaboration that continuously enhance the overall performance of the vessel.

While technological advancements drive the need for collaboration, so too do the ethical considerations surrounding the implications of bioengineering. As living systems enter military applications—a domain where the consequences of failure can be catastrophic—both scientists and engineers must engage in thoughtful discussions about the moral obligations inherent in their work. This could encompass exploring the rights of engineered organisms or the potential ecological impacts of deploying these technologies in combat. By fostering a culture of ethical reflection and interdisciplinary dialogue, teams can ensure that their innovations are responsible and committed to the betterment of both military effectiveness and environmental sustainability.

The multifaceted interactions of various stakeholders also play an integral role in shaping collaborative teams. Military strategists, bioethicists, and legal experts can provide context and insight that enrich discussions and decision-making. By engaging with individuals across different domains, teams can consider how the design of biotech battleships aligns with broader military goals and societal expectations, ensuring that their work is relevant and responsible within the matrix of global security.

Despite the evident advantages of an interdisciplinary approach, the collaborative design process is not devoid of challenges. Differences in language, methodologies, and priorities can hinder progress if not consciously addressed. To avoid these pitfalls, establishing grounded communication protocols and shared terminologies at the onset of a project is vital. This mutual understanding fosters cooperation, creating a unified vision that transcends disciplinary boundaries.

In sum, the successful development of biotech battleships is inextricably linked to the collaboration between scientists and engineers. This dynamic partnership fuels the innovation required to design the sophisticated war machines of the future—ensuring that the integration of biological systems into military applications is not only viable but also ethically sound and responsive to the complexities of life. As we journey into the unknown of intergalactic warfare, it is through this collaborative spirit that humanity can truly harness the power of biotechnology, forging pathways to new frontiers that blend the genius of life with technological advancement.

5. Organic Armor: The Future of Defense

5.1. Developing Bio-Resistant Materials

In the quest for more resilient military capabilities, the development of bio-resistant materials lies at the forefront of innovation in the realm of biotechnology. This subchapter outlines the methodologies and considerations necessary for creating materials that can withstand the harsh realities of intergalactic warfare while integrating living systems into the framework of combat vessels. The fusion of biological resilience with mechanical durability is poised to redefine defense strategies, requiring a multidisciplinary approach that encompasses biological sciences, engineering, and material science.

The foundation of bio-resistant materials is rooted in the understanding of both biological and mechanical properties. Traditional materials, such as metals and composites, serve their purpose well in conventional warfare but are often limited by their static characteristics. As we ponder the future of warfare, the introduction of bio-engineered components into material design illustrates a revolutionary approach. Biological organisms display unique properties, such as self-healing capabilities, adaptive responses to environmental stimuli, and the ability to produce resilient byproducts that can enhance protection against external threats.

At the heart of developing bio-resistant materials lies molecular biology, where genetic and biochemical modifications have the potential to yield materials that outperform conventional protective gear. By engineering organisms to produce materials with specific characteristics—such as enhanced tensile strength, flexibility, or resistance to abrasion—it is possible to create a new class of protective coatings or structures that can better absorb impacts, resist penetration, and even autonomously repair damage. For instance, researchers are exploring the properties of spider silk, renowned for its strength and elasticity, as a template for materials that could significantly enhance the survivability of battleships.

Bio-inspired designs can also leverage the natural world's ingenious solutions to common threats. The study of organisms found in extreme environments—such as extremophiles that thrive in high-radiation areas—fuels the exploration of creating materials that can withstand the rigors of space combat. These organisms have developed cellular mechanisms to protect themselves from extreme conditions, offering invaluable insights into designing materials that can endure the variance in temperatures, pressures, and radiation that accompany interstellar engagements.

Examining the cellulosic structures in certain plants that exhibit remarkable defensive characteristics can pave the way for developing composite materials that combine biological and synthetic elements. Such composites might behave like a typical armor in traditional contexts while retaining properties that allow them to adapt to their environment and dynamically respond to stress. Composite materials that incorporate living cells can provide feedback mechanisms, allowing the vessel to gather data on impacts, environmental stressors, and potential vulnerabilities while remaining protected.

However, the process of integrating living materials into military applications entails a multitude of challenges. Ensuring the stability and reliability of biological components within highly engineered constructs requires rigorous testing and optimization on multiple levels. Researchers will need to establish parameters that dictate how living materials interact with mechanical components during various operational conditions. Factors such as temperature fluctuations, exposure to harsh environments, and mechanical stress can all impact the performance and longevity of bio-integrated systems.

Moreover, bio-security considerations arise when dealing with living organisms on the battlefield. It is imperative to prioritize containment and control to prevent unintended consequences if bioengineered organisms were to escape into ecosystems or undergo unpredictable mutations. Building safeguards into material design—such as kill switches or self-limiting biological processes—can help manage ecological risks while ensuring operational safety.

Part of the innovation process lies in the development of testing frameworks that evaluate bio-resistant materials under simulated battlefield conditions. The design of experiments must closely mimic the potential scenarios these materials might face, including high-impact collisions, abrasions from cosmic debris, and exposure to radiation. Evaluating the performance and durability of these materials will offer pivotal data that informs further iterations, ensuring they fulfill their promises of protection while remaining reliable over time.

Furthermore, the ethical implications of employing bioengineered materials cannot be ignored. As materials designed with living systems come into play, questions surrounding the moral obligation to treat engineered organisms with respect and responsibility emerge. Establishing an ethical framework that governs the use of living systems in military applications is essential for maintaining public trust while enabling innovation. Active engagement with various stakeholders—including scientists, military leaders, ethicists, and the general public—will foster a culture of transparency and collaboration, leading to thoughtful applications of these transformative technologies.

In conclusion, the development of bio-resistant materials stands as a noteworthy frontier in the evolution of military capabilities for intergalactic warfare. Through cross-disciplinary collaboration and the innovative fusion of biological systems with engineered constructs, the potential to reshape the paradigm of defense is enormous. As we harness the strength, adaptability, and autonomous functions of living materials, we must tread thoughtfully, considering the long-term impacts on society, ethics, and the ecosystems we inhabit. The advancements made in creating bio-resistant materials will not only enhance military strategy but redefine our approach to the very essence of life and technology in the context of warfare, ensuring our legacy remains one of responsible innovation.

5.2. Living Armor: Concept and Reality

The concept of living armor, which combines biological components with traditional protective systems, transcends conventional military designs to encapsulate the potential realizations of biotechnology in warfare. As battlefields evolve, so too must the armor that soldiers and vehicles employ. Living armor envisions a layer of protection that can not only withstand physical attacks but also heal, adapt, and respond to environmental threats autonomously.

The foundation of living armor relies upon engineering biological materials that exhibit properties derived from natural organisms known for their resilience and regenerative capacities. For instance, researchers have taken inspiration from the self-healing capabilities of certain amphibians, like salamanders, which can regenerate limbs, and the complex cellular structures of organisms like echinoderms that respond dynamically to environmental stressors. By unlocking these secrets of nature, scientists and engineers can create advanced materials that might self-repair when damaged, enhancing the longevity and operational readiness of combat vehicles.

At the heart of this innovation lies synthetic biology, allowing for the precise manipulation of genetic material. Through techniques such as CRISPR gene editing, materials can be programmed to express specific traits, such as increased tensile strength or the ability to catalyze biochemical reactions vital for repair processes. As a result, living armor can be designed to deploy a healing agent upon sustaining damage, effectively patching vulnerabilities in real-time and maintaining structural integrity on the battlefield.

The integration of living systems into armor presents unique advantages over traditional materials. Conventional armoring relies on fixed properties that often do not respond to changing circumstances, such as impacts from projectiles or environmental extremes. Living armor, on the other hand, can adapt its physical structure and properties in response to threats, potentially thickening in areas under stress or producing biochemical defenses against chemical attacks. This dynamic, responsive nature not only enhances defensive capabilities but also mitigates the need for extensive repairs, preserving operational effectiveness in combat situations.

However, transitioning from concept to reality poses both technical and ethical challenges. Creating living armor that functions reliably within the context of warfare requires rigorous testing and validation under various environmental conditions. Biologists and engineers must collaborate to design experimental protocols that assess the behavior of biological materials during simulated combat scenarios, taking into account factors such as temperature fluctuations, mechanical stress, and exposure to different forms of assaults.

One of the primary concerns surrounding living armor is biosecurity. Ensuring that engineered organisms behave predictably and remain contained is paramount, especially in combat environments where uncontrolled propagation or mutation could have unforeseen consequences. Designing kill switches or self-destruct mechanisms within the engineered organisms can help mitigate these risks, but ongoing monitoring and control will be critical to avoid ecological disruptions resulting from the unintended release of bioengineered life forms.

Additionally, the ethical implications of employing biological materials in military applications must be thoroughly examined. The creation and utilization of living entities for combat raise profound questions regarding the treatment of these organisms, the responsibilities of their creators, and the potential for unintended harm—both to human and non-human life. Defining the moral and ethical boundaries within which living armor operates is essential for fostering public trust and ensuring responsible development.

While promising prototypes have emerged, living armor remains a burgeoning area of research. Military applications could witness a significant transformation, integrating biological constructs seamlessly into modern warfare strategies. Anticipated advancements include materials that not only provide protection but also enhance situational awareness by monitoring environmental conditions and reporting potential risks to personnel—thus creating an intuitive layer of defense that preemptively engages threats.

In summary, the evolution of living armor illustrates an extraordinary frontier where biology and technology converge to redefine defensive strategies in warfare. By harnessing the regenerative capacities of living systems, we stand to gain a profound shift in how we conceive military protection—a paradigm that emphasizes resilience, adaptability, and ethical responsibility. As we continue to explore the realms of biotechnology, it becomes our duty to ensure that innovations in living armor represent not just remarkable technological strides but also a commitment to preserving life and sustainable approaches in the crucible of conflict.

5.3. Flexibility and Adaptation to Threats

In the fast-evolving landscape of interstellar warfare, the flexibility and adaptability of biotechnology stand as fundamental tenets that differentiate future battleships from their traditional counterparts. The essence of these advanced craft lies not only in their biological components but in their inherent capability to respond dynamically to a multitude of threats and challenges. As we venture deeper into the implications of flexible designs and organic systems, we must understand how these characteristics enhance military effectiveness and operational resilience in the face of unpredictable combat scenarios.

Flexibility in the design of biotech battleships is rooted in the very nature of biological organisms, which possess a remarkable capacity for adaptation. Unlike mechanical systems that have fixed functionalities defined by rigid engineering principles, living components imbue these vessels with the ability to adjust to varying conditions, damage, and adversarial tactics. For instance, the incorporation of genetically modified organisms that can sense environmental changes allows for the development of defense mechanisms that activate autonomously. If a ship encounters toxins or harmful radiation, specialized organisms onboard could trigger an adaptive response—either by producing neutralizing agents or by reinforcing structural integrity in compromised areas. Such biological foresight transforms combat readiness, enabling these vessels to operate effectively even in the most hostile environments.

Moreover, the integration of biological systems fosters a holistic approach to warfare where self-healing capabilities become a reality. Imagine a battleship's hull composed of bioengineered materials that mimic the regenerative properties found in certain species. Such materials could not only withstand physical assaults but also autonomously initiate repair processes when damaged. This capability radically reduces downtime for repairs, allowing combat vessels to remain operational without the extensive maintenance that traditional warships require. In a theater of war where every second counts, the ability to quickly bounce back from damage translates into enhanced survivability and effectiveness.

The adaptability of biotech battleships is also reflected in their structural configurations, which can change in response to specific tactical scenarios. Designers envision vessels that can reconfigure their shapes or reduce their profiles to enhance stealth capabilities. For instance, biological materials that can shift based on sensor inputs could effectively render a ship undetectable by enemy radar or visual means. This dynamic adaptability not only emphasizes flexibility but also underscores the importance of environmental context in determining operational effectiveness.

Navigating the complexities of interstellar environments requires strategies that extend beyond conventional parameters. The flexibility of battling challenges in space, such as fluctuations in gravity, radiation exposure, and vacuum conditions, can be immensely improved by integrating organic systems that have evolved to thrive in extreme environments. Research into extremophiles—organisms that endure harsh conditions on Earth—offers insights into bioengineered systems that could be deployed on the surfaces of distant planets or aboard battleships traversing unpredictable routes through cosmic storms.

Training human operators of these biotech battleships involves embracing the complexities of collaborating with living systems. Crews must develop a keen understanding of the biological components onboard, learning to anticipate how these systems will behave under various stressors. This interaction necessitates a new paradigm where training extends beyond traditional military tactics, incorporating biological principles that prepare operators to make informed decisions based on real-time data from living systems. Understanding that their vessel represents a hybrid of biology and technology fosters a mindset attuned to adaptability, enhancing the overall efficacy of military engagements.

However, increased flexibility and adaptability introduce challenges in ensuring reliability and control. The unpredictability of living systems necessitates robust monitoring protocols and responsive AI systems to track biological behaviors. Designing fail-safe mechanisms becomes paramount to mitigate risks associated with deploying organisms in combat scenarios where their reactions could dramatically influence outcomes. Innovations in AI could ensure that living systems and mechanical components are harmonized, permitting adaptable responses while maintaining operational control.

Furthermore, ethical considerations address the moral responsibilities associated with employing biotechnology in warfare. The deployment of living organisms in combat situations invokes discourse around the treatment and rights of bioengineered systems, raising questions about potential ecological impacts and the ethics of creating life for military purposes. Establishing guidelines to navigate these ethical dilemmas will be crucial, fostering a culture of responsibility that aligns military objectives with societal values.

As we integrate flexibility and adaptability into the fabric of future biotech battleships, we embrace a new realm of possibilities where warfare becomes an intricate dance between organic intelligence and mechanical prowess. The potential for crafting living machines equipped to evolve, heal, and respond dynamically in the face of adversity not only transforms our understanding of combat but also urges us to consider the broader implications of merging life with technology. Emphasizing adaptability is paramount—not just for the vessels themselves, but for the strategic frameworks, training methodologies, and ethical considerations that guide their deployment within the cosmos. As we stand on the brink of this brave new frontier, the adaptability intrinsic to biotechnology could very well redefine how humanity confronts the uncertainties of interstellar conflict.

5.4. Testing and Evolution of Biological Coatings

In the field of biotechnology, the testing and evolution of biological coatings represents an exciting frontier, particularly as we turn our gaze toward the conception of biotech battleships designed for interstellar warfare. Biological coatings have emerged as a potent solution for enhancing the protective capabilities of military vessels by integrating systems that can adapt, self-repair, and resist various environmental stresses and threats.

Biological coatings operate on the premise that living organisms possess inherent mechanisms of resilience and adaptation. These coatings often employ various microorganisms or genetically modified cells that can adhere to surfaces and provide protective functions against hostile forces. The journey of developing these biological coatings begins with identifying the right organisms that demonstrate traits beneficial for defense—such as self-healing, microbial resistance, and rapid growth rates. For instance, researchers have explored the potential of biofilms formed by specific bacteria, which can create robust layers on surfaces that not only act as shields but can also adapt their characteristics in response to environmental challenges.

The testing process is critical, requiring comprehensive evaluations of these biological coatings under a range of simulated combat conditions, from extreme temperatures to exposure to corrosive chemicals and projectile impacts. Assessments not only focus on the physical protective capabilities but also on the biological aspects that allow coatings to survive and respond to damage. These tests often involve environmental simulations within laboratories equipped to replicate the stresses and rigors that coatings might encounter in real-world scenarios.

Pioneering studies have documented significant advancements in the efficacy of biological coatings when subjected to aggressive assault tactics. For instance, a group of bioengineers successfully developed a living polymer that incorporates both synthetic components and living microorganisms, which could reinforce its structure when pierced. As damage occurs, the microorganisms detect an environmental change and respond by producing proteins that fill gaps and prevent further breaches. This biotic response exemplifies the self-repairing capabilities integral to the evolution of biological coatings for military applications.

The iterative development of such coatings relies on collecting data from testing and utilizing it to refine both the biological organisms used and the engineering frameworks applied. Researchers continuously evaluate the performance criteria derived from battlefield simulations to improve formulations, ensuring that each generation of coatings not only retains previous resilience but also incorporates new enhancements. For instance, incorporating protective silica beads into a biological coating might enhance its resistance to abrasion while still retaining its self-repair capabilities.

Moreover, as we implement these biological coatings within the structure of biotech battleships, the interactions between the coatings and the ship's surface materials become a focal point for investigation. The compatibility of biological coatings with various substrate materials must be examined, as different surfaces can affect the adherence and the overall functionality of the coating. Engineers often experiment with different surface textures to establish optimal conditions for biological attachment, ensuring that while the coatings perform effectively, they also bond securely to the host materials.

Transitioning from lab tests to field applications further stresses the importance of thorough evolutionary processes. The challenges of deploying biological coatings in unpredictable combat scenarios must be addressed, including how they will react to factors such as changes in atmospheric conditions, gravitational variances as experienced in space, and exposure to alien environmental contaminants. These considerations necessitate ongoing engineering and biological interventions to maintain the integrity and functionality of the coatings as conditions evolve.

Ethical considerations also add complexity to the evolution of biological coatings. As living systems are harnessed for military use, questions of ecological impact surface, particularly concerning potential cross-contamination or unintended interactions with natural ecosystems. Developers must establish protocols to ensure that biological coatings do not propagate outside their intended deployments or disrupt local life forms inadvertently. These concerns necessitate a framework for designing containment and ecological safeguards into the coatings from the outset of their creation.

In summary, the testing and evolution of biological coatings emphasize a deeply interconnected process that blends biological research with advanced materials science. The promising advances in coating technologies showcase the adaptability and resilience of living systems, asserting their role as valuable assets in the technological arsenal of future battleships. As we continue to pioneer these innovations, our understanding of their applications will not only redefine warfare but also guide us toward responsibly navigating the ethical dimensions inherent in engineering living systems for military objectives. This ongoing journey—grounded in science, testing, and ethical reflection—will be essential to advancing the capabilities and functionalities of biotechnological innovations designed for the cosmos, ensuring these biological coatings serve both protective and sustainable purposes in interstellar engagements.

5.5. Comparative Analysis: Traditional vs. Biotech

In the contrasting domains of traditional warfare and biotechnology, a transformative narrative unfolds, painting a picture of future interstellar combat that embodies not only technological advancements but also philosophical shifts in how humanity interprets war, life, and conflict. As we delve into the comparative analysis of these two paradigms—traditional military vessels characterized by rigid, metal constructs versus biotech battleships infused with living components

—we uncover a myriad of distinct attributes, advantages, challenges, and implications inherent in each approach.

Traditional military vessels have long been dictating the dynamics of warfare, founded on mechanical and metallic architectures that emphasize strength, durability, and firepower. The evolution of these ships has consistently been tied to advances in materials science and engineering, with battleships forged from steel and aluminum, reinforced with armor plating and armed with an array of conventional weaponry. The design ethos here revolves around predictability and uniformity; war machines are built to withstand the rigors of battle, operating within strict parameters and predetermined functionalities. Furthermore, operating these ships relies heavily on conventional combat strategies that prioritize hardware over adaptive capability.

Conversely, biotech battleships represent a radical departure from this paradigm, introducing a symbiotic relationship between engineering and biology. Integrated with living systems, these advanced vessels harness the inherent capabilities of life, embodying attributes such as self-repair, adaptability, and responsiveness. Living components are not merely added features; they form the operational core that generates resilience in unpredictable situations, enabling the battleships to react in real time to environmental stimuli and enemy actions. For instance, engineered organisms onboard may autonomously activate defense mechanisms or carry out repairs, circumventing the delays incurred by traditional repair protocols.

The advantages associated with biotech battleships manifest in several domains. Firstly, the sustainability of these vessels heralds a new era in logistics for space warfare. With the capability to recycle matter and generate resources from waste biologically, these ships can sustain themselves during extended missions far from supply chains, a stark contrast to traditional vessels reliant on consistent resupply. Moreover, the deployment of energy-efficient biological processes minimizes the overall environmental footprint, presenting an attractive approach for future warfare across the cosmos.

In terms of combat effectiveness, the flexibility and adaptability of biotech ships introduce a significant tactical advantage. The ability to self-repair damages or dynamically adjust defenses makes biotech battleships formidable contenders on shifting battlefields. Unlike their traditional counterparts, which may require extensive downtime for maintenance, these living machines enhance operational longevity, allowing them to remain engaged with the enemy even under severe duress.

However, the shift toward biotechnology is not without hurdles. There are formidable challenges that accompany the development and deployment of biotech battleships. The most pronounced concern revolves around the reliability and predictability of biological systems, which can exhibit inherent variability due to genetic, environmental, and situational factors. Engineers must tread carefully to ensure that biological systems operate effectively as designed—an endeavor that demands extensive testing and validation processes.

Furthermore, safety and containment protocols emerge as paramount considerations. The potential consequences of engineered organisms escaping into untamed ecosystems or undergoing unintended mutations pose ethical and ecological questions. Robust frameworks must be established to ensure control over these living systems, thus avoiding any adverse impacts on the environments into which they are inserted.

The ethical implications of utilizing biotechnology in warfare also demand careful scrutiny. The creation and deployment of living machines raise profound moral dilemmas regarding the respect owed to engineered organisms. As society grapples with these considerations, the dialogue around the responsible use of biotechnology must evolve, striking a balance between military advancement and ethical stewardship.

Despite these challenges, the comparative analysis reveals that the integration of biology into military applications embodies exciting opportunities for innovation. The realm of biotech warfare prompts shifts in military strategy, emphasizing cooperation between biologists, engineers, and military personnel. Interdisciplinary teams will cultivate collaborative design processes that push the boundaries of what is possible, resulting in increasingly integrated and capable warfare vessels.

The reception of this paradigm shift among military planners and the public also plays a vital role, as perceptions often influence funding and political will. Public understanding and acceptance of biotechnological advancements become imperative in shaping the future landscape of warfare.

In conclusion, the exploration of traditional versus biotech warfare encapsulates a profound narrative—a narrative where the definitions of effectiveness, resilience, and responsibility are redefined against a backdrop of living technologies. Biotech battleships do not merely promise improved combat capabilities; they signify how our understanding of war must evolve as we integrate the complexities of life into our machines. As humanity strides into this uncharted territory of interstellar conflict, our ability to navigate the ethical, logistical, and technical challenges of biotechnology will undoubtedly determine the trajectory of future warfare, reshaping both the cosmos and our identity as stewards of both technology and life.

6. Propulsion Systems: Harnessing Life's Power

6.1. The Basics of Space Propulsion

In the realm of space exploration and interstellar conflict, propulsion systems are crucial for the performance, maneuverability, and efficiency of spaceborne vessels. As humanity endeavors to navigate the vast expanses of the cosmos, the need for innovative and effective propulsion technologies intensifies. In the context of biotech battleships, the principles of space propulsion require careful consideration, as traditional engines face significant challenges in the face of the realities of deep space travel. Understanding the fundamental aspects of propulsion, coupled with advancements in biotechnology, can pave the way for revolutionary developments in military applications.

Space propulsion is fundamentally different from propulsion used within the atmospheres of planets. In the vacuum of space, there is no medium for traditional combustion engines to operate effectively. Conventional rockets rely on the expulsion of gas generated from chemical reactions to produce thrust; however, the efficiency and feasibility of such propulsion systems diminish beyond the lower gravitational confines of planetary bodies. In the absence of atmospheric pressures and with the vast distances between celestial bodies, innovative approaches must be considered.

One of the foundational concepts in space propulsion is Newton's Third Law of Motion: for every action, there is an equal and opposite reaction. This principle is at the core of chemical propulsion, where rockets expel combustion gases at high velocities to generate thrust. While successful in many missions, chemical rockets face inherent limitations, particularly in fuel efficiency and the volume of propellant needed for extended journeys. As a result, research into alternative propulsion systems has gained traction, aiming to provide greater efficiency and adaptability for interstellar engagements.

One promising avenue of exploration includes the development of bio-inspired propulsion systems. Nature has long been a source of inspiration for engineering solutions, with various organisms demonstrating effective locomotion strategies that could inform the design of advanced propulsion methods. For example, certain species of jellyfish utilize a unique pulsating motion to propel themselves through their aquatic environments, effectively utilizing the surrounding water for thrust. This principle could inspire the creation of propulsion systems that harness biological mechanisms, allowing for bioengineered organisms to function as living propulsion units or collaborating mechanically with traditional systems.

Moreover, harnessing microbial processes offers exciting prospects for sustainable propulsion technologies. Research into microbial fuel cells—devices that convert chemical energy from organic matter into electrical energy—presents opportunities for vehicles to generate power from their own waste. In the context of biotech battleships, engineered microbes could provide a renewable source of energy for onboard systems, significantly reducing the reliance on traditional fuel supplies and enhancing the sustainability of long-duration missions.

As humanity explores the potential of biotechnology in propulsion systems, the challenges of achieving effective performance within the constraints of current scientific understanding cannot be overlooked. One of the critical obstacles is ensuring the stability and reliability of bioengineered components under the harsh conditions of space. The biological organisms utilized for propulsion must withstand extreme temperatures, radiation levels, and vacuum environments while maintaining functional integrity. To mitigate these risks, engineers must collaborate with biologists to identify organisms that exhibit resilience and develop methods for supporting their viability in the unique conditions of space.

Additionally, understanding the biocompatibility of materials used in propulsion systems will be essential. Any synthetic components incorporated into biological systems must not inhibit the performance of their living counterparts. This presents opportunities for synthetic biology to play a significant role in developing compatible materials that meet the demands of both mechanical and biological functionalities.

Moreover, the integration of artificial intelligence (AI) into propulsion design could offer exceptional adaptability. AI algorithms could analyze real-time feedback from biological systems, optimizing propulsion according to environmental conditions, energy inputs, and even anticipated maneuvers. This dynamic approach could forge new pathways in how propulsion systems are configured for various mission profiles, enhancing overall efficiency and effectiveness.

The application of these design principles demands comprehensive testing and validation. Prototyping bioengineered propulsion systems warrants rigorous simulation and real-world testing to evaluate their performance under varying conditions. Developing metrics for performance measurement will be crucial, allowing designers to assess energy efficiency, thrust capabilities, and responses to unexpected challenges during flight.

As we move further into the era of biotech battleships, the role of propulsion systems requires collaboration across disciplines—bringing together engineers, biologists, physicists, and military strategists. This interdisciplinary approach fosters innovation, leading to the exploration of uncharted territories and novel solutions that can significantly redefine the nature of warfare in the cosmos.

In summary, the basics of space propulsion underscore the principles that govern propulsion mechanisms while integrating new perspectives from biotechnology. Emphasizing sustainability, adaptability, and efficiency shapes the future direction of interstellar travel and military engagement. This exploration is not merely about thrust and maneuverability; it embodies the intricate relationship between life, energy, and technology, paving the way for a new frontier in warfare where human ingenuity is boldly aligned with the mechanisms of the universe. As we navigate this frontier, the innovations derived from the confluence of life sciences and engineering can propel us toward a future replete with possibilities among the stars.

6.2. Biological Engines: The Next Frontier

In the rapidly advancing field of biotechnology, the integration of biological systems into the design and operation of military vessels presents a remarkable opportunity to redefine interstellar warfare. Grounded in the principles of biological engineering, living armor and its various applications illustrate how innovative approaches can enhance the resilience, adaptability, and overall functionality of future battleships. This venture into developing living armor marks a turning point, pushing the boundaries of traditional defense systems toward an era characterized by dynamic, responsive technologies capable of healing and evolving.

Living armor embodies the synergy between biological materials and mechanical structures, fostering a protective layer that not only withstands physical impacts but also exhibits the extraordinary ability to self-repair. At the forefront of this development lies the exploration of organisms renowned for their regenerative abilities. For instance, examining the cellular structure of certain amphibians that can regenerate limbs informs our understanding of how to create advanced materials capable of healing wounds. Through careful genetic modification and engineering, it becomes feasible to incorporate these biological functions into armor designed for military purposes.

The principles of synthetic biology play a pivotal role in advancing living armor. By employing cutting-edge techniques such as CRISPR gene editing, scientists can craft organisms tailored for specific protective functions. The prospect of embedding cells that can produce protective secretions or rapidly replicate in response to a breach transforms the landscape of military shielding. Living armor is envisioned to deploy biochemical agents upon sustaining damage, effectively patching vulnerabilities in real-time—this dynamic capability stands in stark contrast to traditional armor, which necessitates significant downtime for repairs.

Considering the ecological implications, the development of living armor must address both biosecurity and ethical questions surrounding the manipulation of life forms for military applications. The potential for engineered organisms to escape into the environment or undergo unforeseen mutations necessitates establishing robust containment measures, ensuring these systems remain controlled and do not disrupt local ecosystems. The ethical discourse surrounding the treatment of engineered life forms mandates a framework for responsibility, guiding military entities in their deployment of such technologies.

Integrating living systems into armor introduces a paradigm shift not merely in protective technologies but in broader military strategies. The dynamic nature of living armor fosters enhanced survivability during engagements, allowing battleships to quickly recover from assaults while remaining operational. Furthermore, living armor can adapt to a variety of threats, providing an added layer of versatility in combat scenarios.

Comparatively, living armor challenges long-standing notions of what constitutes military protection, raising philosophical questions about the role of life in warfare. These conversations reflect society's evolving understanding of how technology can interface with the living world, shaping public perception and acceptance of bioengineering in military contexts.

Testing and validation of living armor are paramount to its implementation. Rigorous experimental protocols must replicate battlefield conditions, evaluating not only the physical protective traits of these living materials but also their interactions under various environmental stresses. As research progresses, data gleaned from testing will inform iterative design processes, enabling continuous improvement of living armor's capabilities.

In summary, the concept of living armor represents a remarkable frontier in biotechnology, merging the resilience of living organisms with the structural integrity of traditional materials. This innovative approach offers militaries unprecedented opportunities to enhance survivability, adaptability, and resource efficiency in combat scenarios. As we continue our journey into this realm, fostering interdisciplinary collaboration among scientists, engineers, and strategists becomes indispensable, ensuring that developments in living armor align with ethical considerations and environmental stewardship. The future of military technology reshaped by living systems invites a reconsideration of our relationship with the technologies we create, and it poses a pivotal question: how will we responsibly integrate life with warfare as we journey into the cosmos?

6.3. Sustainable Energy and Biotechnology

As we navigate the evolving landscape of warfare and technology, the intersection of sustainable energy and biotechnology becomes increasingly paramount in shaping the future of military capabilities. In a universe where prolonged missions and resource scarcity are prevalent, integrating sustainable energy solutions into the design and operation of biotech battleships offers not just operational advantages, but also a commitment to environmental responsibility and resource efficiency.

Biotechnology harnesses the unique characteristics of living organisms to create systems that can generate energy sustainably. One prominent approach involves the utilization of biofuel cells, leveraging microbial processes to convert organic matter into usable energy. These systems can metabolize waste produced by crew members, transforming it into biofuels that power various onboard systems. Such an approach not only diminishes the environmental footprint of military operations but also addresses crucial logistical challenges associated with resupply during long interstellar missions.

The development of bioengineered organisms that can produce energy from sunlight or chemical processes offers another exciting avenue for sustainable energy. Photosynthetic microorganisms, for instance, could be employed to convert solar energy into chemical energy, effectively allowing battleships to harness and utilize solar power even in the farthest reaches of space. The ability to establish onboard ecosystems that facilitate this energy conversion presents opportunities for long-duration self-sustaining missions, significantly enhancing operational autonomy.

Furthermore, advancements in synthetic biology enable the design of energy-producing organisms that can adapt to varying environmental conditions. Engineers can modify metabolic pathways within these organisms to optimize energy output based on fluctuating demands, ensuring that the battleship always has the necessary power while minimizing waste. This adaptability is particularly critical in unpredictable combat scenarios, where energy demand can spike unexpectedly.

Sustainability extends beyond energy generation; it encompasses the cyclic use of resources within the living systems onboard the battleships. Closed-loop life support systems mirror ecosystems on Earth, recycling waste products into usable forms—much like nature's nutrient cycles. Such systems can incorporate bioreactors that convert carbon dioxide and waste into oxygen and biomass, creating an environment where the ship's crew can thrive with minimal external support. This self-sufficiency drastically reduces the need for resupply missions, allowing ships to remain operational longer in hostile territories.

Additionally, the integration of biotechnology into energy systems promotes resilience. Living organisms have evolved mechanisms to withstand harsh environments and exploit available resources effectively. By leveraging these biological strategies, military designs can prioritize systems that not only provide substantial energy outputs but are also capable of self-repair and adaptation, enhancing the onboard systems' longevity and reducing maintenance downtime.

The intersections of engineering and biology foster innovative designs that prioritize energy efficiency. For instance, bio-inspired materials developed using principles from nature can optimize energy consumption and minimize waste in various systems. By analyzing how organisms achieve energy efficiency in their habitats, engineers can replicate these strategies in the design of military vessels.

While the promises of sustainable energy and biotechnology are substantial, several challenges loom on the horizon. One notable concern is the reliability of biological systems under varying conditions commonly encountered in space travel. Rigorous testing is essential to ensure that bioengineered organisms can withstand the rigors of interstellar travel and combat environments. Moreover, thorough assessments of how these organisms will interact with mechanical systems must be conducted to ensure operational compatibility and efficiency.

Furthermore, biosecurity remains a critical consideration. Guarding against unintended consequences such as bioengineered organisms escaping into the environment poses significant risks. Developers must institute fail-safe mechanisms that prevent unintended proliferation, ensuring that living systems remain controllable and safe under all conditions.

The ethical implications of harnessing biotechnology for energy generation in warfare also require careful scrutiny. As we ponder the manipulation of life for military objectives, conversations surrounding the rights of engineered organisms and their ecological impacts come to the forefront. Establishing ethical guidelines will be paramount to navigate these complexities and secure public trust in the deployment of biotechnologies in combat scenarios.

In conclusion, the integration of sustainable energy solutions powered by biotechnology stands as a transformative frontier in the design and operation of future biotech battleships. By harnessing the potential of living systems to meet energy demands sustainably, militaries can significantly enhance their operational capabilities while adhering to principles of environmental responsibility. As the research progresses, ongoing collaboration between biologists, engineers, and military strategists will be essential to address the challenges that accompany these innovations, guiding us towards a future where sustainable energy systems fundamentally reshape the nature of warfare in the cosmos. The promise of biotech energies presents a potential paradigm shift—a sustainable yet effective answer to the ever-evolving demands of warfare, environmental stewardship, and the responsible harnessing of life.

6.4. Limitations and Overcoming Challenges

The deployment of biotechnology in warfare is not without its inherent limitations and challenges, which must be carefully navigated to unlock the potential of biotech battleships designed for intergalactic combat. As technology evolves, so too do the complications surrounding its application, and understanding these hurdles is crucial for advancing the field responsibly.

One of the primary limitations stems from the unpredictable nature of biological systems. Unlike traditional mechanical systems, which operate according to fixed principles, biological components can exhibit a high degree of variability. Changes in environmental conditions, such as temperature, radiation, or pressure fluctuations in space, can affect the functions of living organisms onboard. This unpredictability presents challenges for military applications, where reliability and performance consistency are paramount. Engineers and scientists must collaborate closely to develop robust biological models, engage in extensive testing, and continually refine genetic modifications to ensure that living systems can withstand the rigors of combat without compromising functionality.

Another significant challenge lies in ensuring biosecurity and containment of engineered organisms. The introduction of living systems aboard battleships raises concerns regarding possible unintended consequences, such as organisms gaining the ability to proliferate uncontrollably or escape into the environment. These scenarios could have dire ecological implications, leading to potential ecological disruptions or interactions with local ecosystems. To mitigate these risks, strict containment protocols, fail-safe mechanisms, and ethical guidelines must be established. Developing synthetic control systems that can limit the growth or spread of engineered organisms is crucial for ensuring responsible deployment of biotechnologies in warfare.

In addition to ecological considerations, the ethical implications of employing biotechnology in warfare are complex and multifaceted. The manipulation of living systems for military objectives raises moral questions about the rights of engineered organisms, the nature of warfare, and the responsibilities of military entities. Society must engage in open dialogues to establish ethical frameworks that guide the development and use of biotech innovations in a manner that reflects shared values and the intrinsic value of life itself. These discussions become increasingly important in a world where public perception can significantly influence military policy and funding.

Training human operators to work alongside living systems also presents challenges. Future commanders and crew members will need to develop interdisciplinary skills that encompass both techno-logical proficiency and an understanding of biological principles. This necessity underscores the importance of creating comprehensive training programs that foster a deep understanding of the biological components integrated into battleships. By cultivating an operational culture that values adaptability and interdisciplinary collaboration, militaries will be better equipped to leverage living systems in combat.

Moreover, the integration of artificial intelligence (AI) to facilitate human-machine interactions introduces additional challenges. Devel-oping AI systems capable of managing, monitoring, and analyzing the performance of biological components requires careful calibra-tion and testing to ensure reliable operation. Furthermore, ethical concerns regarding the autonomy of AI systems and their role in decision-making must be thoroughly examined, particularly when these systems interact with living organisms.

To overcome these challenges, collaborative efforts across multiple disciplines—biology, engineering, ethics, and military strategy—will be critical. Successful outcomes will hinge on adaptive research methodologies, rigorous testing protocols, and continuous feedback loops that refine both biological and mechanical functionalities. Emphasizing iterative design processes allows for corrections and im-provements based on real-time data and field experiences, ultimately translating to biotech battleships that are robust, reliable, and effec-tive in the complexities of interstellar combat.

A proactive approach is essential in addressing the limitations of biotechnology in warfare. By fostering an environment that encourages innovation while prioritizing ethical considerations, societies can develop responsible frameworks that support the effective and safe integration of biotech systems. The journey toward fully realizing the potential of biotech battleships is one that demands vigilance, interdisciplinary cooperation, and a conscientious commitment to shaping the future of warfare—a future where biology and technology harmoniously coexist as vital elements driving military advancements.

Finally, as we embark on this exploration of biotechnology in warfare, learning from past successes and failures, bridging the gap between research and practical application, and maintaining an ethical compass will be paramount. The roadmap ahead involves not just overcoming present challenges but also envisioning a future where biotech innovations enhance military capabilities while reflecting a profound respect for life and the environment. It is through these efforts that we can ensure that the next generation of intergalactic war machines represents not only technological prowess but also a testament to humanity's ability to harmonize advancement with responsibility.

6.5. Field Tests and Real-World Applications

In the rapidly evolving arena of military technology, the integration of biological systems into the design and operation of biotech battleships not only signifies a transformative shift in warfare strategy but also embodies complex layers of real-world applications that merit careful exploration. As we journey through the implications of these innovations, it becomes evident that testing and field applications serve as the bedrock for validating the potential of biotech designs, ensuring that they meet the multifaceted demands of intergalactic conflict.

The process of field testing biotech innovations is essential for moving from theoretical designs to practical applications. In military scenarios, the stakes are incredibly high; thus, ensuring that these advanced vessels perform consistently and reliably is of paramount importance. Field tests provide critical insights into how biological systems operate under the rigors of combat, revealing the strengths and weaknesses of integrated living components. These assessments typically begin in controlled environments, where prototypes can endure simulations reflecting a range of combat scenarios and spatial extremes.

Through iterative testing, engineers and scientists can identify points of failure and areas for improvement, which in turn inform the design revisions needed for real-world application. For example, if certain bioengineered organisms fail to exhibit the expected self-repair capabilities under simulated impacts, modifications can be made, whether it's changing genetic configurations or rethinking the environmental conditions required for optimal performance.

Real-world applications extend beyond mere performance metrics; they encompass the operational readiness of these biotech battleships in actual combat situations. During military exercises or even theoretical engagements with opposing forces, the interactions between biological systems and traditional military technology can lead to valuable lessons. For instance, engineers can assess how living materials react to weapon impacts or corrosive environments, thus helping to refine the dual-purpose functionality of bio-integrated constructs.

Field applications also address the tactical implications of deploying biotech battleships in the context of strategy and field effectiveness. The ability to adapt rapidly to evolving threats or environmental changes can shift the tides of combat. Observing how crews interact with the living components onboard provides insights into operational logistics and crew training. Understanding human-biology interaction becomes essential—military personnel must be trained not only to operate machinery but also to collaborate with living systems that may behave unpredictably.

Ethical considerations arise prominently throughout both testing and real-world applications, amplifying the need for proactive governance and risk management. The conscious deployment of genetically modified organisms in conflict raises profound questions about the moral implications of utilizing life forms as tools of war. Field tests serve as a litmus test for ethical boundaries; if engineered organisms demonstrate unexpected behaviors that jeopardize ecological balance or civilian safety, these outcomes must be scrutinized. This introspection underscores the necessity for preemptive ethical guidelines prior to large-scale deployment.

Moreover, the challenges associated with maintaining control over living systems form another integral dimension of field testing. The specter of potential ecological disruption due to engineered life forms escaping into the environment must be addressed thoroughly and systematically. Developing containment measures during testing can help safeguard against risks, fostering a culture of responsibility among military stakeholders.

Real-world applications are also informed by cross-sector collaborations, merging military research with insights from biotech industries, academia, and environmental sciences. Collaborative symposia can yield breakthroughs that shape the design and deployment of biotechnology in warfare. Engaging with multifaceted perspectives encourages holistic approaches, enabling innovative solutions that are sound not only technologically but also ethically and ecologically.

As we continue exploring field tests and real-world applications, it becomes clear that the path to successful deployment of biotech battleships hinges on forging robust connections between testing environments and genuine military engagements. The culmination of knowledge gleaned from these experiences paves the way for responsible innovation and the advancement of military capabilities.

Looking ahead, the future of warfare characterized by biotech battleships will demand a collaborative ethos—uniting engineers, biologists, ethicists, and military leaders in a shared endeavor to realize the extraordinary potential of merging biological and technological realms. The lessons learned through field tests and practical applications will not only shape the next generation of war machines but also redefine humanity's engagement with technology, life, and the cosmos. As we navigate the complexities ahead, maintaining a proactive approach to ethics, responsibility, and collaboration will be vital for ensuring these advancements serve the greater good. The transformative nature of these innovations invites consideration, not just in terms of their military applications, but in how they challenge our understanding of conflict, responsibility, and the intricate role of life within the framework of warfare.

7. Weaponry: The Offensive Edge of Biotech Battleships

7.1. Biotechnologically Enhanced Weapon Systems

As humanity strides into the uncharted territories of interstellar warfare, the emergence of biotechnologically enhanced weapon systems signals a transformative shift in military strategy. Unlike traditional armaments that rely solely on mechanical construction, these advanced solutions interlace biological components with cutting-edge technology to create weaponry that is flexible, adaptable, and capable of remarkable precision. This integration of living systems can provide unparalleled advantages in combat scenarios, promising to redefine the capabilities of tomorrow's battleships.

At the heart of these biotechnological weapon systems lies the potential for weapons that can adapt their characteristics and functions based on real-time battlefield conditions. The intrinsic adaptability of biological systems allows for weaponry that can modify its performance parameters, adjusting to environmental changes or enemy tactics on the fly. Imagine a guided missile with the ability to sense incoming signals and self-adjust its trajectory based on shifting wind patterns or obstructions, enhancing its likelihood of success. This level of sophistication not only maximizes effectiveness but also minimizes collateral damage—making strikes more precise and controlled than ever before.

Through genetic engineering and synthetic biology, weapons can be designed to produce or harness biologically derived materials that exhibit unique properties conducive to warfare. Bioengineered projectiles, for instance, could be equipped with neural networks that link to artificial intelligence systems. As a projectile travels through the air, it communicates with the ship and receives data on the target, enabling it to optimize its path, speed, and impact effect during flight. Such weapon systems would significantly enhance operational efficacy in fluid combat scenarios.

Precision weaponry can be further boosted through biologic guidance. Integrated systems composed of organisms capable of sensing and responding to stimuli could lead to a new category of smart munitions. For example, weapons could utilize genetically modified microorganisms designed to detect specific chemical signatures or heat profiles of enemy vehicles. Upon identifying a target—be it organic or metallic—these organisms could communicate their findings back to the weapon system. The result would be a tactical strike unleashing projectiles aimed not only with pinpoint accuracy but also with a layer of biological intelligence. This strategic advantage transforms engagement rules; enemy forces would need to contend not just with physical attacks but also with living, responsive weaponry.

Safety considerations remain paramount as the integration of biotechnologically enhanced weapon systems unfolds. The creation and deployment of living offensive capabilities invoke significant ethical and quantitative challenges, particularly concerning risk management. Understanding the potential repercussions of releasing engineered organisms into combat scenarios is critical. Stringent guidelines and protocols must be established to govern their use—ensuring that such organisms do not inadvertently cause ecological damage, or more crucially, pose risks to military personnel or civilian populations. The implementation of fail-safe mechanisms and monitoring protocols would be essential to maintaining control over these unpredictable living entities.

The potential for innovation within this domain continues to expand exponentially. Future iterations of biotechnologically enhanced weapons may harness advanced capabilities that transcend traditional bounds. For instance, emerging technologies could yield munitions equipped with regenerative biological components that repair themselves after being damaged, allowing for sustained effectiveness throughout extended engagements. These innovations will not only change the landscape of weaponry but could also alter the nature of conflict itself, leading to evolving tactics that leverage the advantages inherent in biological systems.

Moreover, the collaborative design of biotechnologically enhanced weapon systems necessitates a concerted effort between scientists, engineers, and military personnel. This interdisciplinary approach fosters an environment where biological and mechanical innovations coexist, ensuring that designs are optimized for performance while remaining grounded in ethical considerations. The complexities of blending life forms with military hardware underscore the importance of nurturing robust collaborative channels that accommodate diverse viewpoints and expertise—ultimately enhancing the end product's effectiveness and safety.

In conclusion, biotechnologically enhanced weapon systems represent a groundbreaking shift in our approach to warfare. By fusing the adaptability and responsiveness of biological components with advanced technology, we set the stage for a new era of precision and effectiveness in military applications. The road ahead will require careful navigation of ethical, safety, and operational challenges, but the potential for creating living, adaptive weapons offers a tantalizing glimpse into the future of conflict. As we stand on the brink of this revolutionary transformation, the ability to harness the capabilities of life within our systems poses profound questions about humanity's relationship with both warfare and the living world—an inquiry that will guide our innovation toward responsible and effective applications in the cosmos.

7.2. Adaptive Armament: Characteristics and Development

In the realm of intergalactic warfare, the concept of adaptive armament represents a significant evolution in weaponry, integrating biological principles with advanced technology to create systems capable of responding dynamically to various combat scenarios. This innovative approach signifies a departure from traditional mechanical weaponry toward a more fluid and adaptive design ethos that can enhance both offensive and defensive capabilities in the ever-changing landscape of warfare.

At the core of adaptive armament lies the idea of flexibility—systems that can adjust their functions and characteristics in real-time based on environmental conditions and tactical needs. This adaptability can be realized by leveraging genetically engineered organisms that exhibit specific functional traits, allowing weapons to modify their behaviors during engagements. For instance, projectiles might be developed to possess biological sensors capable of detecting the movement or presence of enemy forces, enabling them to alter their trajectories or even change their composition for maximum impact.

The development of adaptive armament encompasses several critical components. First, biological systems can imbue weaponry with self-healing properties, significantly extending the lifespan and effectiveness of munitions. Weapons designed with living materials might be able to repair themselves upon sustaining damage, ensuring that they remain operational even after enduring impacts during a skirmish. This self-repair capability mirrors processes observable in nature, where organisms demonstrate resilience through regenerative mechanisms.

Moreover, biotechnologically enhanced weapon systems can incorporate feedback loops that draw data from their operational environment. By employing artificial intelligence (AI) algorithms, these systems can learn from experiences, allowing them to refine their performance over time. An adaptive armament could analyze battlefield conditions, enemy tactics, and even their own effectiveness mid-operation, leading to optimized responses tailored to the moment. Such capabilities would not only enhance the precision of attacks but also minimize resource waste by ensuring each engagement is conducted with maximum efficiency.

Further experimentation with biologically derived projectiles could yield advancements in weapon efficacy and versatility. For example, bioengineered materials could enable projectiles to deploy secondary effects upon impact, such as releasing biologically engineered agents that can incapacitate enemy systems or reinforce defensive positions. This transformative potential of adaptive armament highlights how biological innovation can introduce novel operational paradigms to traditional warfare.

Despite the promise of adaptive armament, its development is not without significant challenges. Foremost among these is the necessity for rigorous testing and validation to ensure reliability and predictability. Biological systems, while adaptable, can also exhibit variability and unpredictability; ensuring that these systems function consistently under combat conditions is crucial. Addressing this challenge necessitates the establishment of controlled experimental frameworks that can adequately simulate the dynamic conditions of warfare while evaluating the effectiveness of adaptive weapon systems.

Safety considerations are also paramount. The deployment of biotechnologically enhanced weaponry raises questions about containment and the potential for unintended consequences. Carefully designed regulations must govern the use of living systems in combat scenarios, ensuring that the release of engineered organisms does not lead to ecological imbalances or threats to non-combatants. Developing transparent protocols for monitoring and controlling these systems will be essential to mitigate risks and garner public trust in their use.

Ethical considerations further complicate the development of adaptive armament. As society grapples with the moral implications of integrating living systems into warfare, open dialogues surrounding the rights of these engineered organisms and their place in the military domain must be prioritized. Establishing robust ethical guidelines will help navigate the complexities and responsibilities associated with wielding biotechnological innovations, balancing military objectives against the imperative to protect life and maintain ecological integrity.

Looking forward, the potential for adaptive armament in intergalactic warfare reflects a broader vision of merging biological systems with military technologies. As researchers and military strategists embark on this journey, fostering collaboration across disciplines will be critical. By engaging biologists, engineers, ethicists, and military leaders alike, we can harness the full spectrum of knowledge available—ensuring the development of weapon systems that are not only effective but also aligned with our ethical and ecological responsibilities.

In summary, the emergence of adaptive armament signifies a transformative shift in the nature of warfare that integrates biology with weaponry. This evolution promises to extend the capabilities of intergalactic combat systems, emphasizing flexibility, resilience, and precision. As we stand on the cusp of this remarkable frontier, it is our collective responsibility to navigate the challenges and ethical implications of such innovations, ensuring their development serves the greater good while redefining warfare for future generations.

7.3. Precision Weaponry and Biologic Guidance

In the realm of contemporary warfare, the integration of biotechnology into weapon systems heralds a new age of combat lethality and strategic advantage. This chapter delves into the multifaceted domain of precision weaponry and biologic guidance, exploring the transformational potential that living systems offer to traditional military strategies. As the scope of intergalactic warfare expands, understanding the principles and applications of these advanced technologies becomes imperative to grasp how they will reshape combat mechanics.

At the core of precision weaponry lies the ability to deliver ordnance with unparalleled accuracy. Traditional weapons often rely on mechanical methods that, while effective, can lack the fine-tuned responsiveness needed in complex environments. By leveraging biological systems, new contenders emerge—a blend of organic intelligence and mechanical precision that could redefine targeting and strike capabilities.

The concept of biologic guidance involves utilizing living organisms —either engineered or modified—to enhance the intelligent response of weapon systems. These organisms can serve as biological sensors, capable of detecting chemical signatures, physical movements, or environmental changes that holographic and electronic systems may overlook. Imagine a missile equipped with genetically engineered microorganisms that react to heat emitted by enemy machinery; upon detection, the missile would autonomously adjust its course, ensuring an optimal strike without human intervention.

The precision of these biologically guided missiles is not solely based on the organic systems they embody but also on the embedding of artificial intelligence algorithms that interpret data and synchronize with the biological components. By melding machine learning with living sensors, the weapon system can adapt in real-time, enhancing its effectiveness in rapidly changing combat situations. Such firearms not only promise to reduce collateral damage but also increase operational effectiveness, pushing the limits of traditional warfare.

Understanding the dynamics of biological interactions is critical when designing these hybrid systems. The chosen organisms must be compatible with the mechanical apparatus, ensuring that both components communicate seamlessly. Engineers and biologists must collaborate extensively to create interfaces that facilitate these interactions, driven by rigorous testing to validate functional capacities under combat scenarios.

Moreover, the potential for biologically adaptive munitions stretches beyond mere guidance systems. Future innovations may yield projectiles that can change composition or caliber upon release. Drawing inspiration from living organisms that can adapt to their environments, such projectiles could possess polymers capable of altering shape or density as necessary, depending on the target type—be it soft-skinned or armored vehicles. Thus, precision weaponry becomes more than just a means of inflicting damage; it evolves into a strategic instrument capable of responding intelligently to battlefield dynamics.

Yet, as with any technological advancement, developing precision weaponry and biologic guidance systems brings with it a host of considerations. Chief among these is safety. Biological systems inherently come with unpredictability; detailed assessment protocols must be established to monitor the performance and behavior of these organisms in active combat. Ensuring that these living capabilities cannot go rogue—either by self-replicating beyond control or by transmitting unintended responses—will require stringent operational control measures and fail-safes embedded within the weapon systems.

Furthermore, ethical considerations emerge prominently as the integration of living systems into weaponry and warfare becomes a reality. The manipulation of life for military purposes raises questions about the rights of engineered organisms, the moral implications of utilizing living entities as tools for destruction, and the consequences of ecological disruption. Establishing robust ethical guidelines that govern the deployment and use of such weapon systems will be critical for maintaining oversight while advancing military capabilities.

The nature of precision weaponry and biologic guidance also demands a reevaluation of training programs for operators. As personnel engage with advanced systems that harness the capabilities of living organisms, understanding biological principles becomes essential. Future training protocols will need to encompass interdisciplinary knowledge that prepares crew members to interact effectively with both mechanical and organic components, developing a new breed of operator skilled in leveraging hybrid technologies.

Strategic deployment of these weapon systems necessitates a cultural shift within military organizations. Traditional ranks and procedures must adapt to accommodate the interdisciplinary collaboration required for successful integration. By forging pathways for engineers, biologists, military strategists, and ethics experts to work together, militaries can harness the full breadth of potential offered by biotechnologically enhanced weaponry.

In conclusion, precision weaponry and biologic guidance sit at the intersection of biology and advanced military technology, promising to redefine traditional notions of combat effectiveness. As we embark on this exploration of living technologies, we must embrace the complexity and responsibilities that accompany these innovations. By fostering collaborative dialogue, ethical oversight, and rigorous testing, we propel ourselves into an era where skills, strategy, and life converge—ultimately shaping the future of warfare among the stars. The potential for precision in biotechnologically driven combat systems not only creates new tactical avenues but also challenges our understanding of life, responsibility, and the very fabric of war itself.

7.4. Safety Considerations and Risk Management

In the realm of intergalactic warfare, the safety considerations and risk management surrounding the integration of biotech into battle vessels are of paramount importance. The inclusion of living organisms in military applications presents a unique set of challenges that differ significantly from traditional weaponry. As we explore the implications of these advanced designs, it is essential to balance the benefits of biotechnology with rigorous safety protocols and ethical guidelines.

First and foremost, safety considerations in biotech battleships begin with the understanding that the unpredictability of biological systems introduces inherent risks. Unlike conventional machinery operating according to established physical laws, living organisms can exhibit unexpected behavior due to various biological and environmental factors. This variability heightens concerns regarding reliability—especially in combat scenarios where performance consistency is critical. Therefore, thorough testing and iterative design processes must be implemented to mitigate risks associated with biological components. Prototyping and rigorous evaluations under simulated combat conditions are necessary to assess the functionality of living systems under stress, revealing potential vulnerabilities that could compromise operational integrity.

Effective containment strategies are vital in managing the inherent risks associated with employing biological agents in warfare. The potential for genetically engineered organisms to proliferate uncontrollably or escape into the environment poses serious ecological threats. Engineers and biologists must collaborate to design robust containment systems that ensure living components remain confined and regulated during operation. Innovations such as self-limiting genetic circuits and fail-safe mechanisms could serve as critical safeguards, allowing military advisors to deploy these living systems with confidence while minimizing ecological disruptions.

Moreover, rigorous biosecurity protocols need to be established to prevent bioengineered organisms from being weaponized by adversaries or misused beyond intended applications. This involves creating legal frameworks that delineate the acceptable uses of biotechnology in warfare, alongside mechanisms for monitoring compliance and enforcing regulations. By developing comprehensive strategies that govern the deployment and management of biotechnological innovations, military leaders can reduce the potential for misuse while ensuring responsible stewardship of living systems.

Effective training processes also play a crucial role in safety considerations and risk management in biotech battleships. Military personnel must receive specialized training that encompasses the operation of biological systems, fostering an understanding of how to interact responsibly with living components. By equipping soldiers with the knowledge necessary to manage these systems, the military can enhance operational efficiency while ensuring that personnel are prepared for the complexities of engaging with biotechnology.

In this context, the psychological implications of warfare involving living systems cannot be overlooked. As soldiers encounter biologically integrated technologies, the mental challenges posed by operating alongside living organisms require careful consideration. Military organizations must prioritize the mental well-being of personnel trained to use biotech systems, offering psychological support and preparing them to navigate the uncertainties associated with life in warfare. Building resilience in crew members through adaptive training regimens and mental health resources can mitigate the stresses of operating within such unique combat environments.

Ethical considerations demand equal emphasis in the narrative of safety and risk management. The manipulation of life for military objectives raises profound moral questions about the treatment of engineered organisms and their potential consequences. Establishing ethical guidelines is essential, fostering robust discussions about the responsibility associated with developing, deploying, and managing living technologies in warfare. By engaging in dialogue with scientists, ethicists, and military strategists, societies can devise responsible frameworks that position the advancement of biotechnology alongside a commitment to preserving life.

The necessity for transparency with the public cannot be understated. Clear communication regarding how biotechnology will be used in military contexts helps build trust with society. It is crucial to address public concerns surrounding biosecurity and the ethical implications of deploying living systems in warfare. By fostering an environment of informed dialogue, a broader understanding of the benefits and risks associated with biotechnological advancements can be established.

In summary, safety considerations and risk management are integral to the successful integration of biotechnology into battleships designed for intergalactic warfare. A multi-faceted approach combining rigorous testing, containment strategies, comprehensive training, ethical guidelines, and transparent communication will serve to ensure that the promises of biotechnology align with responsible military practices. As we bridge the divide between biology and technology in the pursuit of advanced warfare capabilities, it becomes evident that safety and ethics must be woven into the fabric of these innovations, guiding the evolution of combat as we venture into the cosmos.

7.5. Future Innovations in Biotech Weaponry

In an era marked by rapid advancements in biotechnology, the future of weaponry is poised for a remarkable transformation that could redefine the landscape of warfare. As research and development merge biological systems with traditional military technology, we find ourselves at the threshold of biotechnologically enhanced weapons that promise unprecedented adaptability, precision, and operational capability. These innovations are not mere enhancements of existing weapons but rather a leap into a realm where life itself becomes an integral component of military strategy.

One of the most compelling aspects of these future innovations is the ability to create weapon systems that can learn and evolve. By integrating living organisms into targeting systems, weaponry could be designed to respond intelligently to real-time battlefield conditions. For instance, imagine a missile that utilizes genetically modified microorganisms capable of sensing heat signatures, allowing it to home in on a target with unparalleled accuracy. In such a scenario, the organic components not only enhance the missile's guidance systems but also allow for autonomous adjustments during flight—drastically increasing the likelihood of a successful strike while minimizing collateral damage.

Beyond precision, the adaptability of biotechnologically enhanced weapon systems offers significant operational advantages. Traditional weapons are generally limited by fixed capabilities, requiring designers to predict and account for all possible combat scenarios in advance. In contrast, enhanced weaponry harnesses biological systems' ability to react and adapt to unforeseen circumstances. This adaptability could prove invaluable in fluid combat environments, where conditions shift dramatically in response to enemy maneuvers or environmental factors. With such capabilities, military planners could deploy strategies that leverage the inherent resilience of organic components, allowing support units to adapt their role based on evolving battlefield dynamics.

Moreover, the fusion of biology and technology extends to creating new types of munitions that can regenerate or repair themselves after sustaining damage. Drawing inspiration from nature, scientists explore materials that mimic the healing properties of various organisms. By embedding these regenerative capabilities into projectiles, weapons could maintain their effectiveness throughout engagements, reducing the logistical burden associated with resupplying physical assets. As these technologies mature, we may witness the emergence of entirely new paradigms of engagement in warfare—where the concept of "defeat" morphs into an opportunity for recovery and resilience.

However, the potential benefits of biotechnologically enhanced weapon systems must be viewed within the context of ethical responsibility and ecological stewardship. Engaging with living systems in military applications raises profound moral questions surrounding the treatment of engineered organisms and the potential risks of their deployment. Developers of such technologies must establish comprehensive guidelines to govern their use, ensuring that the manipulation of life aligns with principles of respect and ecological balance. The military's integration of these capabilities should not overshadow the pressing need for responsibility.

Safety protocols will play a crucial role in the development and implementation of these weapon systems. Effective containment mechanisms must be designed to prevent the unintended release of engineered organisms into the environment. These procedures will become increasingly important in conflict scenarios, where the risks associated with unanticipated biological behaviors could have significant consequences.

Public perception surrounding the use of biotechnology in warfare presents yet another hurdle to navigate. As societies grapple with the implications of deploying living systems as weapons, transparency and dialogue will be essential for fostering trust. Engaging communities in conversations about the goals, benefits, and risks associated with biotechnologically enhanced weapon systems will be necessary for gaining acceptance and support.

Additionally, the speed of technological advances necessitates agile training programs for military personnel. Future commanders and operators must be conversant with biological principles and competent in managing living systems that may exhibit unpredictable behavior. This requires developing robust training modalities that emphasize both technical proficiency and biological understanding while enhancing adaptability to organic interactions.

As we map the evolution of biotechnologically enhanced weaponry, it becomes clear that the future is rife with possibilities. The integration of living systems into military applications signals the dawn of a new era characterized by unprecedented opportunities and challenges. This journey towards innovation necessitates a commitment to ethics, transparency, and interdisciplinary collaboration. Ultimately, the successful realization of biotechnologically enhanced weaponry will shape not only the future of warfare but also our understanding of the delicate relationship between life and technology in a universe where the boundaries continue to blur.

As we continue to contemplate the implications of these innovations, we invite ourselves to ponder how we will wield the power of biotechnology in our quest for security and stability among the stars, understanding that the intersections of life and technology may hold the keys to our future—one that must be approached with both awe and responsibility.

8. The Crew and Command: Human and Organic Interactions

8.1. Training Requirements for Biotech Operators

In the age of biotechnology, the role of operators in managing complex systems—especially those blending organic and mechanical components—is pivotal. Training requirements for biotech operators are not merely an extension of traditional military training but a multidimensional program that encompasses a deep understanding of biological systems, technical skills in operating advanced weaponry, and the ability to adapt to rapidly changing conditions on the battle-field. As the military transitions to incorporating living organisms into its arsenal, the competencies required for operators must expand to reflect this new paradigm.

To begin, operators must develop a solid foundation in the biological sciences. Understanding the principles of genetics, microbiology, and ecology will be critical for anyone tasked with commanding a biotech battleship. This foundational knowledge empowers operators to manage living systems effectively, allowing them to interpret how biological organisms behave under various environmental stresses and combat conditions. Training programs should include coursework in cellular biology and genetic engineering, providing operators with the skills they need to diagnose and troubleshoot issues that may arise from biological systems on board.

Moreover, operators must develop technical skills to interface with advanced machinery integrated with biological components. This requires familiarity with both the engineering aspects of the battleship's mechanical systems and the biological functions of the organisms involved. Operators will need training in bioengineering principles, equipping them with the expertise to understand how to work with bio-integrated systems and ensure the smooth functioning of machinery reliant on biological inputs. For instance, they must know how to monitor and adjust the environmental conditions essential for the organisms' viability within the ship, such as temperature and humidity levels, to optimize performance.

Hands-on practical experience will also be essential. Simulated training exercises that mimic real-world scenarios can help operators develop the leadership and decision-making skills necessary for high-pressure situations. These simulations should encompass both combat operations and the management of biological systems. For example, operators may face situations requiring them to determine the best course of action in the event of a biological system malfunction during an engagement, assessing the situation and working quickly to implement corrective measures to ensure operational continuity.

Additionally, considering the unpredictability of living systems, operators need to cultivate adaptability and resilience. Rigorous psychological preparedness training can enhance their ability to respond to unforeseen challenges that arise from the inherent variability of biological organisms. Such training may include resilience workshops, crisis management drills, and exercises in adaptive leadership. By fostering a mindset that embraces flexibility and problem-solving, operators will be better equipped to make critical decisions in rapidly evolving combat environments.

The interplay between human operators and artificial intelligence (AI) systems introduces another layer of complexity. Operators will work closely with AI-based systems designed to enhance operational efficiency, providing recommendations based on real-time data from biological sources. Consequently, operators must be trained to understand AI's functionalities and limitations, granting them the ability to manage intuitively the cooperation between organic and mechanical components effectively. This will involve ongoing training in data analytics and the operation of AI interfaces, equipping operators with the skills to interpret insights and make informed decisions that incorporate both biological capabilities and AI-generated support.

Moreover, interdisciplinary collaboration will be encouraged among operators, biologists, and engineers within the military framework.

Operators will need to cultivate communication and teamwork skills that allow them to fluidly engage with experts from various fields. Effective collaboration will ensure that the design and operation of biotech battleships benefit from cumulative knowledge—bridging the gap between biological understanding and mechanical operation.

Ethical training should also be integrated into operator programs, emphasizing the moral implications of wielding biotechnological advancements in combat. Operators must reflect on the responsibilities associated with managing life forms engineered for military purposes and engage in discussions about the potential for ecological impact and the treatment of living systems. Cultivating an ethical mindset will empower operators to navigate the complexities of using biotechnologies in warfare, grounding their actions in principles of responsibility and care for life.

In summary, the training requirements for biotech operators extend far beyond traditional military education. A comprehensive approach must intertwine biological sciences, technical training, practical experiences, adaptability, interdisciplinary collaboration, ethical considerations, and psychological preparedness. As the future of warfare unfolds, operators will become adept at managing intricate systems, ensuring that biotechnologically enhanced battleships can fully realize their potential while operating effectively and responsibly in the vastness of space.

8.2. Human Interaction with Biological Systems

In the context of battleships that merge biological systems with military technology, human interaction with these biological constructs represents a pivotal aspect of operating and optimizing such complicated systems. As we evolve into an age dominated by biotech warfare, understanding how humans interface with living technologies becomes crucial not only for operational success but also for ensuring ethical and responsible usage of biotechnology in combat scenarios.

To begin with, human operators must undergo extensive training that encompasses knowledge of both the biological systems they will be working with and the mechanical aspects of the vessels. This training should integrate principles of biology, genetics, and ecology, offering operators insights into how biological organisms function under varying conditions. Familiarity with these concepts enables operators to recognize the signs of distress or dysfunction in engineered organisms, ultimately allowing them to respond appropriately to prevent system failures.

In addition to foundational knowledge, operators will need advanced practical skills to manage complex systems effectively. Simulated training exercises are essential for preparing personnel to operate in environments where human decisions may directly affect the performance of living technologies. These simulations can mimic the unpredictable challenges faced in combat, requiring operators to make quick, informed choices while collaborating with both human crew members and biologically integrated systems. Training should place a strong emphasis on teamwork and communication, promoting collaborative decision-making processes that leverage the strengths of both human and biological participants.

Moreover, as biotechnologically integrated ships introduce live components that act autonomously or semi-autonomously, operators must develop acute situational awareness. This includes understanding the behaviors of the biological systems onboard and how these behaviors may shift based on environmental stimulus or combat conditions. Operators also need to be versed in the integration of artificial intelligence systems that govern interactions between humans and the living components. Knowing how to interpret AI-generated insights and data from biological sensors allows operators to make tactical decisions informed by real-time information.

Effective human interaction with biological systems also hinges on the psychological dimensions of warfare with living machines. As operators engage with biotechnologically enhanced technologies, they may experience unique pressures associated with managing life forms in combat settings. Developing psychological resilience and coping strategies is essential to ensure that operators can navigate these complexities without compromising their decision-making abilities. Military programs should offer support mechanisms, fostering mental well-being while equipping personnel with the tools needed to adapt to rapidly evolving encounters in battle.

Ethical considerations should underlie the approach to human interaction with biological systems as well. Operators must acknowledge their responsibilities in utilizing engineered organisms for military objectives, reflecting on how their actions impact not only their operational success but also ecological constraints and the integrity of living systems. Training should include discussions surrounding the ethical implications of using biotechnological advances in warfare, fostering a culture of responsibility and respect for life that infuses decision-making processes.

Furthermore, collaborative design and operational techniques between soldiers and biologists or engineers can enhance the efficacy of biotech battleships. By maintaining open lines of communication, operators can work alongside scientists that understand the biological functions of the organisms embedded within the systems. Joint problem-solving exercises in training can simulate scenarios where operators might need to rely on biological insights to make quick decisions, promoting a sense of partnership and shared responsibility for the vessel's success.

The development of support frameworks that connect operators with experts in biology, psychology, and ethics is essential in fostering a comprehensive understanding of the complex interactions between humans and biological systems. These multidisciplinary partnerships create an environment where operators can seek guidance and resources that enhance their performance while aligning with ethical considerations that reduce risks associated with deploying living systems in warfare.

In summary, human interaction with biological systems aboard biotech battleships is a multifaceted endeavor that necessitates comprehensive training, situational awareness, psychological resilience, and ethical responsibility. As biotechnological innovations redefine warfare, ensuring that operators can effectively manage living systems will be paramount to operational success and societal acceptance of these advanced military technologies. The evolving landscape calls for ongoing dialogue, research, and professional collaboration as we navigate the symbiotic relationship between humans and living technologies, ultimately shaping the future of interstellar warfare.

8.3. AI Integration and Command Structures

AI integration in the command structures of biotech battleships represents a groundbreaking evolution in military operations at a time when the boundaries of warfare are being redefined by living technologies. The introduction of AI into military frameworks is not merely a technological enhancement; it fundamentally alters the operational dynamics, command hierarchies, and decision-making processes on board these complex war machines. In a context where biological systems interface seamlessly with mechanical structures, establishing AI-based command systems poses both remarkable opportunities and significant challenges.

At the heart of AI integration lies the potential for operational efficiency and enhanced situational awareness. Traditional command structures often rely on a hierarchy of human decision-makers who assess vast amounts of information to make tactical choices. However, the complex and dynamic environments of interstellar combat necessitate rapid responses and insights that can be efficiently derived from extensive data processing. AI systems can analyze incoming information from various biological sensors, mechanical systems, and environmental inputs, synthesizing this data to provide commanders with actionable intelligence instantaneously. This capacity allows military personnel to make informed decisions rapidly, adapting to the fluidity of battle and enhancing overall effectiveness.

Moreover, AI can facilitate more collaborative command structures by acting as a bridge between human operators and the biological systems aboard biotech battleships. When living organisms are integrated into military operations, their responses and behaviors become critical factors. AI systems can monitor these biological systems in real time, interpreting their physiological states and predicting how they will react to stimuli based on collected data. This capability permits command teams to adjust tactics and strategies proactively, aligning human judgment with organic responses to threats and environmental changes.

However, the integration of AI into command structures raises critical concerns about reliability, accountability, and ethics. As systems become more automated and AI assumes a more central role in decision-making, ensuring that command hierarchies remain accountable becomes paramount. There lies the risk of over-reliance on AI systems, which could inadvertently lead to detrimental consequences if the AI misinterprets data or executes commands without human oversight. Establishing safeguards that maintain human input while leveraging AI's analytical capabilities will be necessary to promote a balanced command structure.

The nature of human interaction with AI in the context of biological systems introduces another dimension to command structures. Operators must develop nuanced skills to engage with AI effectively, understanding both its capabilities and limitations. Training and education programs will be essential in equipping military personnel with the knowledge required to harness AI for operational success, fostering familiarity with AI interfaces that manage biological responses while allowing for rapid decision-making during engagements.

Furthermore, ethical considerations surrounding AI integration into command structures must be a priority. The implications of AI making autonomous decisions regarding the lives of engineered organisms—or the environment—demand careful scrutiny. Establishing ethical frameworks that govern AI's role in military operations is essential to navigate the potential risks associated with delegating decisions to non-human entities. Public trust in military institutions hinges on transparency, ensuring decisions made by AI uphold the values of responsibility and accountability.

The integration of AI within the command structures of biotech battleships also necessitates a significant cultural shift within military organizations. Emphasizing the importance of adaptability and interdisciplinary cooperation will be crucial as personnel navigate the complexities of operating within environments where humans, technology, and biology intersect. Fostering a culture of collaboration —drawing on the expertise of biologists, engineers, ethicists, and military leaders—will be vital in enhancing the operational agility of these systems.

The operational complexities introduced by the interplay of AI and living systems also present opportunities for continued learning and innovation in military command structures. Each engagement will serve as a valuable learning experience, providing data and insights that can be fed back into AI systems, leading to continual improvement in decision-making processes and operational strategies over time.

In summary, AI integration into the command structures of biotech battleships brings forth transformative possibilities for military operations, allowing for rapid decision-making, enhanced situational awareness, and collaboration between humans and biological systems. However, navigating the challenges of reliability, accountability, ethical implications, and cultural shifts within military organizations remains paramount. As we stand on the brink of this new era in warfare, a commitment to responsible innovation will ensure that the collaboration between AI and biological systems serves not only operational goals but also aligns with the fundamental values of our society. The future of intergalactic conflict lies in our ability to effectively harmonize the power of AI with the organic complexities of life, ultimately reshaping our perceptions of warfare amid the stars.

8.4. Challenges of Interdisciplinary Operation Teams

The advancement of interdisciplinary operation teams in the context of biotech battleships represents both an exhilarating opportunity and an array of challenges that must be tactically navigated. The integration of diverse scientific fields—encompassing biology, engineering, ethics, military strategy, and logistics—forms the backbone of a successful biotech-focused military operation. However, the inherent complexities of managing such multifaceted teams can create hurdles that impede progress and effective collaboration. Understanding and addressing these challenges is critical to ensuring that the full potential of biotech innovations is realized in future warfare.

One of the foremost challenges facing interdisciplinary operation teams is the communication barrier that often arises between specialists from differing backgrounds. Each discipline possesses its own lexicon, methodologies, and implicit assumptions, which can result in misunderstandings and misalignments when attempting to achieve common objectives. For instance, while engineers may focus on performance metrics and mechanical reliability, biologists might prioritize the health and adaptability of living systems. This divergence can lead to tensions during project development, with potential conflicts emerging concerning design priorities or operational feasibility. It is imperative for teams to cultivate an environment of open communication, establishing shared terminologies and frameworks that facilitate effective dialogue. Regular collaborative workshops that encourage cross-disciplinary interactions can help break down siloes of expertise and promote a shared understanding among team members.

Another significant hurdle is the alignment of individual and organizational objectives across various disciplines. Biotech warfare development involves stakeholders with varying motivations and perspectives. Engineers may be driven by technological advancement and operational efficiency, while biologists might seek to uphold ethical standards within the deployment of living systems. Additionally,

101

military strategists may prioritize mission success at any cost, leading to potential friction. Navigating this intersection requires a leadership approach that emphasizes a unified vision, encouraging all members of the team to invest in and commit to shared goals. Establishing cross-functional leaders who can bridge these disparate interests and mediate conflicts will be crucial in maintaining cohesion.

Furthermore, practical challenges arise when teams endeavor to integrate biological systems into mechanical designs. These operations often demand rapid iteration and prototyping, prompting engineers and scientists to work closely together throughout the design process. For instance, while an engineer may design a system intended to house bioengineered organisms, unexpected biological behaviors could necessitate design adjustments, leading to delays. Establishing adaptive project management methodologies that allow for continuous feedback and flexibility in design frameworks can greatly enhance the workflow. Employing agile design principles, which prioritize iterative development and real-time problem-solving, can empower teams to respond effectively to the challenges posed by integrating various systems.

Resource allocation is additionally a challenge that interdisciplinary teams face. Biotech innovations frequently require substantial investments in research and development across diverse fields, yet funding streams may be limited or compartmentalized by disciplinary boundaries. Mobilizing support from external sources—including governmental bodies, academic institutions, and private sector partnerships—can provide essential financial backing for collaborative R&D. However, competing priorities within these funding entities can complicate the establishment of joint initiatives. Creating clear proposals that outline the overarching benefits of interdisciplinary collaborations can serve to attract investment and foster supportive environments for these endeavors.

Human resource considerations cannot be understated either. The complexity of operating biotech battleships necessitates not only technical expertise but also individuals with strong interpersonal skills who can adapt to diverse work culture and communication styles. Investing in training programs that develop both hard and soft skills will be crucial to ensuring teams are well-equipped to navigate the intricate dynamics of interdisciplinary collaboration. Fostering a culture of lifelong learning that encourages personnel to engage with fields adjacent to their own expertise will help cultivate versatility and adaptability among team members.

Common ethical dilemmas arising from the integration of biotechnology in military settings can also strain interdisciplinary teams. Differing ethical views on the manipulation of life forms can lead to considerable discord and hesitance regarding the development and deployment of living technologies. Inclusivity in decision-making processes, where bioethicists play a significant role alongside scientists and military personnel, will be vital in fostering consensus and accountability within teams. Establishing ethical guidelines early in the project lifecycle can help shape discussions and decisions surrounding the responsible application of biotechnologies, ultimately strengthening team cohesion across disciplines.

In conclusion, while the challenges faced by interdisciplinary operation teams in the context of biotech battleships are manifold, they are not insurmountable. By promoting effective communication, aligning objectives, adopting agile methodologies, securing necessary resources, fostering a culture of adaptability, and establishing a framework for ethical oversight, teams can effectively navigate the complexities inherent in integrating biological systems into military applications. The potential for groundbreaking innovations that emerge from collaborative efforts in this sphere is immense, and addressing these challenges serves to position interdisciplinary operation teams as the vanguard of future intergalactic warfare. By cultivating adaptive, inclusive, and well-coordinated teams, military organizations can unlock the transformative power of biotechnology and ensure a robust response to the demands of tomorrow's battlefields.

8.5. Psychology of Warfare with Living Machines

In the unfolding narrative of intergalactic warfare, the psychology of warfare with living machines emerges as a critical theme, transcending conventional military strategies and prompting a fundamental reevaluation of how we engage with living systems as instruments of conflict. As humanity strives to innovate in the realm of biotechnology, the implications for both operators and adversaries become increasingly profound—inviting a deeper understanding of the psychological dynamics at play when machines integrated with biological components are deployed in wartime scenarios.

The human psyche has been shaped by millennia of warfare, marked by the engagement of standardized machines and strategies rooted in rational decision-making and tactical calculus. However, with the advent of biotech battleships—vehicles that intertwine the dynamism of living organisms with mechanical precision—this paradigm shifts dramatically. Operators must come to terms with the fact that they are not merely engaging with machines but are also involved in intricately entwined relationships with living systems that possess their own behaviors, responses, and needs. This interplay fundamentally alters command philosophies, leading to the development of new psychological paradigms that address the nuances introduced by living machines.

To begin understanding these psychological dynamics, we must consider the emotional impact on operators entrusted with managing living technologies. The introduction of biologically integrated systems requires personnel to navigate the complexities of both machine mechanics and biological interactions. This dual engagement necessitates higher levels of emotional intelligence as operators learn to interpret the 'moods' and 'states' of the living components within their command. The ability to empathize with biological systems translates into improved decision-making in critical moments, enhancing the overall effectiveness of military actions. Operators may find themselves developing attachment to the living systems they manage, fostering a sense of responsibility to ensure their well-being

—a sentiment that evokes a new ethos of stewardship among military personnel.

Moreover, the presence of living machines can evoke varying degrees of anxiety and uncertainty about operational control. The unpredictable nature of living systems introduces challenges that traditional mechanistic systems do not, potentially leading to feelings of helplessness during engagements. Operators may grapple with the tension of relying on biological components that do not adhere to predictable protocols or algorithms. This psychological burden underscores the importance of comprehensive training and preparation, equipping personnel with the tools needed to contend with the complexities that living technologies present, and alleviating anxiety through understanding and familiarity with their operations.

The concept of "trust" takes on new dimensions as well. Trust in traditional systems is often rooted in predictable performance; however, with biologically integrated applications, operators must learn to develop trust in systems that operate more like independent entities. Effective command structures must foster an environment where personnel build rapport with the living technologies, nurturing adaptability and resilience in the face of uncertainty. By continually assessing the health and performance of organic components, operators can gain insights into their behaviors, leading to greater confidence in decision-making processes—ultimately creating a virtuous cycle of understanding and control.

Furthermore, the dynamics of combat engagement shift as adversaries are introduced to the psychological dimensions of living machines. The visual impact of confronting a biotech battleship equipped with self-repairing capabilities or adaptive weapons systems can profoundly affect enemy morale. The possibility of facing unpredictable biological agents can evoke fear, undermining the psychological resilience of opposing forces. The awareness that their actions may provoke autonomous reactions from living machines brings an element of unpredictability that traditional warfare lacked. This new mental landscape can alter strategies and tactics employed by both sides, leading to an arms race not only in technology but also in psychological warfare.

To navigate these psychological complexities as intergalactic warfare evolves, further research into the cognitive implications of interacting with biological systems must be prioritized. Understanding the human responses to engaging with living machines—from fear and anxiety to attachment and empathy—can inform the design of operational protocols and command structures. This psychological groundwork will become critical in ensuring that operators are not only well-prepared to interface with living organisms but are also psychologically equipped to perform effectively in high-stakes combat environments.

Additionally, ethical considerations will weave through the psychological landscape of warfare with living machines. The implications of utilizing engineered organisms for conflict call for careful reflection on moral responsibilities. Warfare has always been fraught with difficult decisions, but engaging with living systems introduces questions surrounding the rights of engineered organisms and the ecological impact of their deployment. Soldiers must be trained to navigate these ethical dilemmas, further enhancing their psychological preparedness to engage thoughtfully with the implications of their actions.

In summary, the psychology of warfare with living machines embodies a transformative journey for operators and military strategists alike. The integration of biological systems into military applications compels us to reconsider our understanding of combat dynamics, emphasizing the emotional and ethical dimensions that accompany the deployment of living technology. As we advance into this brave new era of intergalactic conflict, developing training programs, command structures, and ethical frameworks that integrate psychological insights will be vital in shaping responsible and effective military practices. Ultimately, comprehending the intersection of biology and technology in warfare not only enhances operational success but also challenges us to reflect on our responsibilities as stewards of both innovation and life itself.

9. Life Support Systems: Sustainability in Space

9.1. Biological Life Support Mechanisms

In the context of developing future intergalactic war machines, the adoption of biological life support mechanisms represents a crucial advancement that intertwines sustainability with combat readiness. As humanity ventures further into the depths of space, the challenges of sustaining life in an environment devoid of natural resources demand innovative solutions that synergize biological systems with engineering principles. This subchapter will delve into the intricacies of biological life support mechanisms, highlighting their significance, functionality, and the broader implications for warfare and long-term space exploration.

Biological life support mechanisms are designed to create self-sustaining ecosystems that can maintain human life by recycling air, water, and nutrients while minimizing the need for external resupply. At the heart of these systems lies the integration of engineered organisms that can perform critical functions, such as photosynthesis, waste recycling, and carbon dioxide removal, mimicking the intricacies of Earth's ecosystems which have evolved over millennia to sustain life.

One of the most promising candidates for biological life support systems is the use of photosynthetic microorganisms—specifically, genetically modified algae and cyanobacteria. These organisms can harness solar energy to produce oxygen while simultaneously consuming carbon dioxide. By cultivating these microorganisms within bioreactors aboard biotech battleships, it becomes possible to create a sustainable and closed-loop environment. This process not only regenerates breathable air but also contributes to the overall energy balance of the vessel, reducing dependency on traditional energy sources.

In addition to providing oxygen, these organisms can be engineered to produce biomass that could serve as food for crew members or as a raw material for further bioconversion processes. Integrated bioproduction systems can transform organic waste generated by the crew into energy-rich feedstock—ensuring a continuous, circular flow of resources within the ship. Such capabilities drastically alleviate logistical strains during long missions where resupplies would be impractical, allowing crew members to focus on their operational duties rather than existential concerns.

Water recycling systems must also be engineered to work synergistically with biological life support mechanisms. Utilizing biofiltration and microbial degradation processes, these systems can purify wastewater through biological means. For instance, bioengineered bacteria capable of breaking down organic molecules can be employed to process human waste, freeing up essential resources while simultaneously producing clean water. Through these integrated assemblies, biotechnology facilitates efficient waste management and resource recovery—forming the crux of sustainable life support solutions in extraterrestrial settings.

As we explore the environmental controls inherent in biotech ships, the role of various biological organisms becomes evident. An optimal onboard environment involves carefully balancing temperature, humidity, and atmospheric pressure—all critical factors that directly impact the health of both crew and biological systems. Engineers will need to design systems capable of dynamically adjusting environmental parameters in response to real-time monitoring data, ensuring that both humans and living components thrive together. This level of integration requires advanced sensor networks to provide continuous feedback and enable automated adjustments, reflecting the symbiotic relationship at the heart of these innovative vessels.

However, the integration of biological life support mechanisms does not come without challenges and risks. The health of the onboard ecosystems must be continually monitored to prevent biological imbalances that could threaten crew safety or operational efficiency. Should a specific organism within the ecosystem falter or become invasive, it could lead to catastrophic breaches in life support systems.

Proactively addressing these potential issues will require ongoing research into the stability of engineered organisms, their interactions, and the overall dynamics of closed ecological systems.

Moreover, ethical considerations remain integral to the deployment of biological life support mechanisms. The use of genetically modified organisms invokes complex questions regarding their treatment, rights, and implications for sustainability. Developing ethical guidelines rooted in responsible stewardship of living systems will encourage military organizations to approach biotechnology with the care and respect it warrants.

As we contemplate the future prospects for sustainable space living, the advancements offered by biological life support mechanisms signify a remarkable convergence of technology and biology. Not only do they enhance operational efficiency in biotech battleships, but they also establish new paradigms for human existence in space. The embrace of living systems as integral components of survival reflects a broader understanding of our responsibilities as stewards of both technology and life.

In conclusion, biological life support mechanisms stand at the forefront of innovations designed to enable sustainable life aboard the battleships of the future. By harnessing the power of engineered organisms to support human life, combat environmental challenges, and ensure operational readiness, we are set to redefine the very essence of warfare in the cosmos. As we continue to explore this transformative potential, we must approach these advancements with curiosity, responsibility, and a commitment to fostering a harmonious relationship with the living systems that sustain us among the stars.

9.2. Environmental Control within Biotech Ships

In the context of developing efficient and sustainable interstellar warfare, environmental control within biotech ships emerges as a paramount concern encompassing life support, ecological balance, and resource management. The design of biotech battleships—which integrate biological systems to enhance operational capabilities—

must take into account not just the utilization of living organisms, but also their impact on the crew, the ship's environment, and, ultimately, the success of military missions in the cosmos.

The primary challenge lies in creating a closed-loop system that effectively maintains a habitable environment for humans while simultaneously leveraging biological processes to optimize the ship's operations. At the heart of this endeavor is the understanding that biological systems can be harnessed not only to manage life support but also to assist in broader ecological functionality onboard the vessel.

Initially, environmental management can focus on oxygen production and carbon dioxide removal—key factors essential for sustaining human life in the confined spaces of a biotech battleship. The integration of photosynthetic organisms, such as algae or cyanobacteria, possesses incredible potential to achieve this goal. These organisms utilize sunlight to produce oxygen while absorbing carbon dioxide, thus contributing to a balanced atmospheric composition. By cultivating these organisms within bioreactors intelligently designed to maximize light exposure and growth rates, engineers can establish a sustainable oxygen supply that adapts to variations in crew activity levels or atmospheric demands.

Furthermore, waste management is a significant component of maintaining ecological balance within the ship. Biodegradable waste generated by the crew can be repurposed through biological processes, such as anaerobic digestion, to yield biogas—an effective energy source that can power various systems onboard. The digestion process can also produce nutrient-rich byproducts that could be used to cultivate a secondary crop of microorganisms or even genetically engineered plants, reinforcing the principle of waste recycling as a means of resource conservation. This closed-loop system not only reduces the burden of resupply missions but also transforms waste into valuable resources, promoting sustainability.

In addition to managing atmospheric composition and waste, water recycling becomes a focal point of environmental control. Advanced biofiltration systems using engineered bacteria can effectively purify wastewater generated from different sources, such as food preparation or hygiene practices. These organisms break down organic materials, converting wastewater into clean, potable water, thus ensuring a reliable supply—crucial for long-duration missions. The purity and quality of recycled water obtained from these biological systems may even surpass that of traditional mechanical filtration methods, offering an added layer of safety for crew health.

The ecological integrity of the ship's environment further necessitates the consideration of temperature and humidity controls. Living organisms thrive within specific ranges of environmental conditions; thus, effective management of these parameters becomes vital. Sensor networks equipped with real-time monitoring capabilities should be deployed to assess not only the atmospheric conditions that affect human crew members but also those that impact the organisms integrated into the ship's systems. Drawing upon this data, automated systems can modulate conditions to maintain optimal habitats for both people and biological organisms alike.

However, managing this complex biosphere onboard presents inherent challenges. The balance between mechanical reliability and biological unpredictability requires ongoing research, testing, and iteration to ensure that these intertwined systems operate harmoniously. For instance, the biological organisms that contribute to air and water recycling must remain healthy and productive, thus necessitating a thorough understanding of their life cycles and interactions. Developing protocols for regular assessments, maintenance, and potential interventions will be crucial in preventing ecological imbalances that could compromise the functionality of life support systems.

Moreover, risk management procedures must address the potential impacts of introducing engineered biological systems into warfare contexts. The unpredictability of biological organisms poses specific challenges; operators must remain vigilant to ensure that living components do not introduce unforeseen complications or dangers during combat. Containment measures, fail-safes, and thorough monitoring of biological systems become paramount in preserving ecological integrity while safeguarding crew safety.

From an ethical perspective, discussions regarding the deployment of living systems in combat scenarios must also consider their rights and treatment. Engineers and military strategists must engage with bioethicists to craft guidelines that govern the responsible usage of these organisms in warfare, considering the broader implications on ecosystems and biodiversity. Establishing principles that emphasize respect for life, even in engineered forms, will reinforce responsible innovation.

In conclusion, environmental control within biotech ships demands a holistic approach that encompasses life support systems, resource management, and ecological balance. The synergy of biological processes serves not only to sustain crew members but also to optimize operational efficiency and support long-duration missions in space. As we design and deploy these innovative battleships, we must remain cognizant of the intricacies involved in managing these intertwined systems, fostering a culture of responsibility, ethical stewardship, and continuous learning. Ultimately, the future of interstellar warfare is not just about creating formidable machines; it is about understanding how we can harmonize life and technology to navigate the cosmos responsibly. The ability to cultivate living environments tailored for human and biological coexistence aboard these vessels will pave the way for sustainable operations that extend the potential of humanity among the stars, reflecting our commitment to both innovation and ecological integrity.

9.3. Maintaining Health in Biologically Integrated Ships

Maintaining health in biologically integrated ships is a complex endeavor that intersects diverse fields such as biology, engineering, ethics, and psychology, shaping operational effectiveness and crew welfare. The successful integration of living systems into the fabric of military vessels requires meticulous planning and execution, ensuring that both biological organisms and human operators can thrive in the unique challenges posed by interstellar travel.

At the core of maintaining health on biotech battleships lies the establishment of robust life support systems that not only ensure the physical well-being of the crew but also support the operational health of the biological components onboard. Understanding the physiological needs of living organisms is essential; engineers and biologists must collaboratively design systems that replicate the necessary environmental conditions these organisms require to function optimally. Factors such as temperature, humidity, nutrient availability, and waste management will be crucial components of these systems. The presence of genetically modified organisms capable of processing waste and recycling resources offers an unparalleled advantage, transforming potential liabilities into vital contributions to the onboard ecosystem.

Nutritional health is another significant consideration. Just as the crew relies on carefully balanced diets to maintain physical health, the engineered organisms integrated into the ship must also receive appropriate nutrients to sustain their functions. The development of closed-loop systems wherein biological waste is converted into viable nutrients for organisms presents opportunities to enhance overall health on the ship. Such systems not only optimize resource use but reduce dependency on external supplies—central to the operational sustainability of long-duration missions in hostile environments.

To complement biological life support systems, monitoring health through real-time diagnostics becomes pivotal in maintaining overall system health. Deploying sensor technologies capable of tracking physiological changes in both crew members and biological organisms allows teams to promptly respond to issues as they arise. By establishing a feedback loop whereby monitoring data informs operational decisions, command can ensure a synergistic balance is always maintained, preventing crises that could jeopardize mission objectives.

Psychological health is equally critical in the context of maintaining well-being aboard biologically integrated ships. Human operators may experience unique bonding dynamics with living systems, which can range from attachment and empathy to anxiety and stress. Training and support programs must recognize these complexities, empowering personnel with strategies to navigate their interactions with engineered organisms. Promoting mental resilience will foster a culture of awareness, promoting mental well-being while enhancing the operational efficacy of the crew.

Ethical responsibilities accompanying the deployment of living systems present profound implications for the health maintenance processes aboard biotech battleships. Commanders must remain cognizant of their duty to treat engineered organisms with respect and care, mirroring the principles used with human crews. Establishing guidelines for how living systems are monitored, maintained, and utilized in combat will demand interdisciplinary conversations involving biologists, ethicists, and military strategists.

Another vital element involves stress testing the systems in scenarios that simulate the unpredictability of space warfare. The integration of new technology could introduce unexpected stressors or impairments, necessitating ongoing evaluations of how biological systems and the crew adapt. Conducting drills that prepare personnel for crises involving both human and biological components will ensure that operators are ready to adjust quickly under pressure, fostering resilience and adaptability among crew members.

In conclusion, maintaining health in biologically integrated ships is a multifaceted challenge encompassing environmental control, nutritional management, psychological resilience, ethical considerations, and ongoing monitoring. As militaries embrace biotechnological advancements, ensuring that both living organisms and human operators can thrive in the demanding conditions of space travel demands comprehensive strategies that intertwine advanced engineering, biology, psychological support, and ethical frameworks. By prioritizing holistic health within the operations of biotech battleships, we shall unlock the full potential of these remarkable vessels and their integrated living systems. The future of interstellar warfare will hinge not only on technological innovation but also on cultivating a profound respect for life, fostering sustainable operations amid the stars.

9.4. Impact of Interstellar Travel on Biology

The advent of interstellar travel introduces a myriad of complex biological implications that could redefine our understanding of life itself. As humanity seeks to expand its reach beyond Earth, the effects of long-duration spaceflight on biological systems become increasingly critical. This exploration not only raises questions regarding the health and well-being of human crews but also impacts the biological entities we intend to utilize in the design of future biotechnology-integrated battleships.

The first and foremost consideration is the physiological impacts of space travel on human beings. Prolonged exposure to microgravity affects muscle and bone density, cardiovascular function, and immune system performance. It is crucial to understand these biological changes to devise effective countermeasures that enhance human resilience during extended missions. Biotechnology could play an integral role in this context; for example, engineered microorganisms might be utilized to support the human microbiome or to produce essential nutrients that are depleted during spaceflight. Additionally, advancements in gene therapy might address physiological degradation by optimizing cellular health and function under new conditions.

Furthermore, the detrimental effects of radiation in space cannot be understated. Cosmic rays and solar radiation present significant threats to not only human health but also the viability of organic components onboard biotech battleships. Understanding how various biological systems respond to radiation will drive innovations for biological shielding and enhancement strategies aimed at bolstering resilience against such hazards. Through research into extremophiles

—organisms that thrive in extreme environments—scientists may uncover mechanisms that could be harnessed to protect future crews and biotechnological components.

The emotional and psychological impacts of interstellar travel also present vital considerations for expedition planning. Long periods in confined environments can lead to psychological stressors that might disrupt team dynamics and hinder operational efficiency. Childhood development studies reveal how environments significantly influence emotional well-being; similarly, managing the psychological health of crew members on long missions will demand innovative interventions. This might involve incorporating biofeedback mechanisms or utilizing living systems that promote mental well-being, such as plants that enhance air quality and foster a sense of nature onboard.

Biological adaptation over time also emerges as a notable consideration in the context of interstellar travel. As crews venture beyond the confines of Earth, natural selection could introduce significant evolutionary pressures on living organisms intended for use in space missions. Understanding these adaptive dynamics will be critical when engineering organisms for specific functions, as their behavior and survival may shift far beyond initial projections. This highlights the importance of adaptability in design, as biotech battleships will need to accommodate these dynamic biological changes over time.

The implications extend to ethical considerations as well. As humanity's reach expands into the stars, our responsibilities toward engineered organisms must evolve accordingly. Treating these life forms with respect and care echoes broader discussions about our stewardship of biological resources, and the moral imperative to consider the rights and welfare of the living beings aboard our technologically advanced vessels. The creation of robust ethical guidelines surrounding the deployment of biotechnological innovations in combat will be paramount in fostering a culture of responsible innovation.

The outcomes of interstellar travel will inevitably influence our understanding of life and existence as a whole. Integrating biological systems with mechanical technologies prompts profound inquiries regarding identity, adaptation, and what it means to be alive. As we navigate this brave new frontier, we must remain vigilant in exploring the biological implications of resistance and resilience—not only in our battle systems but also in our definition of who we are as a species among the stars.

In conclusion, the impact of interstellar travel on biology encompasses a multifaceted landscape that requires careful examination and thoughtful consideration. The convergence of biotechnology with human health, psychological well-being, and ethical stewardship presents an extraordinary opportunity to redefine our approach to warfare and space exploration. By addressing these challenges with collaborative foresight, we can realize a future where the complexities of life are harmoniously integrated into our endeavors across the cosmos, reshaping our legacy as both explorers and protectors of life in all its forms.

9.5. Future Prospects for Sustainable Space Living

In contemplating the future prospects for sustainable space living, particularly in the context of biotech battleships, we find that the intersection of advanced biotechnology, ecological sustainability, and military strategy offers a dynamic and transformative blueprint for how humanity may inhabit and operate in the cosmos. The rapid advancement of biotechnology presents a unique opportunity to create living machines that not only serve as vessels in combat but also establish self-sustaining ecosystems that meet the challenging demands of deep-space exploration and warfare.

Central to this vision is the concept of closed-loop life support systems, wherein engineered biological organisms are deployed to maintain a habitable environment. By harnessing the power of photosynthetic microorganisms, such as algae and cyanobacteria, biotech battleships can produce oxygen, recycling carbon dioxide generated by crewmembers, thus creating a sustainable atmosphere. This shift from dependence on finite supplies to biological regeneration signals a new era in long-duration missions that could last months or years, enabling crews to operate efficiently far from Earth.

Furthermore, waste management systems integrated with biological processes can effectively convert organic waste into usable resources. The notion of utilizing engineered bacteria to break down and repurpose biological waste into vital nutrients emphasizes the benefits of recycling both for sustainability and resource efficiency. This operational model fosters a culture of responsibility, aligning military endeavors with ecological stewardship—a critical consideration as humanity sets its sights on traversing the stars.

In addition to life support, the design of these vessels must also address broader ecological implications. The importance of environmental control and management cannot be overstated, as biological life support ecosystems must be carefully regulated to maintain harmony. This necessitates advanced monitoring systems capable of dynamically adjusting conditions—temperature, humidity, and nutrient levels—designed for optimal performance not just for humans but also for the engineered organisms that sustain life aboard.

The psychological aspects of living and operating within a biotech battleship also present unique insights into future prospects. Crews must adapt to the understanding that they are cohabiting with living systems that possess their own needs and characteristics. Training programs will need to incorporate not only technical proficiency but also an awareness of the biological interdependencies at play, fostering a sense of agency and responsibility toward the living systems that enhance their own survival.

Crucially, the ethics of employing biotechnological advancements in warfare impose limitations on how these sustainable practices may be framed. The deployment of living systems in combat raises significant ethical questions regarding responsibility for decision-making, the treatment of bioengineered organisms, and ecological impacts. Developing robust ethical guidelines around biotechnology applications will become indispensable for maintaining legitimacy and societal support.

As we venture into this new frontier of sustainable space living, the innovation of biotech battleships also calls for a reevaluation of military strategies that incorporate sustainability into operational doctrine. The development of vehicles capable of thriving within their self-sustaining ecosystems allows for strategies that prioritize resilience and resource optimization, particularly in engagements where supply lines may be severed or unavailable.

The exploration of sustainable space living also entails collaboration across disciplines—scientists, engineers, military leaders, and ethicists must converge to inform wide-ranging perspectives. This collaborative ethos fosters a culture of innovation while ensuring that ethical considerations remain central to the development process. Addressing the societal implications of biotechnology in warfare will help mitigate potential resistance and foster a shared vision of responsible advancement.

In summary, the future prospects for sustainable space living, specifically through the lens of biotech battleships, reveal a unique opportunity to harmonize technology with ecological responsibility. The ability to create living ecosystems integrated within military vessels not only enhances operational sustainability but also reflects humanity's growing understanding of its responsibilities in the cosmos. As we look toward the stars, the emphasis on sustainability, ethical stewardship, and innovative design will play a crucial role in shaping a new era of exploration and conflict that embraces life in all its forms. As we navigate this path, the potential to redefine how we understand warfare through sustainable practices will be instrumental in forging a future that respects both the technological and living systems in our pursuit of resilience among the stars.

10. The Cold Equation: Calculating Efficiency and Survival

10.1. Measuring Energy Efficiency of Biotech Mechanics

Measuring the energy efficiency of biotech mechanics plays a crucial role in the development of future biotech battleships and their operational capabilities. As these vessels begin to redefine the landscape of interstellar warfare, understanding how to optimize energy consumption while maximizing performance is paramount. This task involves examining the unique requirements of biological systems in conjunction with mechanical components, creating pathways for enhanced sustainability, and ensuring that every aspect of functioning within a biotech battleship contributes positively to its energy efficiency.

Energy efficiency encompasses not only the consumption of energy but also the generation and recycling processes within these hybrid systems. As we design biotech battleships, it is essential to integrate biological organisms capable of harnessing various energy sources effectively. These organisms could potentially utilize solar energy through photosynthesis, chemical energy derived from metabolic processes, or waste products generated by the crew. The ability to transform available resources into usable energy forms adds an invaluable layer of resilience for the vessel, ensuring that it can function autonomously during extended missions.

The first step in measuring energy efficiency involves evaluating how these biological systems convert resources into energy. For instance, bioreactors housing genetically modified algae might be designed to optimize light absorption and growth rates while maximizing oxygen production and carbon dioxide consumption. By tracking the metabolic rates of these organisms under different environmental conditions—such as variations in temperature, light intensity, and nutrient availability—we can develop performance benchmarks that inform operational efficiency within the battleship's life support systems.

Additionally, assessing energy expenditures associated with maintaining stable conditions for biological growth is critical. Humans and onboard organisms both depend on regulated environmental parameters like temperature, humidity, and atmospheric pressure. By modeling how much energy is consumed through mechanical systems used to uphold these parameters—such as heating, cooling, or ventilation—we can develop strategies to optimize energy use. Innovations like employing bio-based insulation materials or using waste heat from machinery could minimize energy loss, contributing to a more efficient operational framework.

Moreover, we must consider how integrated energy systems—where mechanical and biological components coalesce—can enhance overall efficiency. For example, developing microbial fuel cells that convert organic waste into electrical energy demonstrates a dual benefit: effective waste management while providing power to essential systems aboard the battleship. By analyzing the energy transitions from waste to energy generation, we can refine designs that maximize resource use with as little energy expenditure as possible.

The measurement of energy efficiency also includes monitoring energy losses within the systems. Traditional machines often experience energy dissipation due to mechanical friction, inefficiencies in energy conversion, and waste heat generation. Likewise, biological systems can introduce unique sources of energy loss, such as metabolic inefficiencies or the thermodynamic costs of maintaining homeostasis. Employing avenues such as smart sensors and AI-driven management systems can facilitate ongoing monitoring and analysis of energy usage patterns, allowing commanders to adapt strategies or processes to mitigate losses and improve overall efficiency.

In navigating these complexities, establishing performance metrics for energy-efficient designs is essential. Creating benchmarking tests and standardizing energy consumption measurements will enhance our ability to assess various configurations of bio-integrated systems. Metrics may cover a range of factors—from basic energy inputs and outputs to overall system resilience and longevity—enabling continuous evaluation and improvement in energy efficiency as the designs evolve.

Furthermore, addressing the sustainability of energy sources used within biotech battleships is critical for long-term operational efficiency. As we engage with living systems, it becomes imperative to ensure that the breeding, cultivation, and maintenance of these organisms do not deplete available resources or compromise their performance. Sustainable practices in sourcing nutrients and energy can create equilibrium that bolsters both efficiency and ecological integrity, reinforcing the idea that resource-conscious innovation is vital as we expand the scope of warfare.

In conclusion, measuring energy efficiency within the context of biotech mechanics is foundational as we push towards new frontiers in interstellar warfare. Integrating biological systems into battleships has the potential to redefine operational paradigms, engendering self-sustaining environments capable of thriving in hostile conditions. By focusing on optimizing energy consumption through thoughtful designs and processes, we can create pathways toward enhanced performance, sustainability, and efficiency in the futuristic landscape of military operations. This endeavor will not only elevate the capabilities of biotech battleships but also reflect a broader commitment to responsible practices and advancements that honor the intricate connection between technology and life.

10.2. Survivability of Bio-integrated Constructs

In examining the survivability of bio-integrated constructs, it becomes evident that the evolution of biotechnology is transforming the design and functionality of future war machines. As we venture into an era where living organisms are interwoven with mechanical systems, the capacity for these biotech battleships to endure the rigors of interstellar combat hinges on their inherent adaptability, resilience, and effectively engineered biological components. This discussion not only outlines the mechanisms that promote survivability but also highlights the numerous challenges that must be navigated to ensure these hybrid constructs succeed in their missions.

The primary advantage of bio-integrated constructs lies in their ability to self-repair—a trait that embodies the resilience of living systems. Just as certain organisms can regenerate damaged tissues, bioengineered materials can be designed to respond dynamically to breaches or damage. This capacity may involve incorporating living cells within structural components, which can release healing agents or undergo regenerative processes upon detecting distress. For instance, a vessel's hull could be embedded with engineered micro-organisms capable of synthesizing materials that patch holes or absorb moisture, significantly reducing the frequency and extent of repair operations. Such self-healing features fundamentally alter the logistic challenges previously faced in traditional warships, offering the prospect of extended operational life without extensive downtime for repairs.

Moreover, the adaptability of bio-integrated constructs enhances their survivability in unpredictable combat scenarios. By harnessing genetic engineering techniques, living systems can be tailor-made to exhibit certain defenses or adaptations in reaction to environmental stimuli, damage, or adversarial tactics. For example, biosynthetic materials might change their properties—such as stiffness, flexibility, or strength—based on the object's exposure to thermal conditions or the stress of impacts. The ability to remain functional and resilient amid attacks allows these bio-integrated systems to address threats in real-time and respond appropriately, thus enhancing their survivability on the interstellar battlefield.

However, the integration of biological systems also introduces unique challenges that can hinder the resilience of these constructs. The variability inherent in living organisms can lead to unpredictable behaviors, necessitating constant monitoring and assessment of their vitality. Factors such as environmental fluctuations, radiation exposure, and collision forces must be accounted for, as these can affect the performance and stability of biological components. The increased complexity of managing living systems heightens the demand for sophisticated monitoring systems—those capable of sensing biological responses and relaying crucial data to operators. These systems must function autonomously, minimizing human intervention while providing reliable, actionable insights that promote informed decision-making.

Maintaining the health of the biological components is another essential factor in ensuring the survivability of bio-integrated constructs. The health and welfare of engineered organisms must be prioritized —and this requires ongoing assessments, optimal environmental conditions, and appropriate resource inputs. Implementing life-support systems that can efficiently recycle nutrients and manage waste is vital to sustaining biological health onboard, thereby creating an environment conducive to maximum performance. Any imbalances within these ecosystems could compromise overall system resilience and hinder operational capabilities, highlighting the necessity for a well-rounded understanding of biological needs.

In addition to these engineering and biological considerations, ethical dimensions surrounding the use of living systems in warfare profoundly impact survivability. As military entities embrace the power of biotechnology, they implicitly assume responsibilities toward the life forms they engineer. Ethical frameworks must govern the development, deployment, and management of these organisms aboard biotech battleships, ensuring that their manipulation aligns with broader societal values and moral imperatives. Striking a balance between military objectives and ethical stewardship is essential—a task that requires continuous dialogue and cooperation among scientists, military personnel, ethicists, and the public.

Equally important is the cultural dimension associated with the deployment of bio-integrated constructs. Operators tasked with managing living systems must be trained not only in technical and tactical skills but also in understanding the nuances of interacting with biological organisms. Training programs that emphasize collaboration between human and living technologies will foster an operational culture where respect for life underpins mission objectives. Empowering personnel to engage responsibly with engineered organisms will enhance operational efficacy while also promoting a sense of accountability toward the life systems that contribute to their survival.

In summary, the survivability of bio-integrated constructs stands at the intersection of innovation, resilience, adaptability, and ethical considerations. By optimizing the integration of biological systems within military applications, we can enhance operational performance while addressing logistical challenges associated with traditional designs. As we embark on creating the battleships of the future, our commitment to fostering harmonious interactions between human operators and living systems will determine not only their effectiveness in combat but also the legacy we leave behind in our exploration of life and technology's frontiers. By navigating the complexities of bioengineering responsibly, we stand poised to redefine the nature of warfare in the vast expanses of the cosmos.

10.3. Cost-Benefit Analysis of Biotech Designs

Cost-benefit analysis of biotech designs plays a critical role in assessing the practicality, efficiency, and potential returns of integrating biological systems with military technology for future warfare. As we journey further into an era characterized by rapid advancements in biotechnology, understanding the balance between the benefits derived from these innovations and their associated costs becomes imperative. This analysis allows military strategists and policymakers to make informed decisions regarding resource allocation, operational sectors, and long-term sustainability in intergalactic conflict scenarios.

To begin this analysis, we must first catalog the explicit benefits of incorporating biotech designs into warfare. Key advantages include improved adaptability, resilience, and operational efficiency. Biotech battleships, integrated with engineered biological systems, have the inherent capability to self-repair, regenerate resources, and optimize energy consumption—enhancing the overall combat effectiveness of military forces. For instance, self-healing materials could drastically reduce downtime for repairs, translating to extended operational capabilities and reduced logistical burdens associated with traditional maintenance.

Additionally, the implementation of biological life support systems can promote sustainability during long-duration missions. Engineering organisms capable of recycling waste products into vital nutrients and energy minimizes the need for resupply missions. These closed-loop systems not only ensure the survival of crews but also align military operations with environmental sustainability, thus enhancing public perception and acceptance of military actions that utilize biotechnological advancements.

Yet, alongside these benefits must be a thorough evaluation of the costs associated with the development, integration, and maintenance of biotech designs. Investing in biotechnological research and development often entails significant financial commitments, demanding resources for interdisciplinary collaboration, facility upgrades, and extensive testing protocols. The uncertainty inherent in working with living organisms—whose behaviors may be unpredictable—creates risks that can lead to potential failures or miscalculations. These challenges must be factored into the analysis to present an accurate overall cost picture.

Financial impacts also extend to regulatory compliance and ethical oversight, which could require additional resources to navigate the complexities surrounding the use of living systems in military contexts. The establishment of legal frameworks and ethical guidelines necessitates funding for policy development, training personnel, and ensuring adherence to laws governing biotechnology in warfare. Failure to adhere to these frameworks can invoke public backlash, potential litigation, and ultimately undermine the mission objectives.

Furthermore, measuring the potential outcomes of integrating biotech designs requires benchmarking against existing technologies. Comparing the operational performance of biotech constructs with conventional weaponry can yield significant insights into their effectiveness and long-term viability. Computational models, supported by empirical data from testing, can inform the cost-benefit analysis by illustrating potential scenarios wherein the two categories may offer distinct advantages or disadvantages.

The assessment of costs and benefits must also account for ongoing maintenance and support requirements. Biotech systems, particularly those involving live organisms, demand consistent monitoring, adjustment, and potential intervention—a factor not typically required for traditional machinery. Understanding these operational demands can help military planners determine personnel needs, training provisions, and support systems necessary to maintain the functionality of biotechnological innovations.

As we engage in this comprehensive analysis, it is vital to anticipate the potential for conflict arising from public perception, ethical considerations, and societal pushback against the militarization of biotechnological advancements. The integration of living systems in warfare poses dilemmas that extend beyond quantification of costs and benefits; they demand critical reflection on the moral and ethical implications of such actions—a reality that must be factored into the overall assessment.

Implementing cost-benefit analysis in biotech designs ultimately serves as a strategic tool for prioritizing military investments and sparking discussions on the future directions of warfare technology. As we stand at the crossroads of innovation and responsibility, embracing this analytical approach allows us to assess how best to navigate the complexities of interstellar conflict while fostering a commitment to ethical stewardship and ecological integrity. By balancing the promise of biotechnological advancements with pragmatic assessments of their implications, we can chart a path forward that not only enhances our military capabilities but reconciles with the moral obligations we bear toward life itself.

10.4. Modeling and Simulations in Design Processes

In the realm of military applications, modeling and simulations in design processes become critical aspects of developing biotech battleships, especially as integration of biological systems with traditional engineering progresses. The complexities inherent to this fusion demand sophisticated methodologies to predict, analyze, and optimize performance across various interconnected systems—an endeavor that directly affects operational readiness and battle efficacy.

Modeling serves as a preliminary step in understanding the behavior and interactions of living organisms within a mechanical framework. It allows designers to create virtual representations of biological functions, environmental influences, and mechanical responses. By employing computational models that simulate biological processes, engineers can gain critical insights into how these hybrid systems might respond under different wartime conditions, including extreme environmental factors and stressors akin to those encountered during interstellar engagements.

One essential aspect of modeling involves the formulation of dynamic systems that can account for variables such as metabolic rates of biological entities, nutrient cycling, and waste management. By leveraging input parameters derived from empirical research on biological systems, engineers can build simulations that predict the operational limits and efficiencies of these systems under various scenarios. For instance, modeling the growth rates of bioengineered algae utilized for oxygen production can guide designers in determining the scale of bioreactors needed to sustain a crew during extended missions. Such predictive capabilities help establish the balance necessary for maintaining the ecological integrity of life support systems.

Simulations address both mechanical and biological elements, serving to enhance the survivability, adaptability, and overall functionality of biotech battleships. Environmental conditions under which these vessels will operate can be mimicked using simulations that explore how climate factors, cosmic radiation, and gravitational stresses can affect biological systems onboard. Establishing optimal parameters for environmental control ensures biological components can thrive while also functioning effectively, providing critical resources for human crews.

Incorporating AI into these modeling and simulation processes can significantly enhance decision-making capabilities. AI can analyze extensive datasets produced from simulations to recognize patterns and provide actionable insights for design adjustments. For example, machine learning algorithms can identify relationships between biological health and environmental factors, leading to predictive maintenance protocols that proactively address any deviations from optimal performance.

Testing becomes an integral part of the modeling process, allowing for the validation of predictions and design iterations. High-fidelity simulations must undergo rigorous validation against real-world experimental results—ensuring that the models accurately replicate biological behaviors and mechanical responses to evolving combat conditions. Utilizing feedback from field experiences can facilitate continuous refinement of models, enhancing their reliability and accuracy.

Furthermore, the role of interdisciplinary collaboration cannot be overstated in modeling and simulations. The integration of insights from various fields, including biology, engineering, ethics, and psychology, fosters innovative approaches to designing biotech battleships. Engaging biologists knowledgeable in genetic modification can provide critical context for understanding organism behavior, while engineers bring design expertise required to harmonize biological and mechanical elements. Establishing a collective framework encourages cross-pollination of ideas and enhances the overall efficacy of the modeling processes.

As advancements continue, ethical considerations must be woven into the fabric of modeling and simulations. The introduction of living systems into warfare underscores the need for responsible innovation, compelling teams to question the potential environmental and societal implications of their designs. Collaborative dialogues emphasizing ethical principles can help establish guidelines that govern the impact of biological systems on both human operators and the ecosystems they inhabit.

Constraints associated with these modeling and simulations also provoke essential discussions about the reliability of predictions derived from biological systems that may exhibit variability. Understanding known limits within biological performance and integrating these constraints into modeling ensures that design processes account for uncertainties and instills confidence in operational readiness.

In conclusion, the application of modeling and simulations in design processes is essential for integrating biotechnology into military applications, particularly in the pursuit of developing biotech battleships. By engaging in sophisticated modeling techniques and collaborative endeavors, future military innovations can strategically harness the capabilities offered by living systems while ensuring a sustainable, responsible approach to modern warfare. The adoption of these methodologies will not only enhance operational effectiveness on the battlefield but also reshape our understanding of how biotechnology intersects with engineering as we navigate the complexities of interstellar conflict.

10.5. Benchmarking Against Traditional Technology

In an era where technology and biology coalesce to reshape the landscape of warfare, the process of benchmarking biotech battleships against traditional technology serves as both a critical evaluation technique and a forward-looking strategy. As we explore the efficacy, advantages, and limitations of biologically integrated war machines relative to conventional counterparts, we uncover deeper insights into the future of interstellar combat. This assessment involves comparing not only mechanical performance and efficiency but also the sustainability, durability, adaptability, and ethical implications of these pioneering constructs.

Starting with performance metrics, traditional warships have thrived for centuries on mechanical reliability, relying on predictable systems built from heavy metals and advanced alloys. These vessels have been designed for endurance, leveraging the principles of mechanical engineering to withstand high-stress environments and endure long engagements with minimal failure. However, traditional technologies often require extensive logistical support, regular maintenance, and significant resource consumption. The rigid frameworks that characterize conventional designs can hinder adaptability—a crucial quality in modern warfare where threats can emerge unexpectedly and evolve rapidly.

In contrast, biotech battleships are designed with biological resilience and adaptability at their core. Living systems enable these vessels to not only self-repair but also respond dynamically to changing combat conditions. This flexibility can enhance survivability during engagements, allowing these advanced ships to recover from damage autonomously. As we benchmark the two paradigms, we must consider the implications of each design philosophy. Traditional systems, while reliable, often lack the ability to adapt in real-time, whereas the biological constructs prioritize the capacity to learn and evolve, which offers a transformative edge in maneuverability and defense against novel threats.

Evaluating energy efficiency presents another key differentiation between biotech and traditional designs. Conventional warships consume fuel in considerable quantities, driving the need for robust supply chains and logistical management. By contrast, biotech battleships can harness biological processes for resource generation through waste recycling and energy production from renewable sources. This sustainability not only enhances operational longevity but aligns with broader societal values regarding ecological stewardship, thereby addressing public concerns over the environmental impact of military operations. The ability to recycle resources could place biotech fleets at a strategic advantage, as they would be less reliant on constant re-supply from Earth or other bases.

When discussing deployment versatility, biotech battleships can excel in roles traditionally difficult for standard vessels. Integration of biological units allows for more multifunctional designs—combat is no longer strictly about offensive capabilities; it includes dynamic defense mechanisms, reconnaissance through living sensors, and adaptability to shifting threats, thus knitting together warfare strategies that encompass intelligence, protection, and engagement. Traditional technologies may struggle to keep pace with these novel methodologies, leading to tactical obsolescence in rapidly changing theaters of conflict.

However, the challenges associated with bio-integrated constructs must not be overlooked. The unpredictability inherent in living systems introduces risks that conventionally engineered machines do not confront. Variability in biological behavior can complicate operational strategies, where a living organism's response to environmental factors may be unpredictable. This necessitates extensive testing and continuous monitoring—critical components that require resources and strategic foresight to mitigate the risks associated with deploying living systems in high-stakes engagements. Traditional ships, while mechanical, offer more predictable performance and extensive historical data for decision-making, establishing conventions for understanding risk versus reward.

As we incorporate these considerations, it is also vital to address ethical implications surrounding the use of biotechnology in warfare. Unlike traditional warfare, which has a well-defined moral and legal framework, the integration of living systems enters a complex legal landscape influenced by public perception, societal values, and ecological concerns. The creation and deployment of organisms engineered for combat requires robust ethical frameworks that contemplate the rights of these life forms and the responsibilities of military entities. This dimension is not typically associated with conventional technology, highlighting a unique dichotomy that underscores the moral responsibilities introduced by bio-integration.

In conclusion, benchmarking biotech battleships against traditional technology illuminates the shifting paradigms of warfare, revealing the advantages and challenges of integrating living systems into military design. By examining performance metrics, sustainability, adaptability, and ethical concerns, we can elucidate the pathways toward crafting advanced and resilient war machines. The road ahead is paved with opportunities and challenges, calling for careful evaluation as we traverse the exciting frontier of biotechnology and its implications for the future of interstellar combat. Understanding these dynamics will empower military planners, scientists, and policymakers to strategically navigate this burgeoning landscape, ensuring that innovation aligns with humanity's broader aspirations and ethical responsibilities in a rapidly evolving universe.

11. Strategic Deployment of Biotech Battleships

11.1. Roles and Missions in Intergalactic Defense

In the context of intergalactic warfare, where strategies evolve to meet the complexities of integrating biotechnology into military design, the roles and missions in intergalactic defense become paramount. The forward-thinking deployment of biotech battleships suggests a future in which organisms and machines operate in synergy, enabling forces to adapt and respond effectively amidst the challenges of combat in the vastness of space.

To begin with, the primary role of biotech battleships lies in their enhanced adaptability and resilience. Traditional military technologies have often struggled to account for the unpredictable nature of warfare, where threats can emerge suddenly and evolve rapidly. By leveraging the inherent properties of living systems, biotech battleships can respond dynamically to multiple combat scenarios. For instance, equipped with bioengineered organisms, these vessels can automatically detect and neutralize biological or chemical threats, altering their defensive strategies in real time. This unique capability gives them a distinct advantage over conventional craft, allowing them to remain highly functional and effective in the unpredictable and rapidly changing environments of interstellar conflict.

Biotech battleships are also well-suited for long-duration missions, where sustainability becomes a central concern. The ability to recycle resources such as air, water, and waste through biological processes means that missions can be extended without relying on supply ships for resupply. As conflicts may occur far from established bases, deploying forces equipped with living systems enables them to function autonomously for longer periods. This capacity to act in self-sustaining modes aligns with modern military strategies prioritizing prolonged operational capabilities, particularly in engagement scenarios involving dispersed forces or remote locations.

Moreover, these vessels can be tailored for specialized missions, such as reconnaissance or environmental monitoring. Biotech battleships equipped with living sensors can gather real-time intelligence on enemy movements, terrain, or celestial phenomena, providing crucial insights for strategic decision-making. This intelligence-gathering role not only enhances situational awareness but also supports more effective planning and execution for upcoming engagements.

The missions related to intergalactic defense are also evolving to encompass humanitarian roles. Biotechnologically integrated vessels could be used in disaster relief operations, leveraging their ability to generate resources and maintain life support for civilian populations impacted by conflict. The deployment of living systems capable of purifying water, generating food, or providing medical assistance can be invaluable in scenarios where humanitarian aid is desperately needed.

From a strategic perspective, fleet formations involving biotech battleships can enhance defensive postures. The integration of broader ecosystems within fleets means that tactics can adapt based on biological inputs—the vessels can operate not just as individual units but as participating members in a cohesive biological network. For instance, if one ship experiences damage, the remaining vessels could redistribute resources, allowing the injured ship to recover more efficiently, showcasing true interdependence in operation.

Communication within these fleets takes on a new form as well. Biologically integrated command structures can incorporate communication channels that flow not only through electronic means but also through biological signaling, creating a hybrid approach where decisions are informed by data from both machines and living systems. These channels facilitate rapid adjustments during engagements, allowing for seamless coordination among various message units—whether human or biological.

Integrating biotech battleships with traditional fleets raises the need for interoperability. Understanding that both conventional and biotech vessels may play complementary roles in missions allows for optimized strategic deployment. Developing protocols for joint operability ensures that communications, logistics, and operational strategies are harmonized across the fleet spectrum, fostering a cohesive approach to intergalactic defense.

As we look toward the future, the outlook for roles and missions in intergalactic defense becomes increasingly intertwined with responsible innovation and ethical considerations. The deployment of living systems in warfare demands a commitment to ensuring that the introduction of biotechnology contributes positively to societal values and ecological sustainability. By navigating the complexities of intergalactic conflict through the lens of biotechnology, military planners can forge a new narrative that emphasizes adaptability, resilience, and cooperation—ultimately redefining how humanity engages with both technology and life among the stars.

In summary, the roles and missions in intergalactic defense, as shaped by the introduction of biotech battleships, hold remarkable potential for innovative warfare approaches. By harnessing the adaptability and sustainability offered by living systems, military units can thrive in the challenges of deep space. The confluence of biology and technology in warfare presents us with new opportunities to rethink strategies, operational limits, and ethical responsibilities, paving the way for a multifaceted and dynamic future in interstellar conflict.

11.2. Fleet Formations and Tactics with Biotech Ships

The multifaceted landscape of warfare is undergoing a profound transformation with the introduction of biotech ships, where the integration of biological systems redefines not only the mechanics of combat but also the strategies and tactics employed in intergalactic defense. The deployment of these vessels necessitates a comprehensive understanding of fleet formations and battlefield strategies, taking into account the unique properties of living organisms and their interactions within military frameworks.

In the realm of fleet formations, biotech ships present intriguing possibilities that extend beyond traditional naval tactics. The synergy between mechanical and biological elements allows for a dynamic approach to formations that can adapt in real time to an evolving battlefield. When organized in formations, biotech ships can leverage their biological enhancements to function cooperatively, establishing a living network that enhances situational awareness and responsiveness. For instance, formations may employ bioengineered sensors embedded in the vessels' exteriors, providing real-time data back to a centralized command unit. This interconnectedness not only fosters effective communication within the fleet but allows for instantaneous decision-making based on shared biological insights, creating a tactical edge over conventional fleets.

The adaptability of biological systems aligns perfectly with the idea of fluid, non-linear tactics that characterize modern warfare. Traditional fleet formations can be rigid and predictable, but biotech vessels equipped with living components could maneuver fluidly, breaking formation to adapt to instantaneous tactical demands. They could engage in evasive actions that living systems employed in nature often exhibit, effectively mirroring the agility of organisms in reaction to environmental challenges. The incorporation of bioadaptive strategies would also facilitate a nuanced response to enemy formations, with vessels capable of responding autonomously to threats based on biological 'instincts' programmed into their operational matrix.

In combat scenarios, the strategic utilization of biotech capabilities can provide a significant advantage. For instance, a fleet of biotech ships could simultaneously engage in asymmetric warfare, deploying specialized bioweapons designed to incapacitate or deceive enemy forces. Utilizing weaponry that incorporates living organisms could enhance offensive capabilities, allowing ships to unleash bioengineered projectiles that contain adaptive agents. These projectiles could identify and exploit vulnerabilities in enemy defenses, altering their behavior to ensure more effective strikes. Such versatility not only enhances strike capabilities but introduces an element of unpredictability that can undermine enemy tactics.

Furthermore, the potential for biotech ships to engage in defensive maneuvers through biological means reinforces their operational viability. Living systems aboard the vessels may be engineered to produce defensive compounds or secretions that counteract enemy attacks, thereby reinforcing the vessel's environmental resilience. This capability aligns with modern warfare's shift toward force multipliers—vessels that can leverage biological resources to create layers of defense that hinder enemy offensives.

However, strategic deployment in the context of warfare involving living systems encompasses ethical and ecological considerations that must be acknowledged. The integration of biological organisms into combat scenarios necessitates an ethical framework surrounding their use. Military leaders must navigate the implications of deploying living systems in scenarios where their survival and rights are of concern. Developing robust guidelines that balance military objectives with ethical stewardship is essential to ensure responsible tactics and maintain credibility on the interstellar stage.

As we consider the future of fleet formations and tactics with biotech ships, it is vital to foster interdisciplinary collaborations among engineers, biologists, ethicists, and military strategists. The sharing of knowledge and insights across these domains will yield innovative approaches toward integrating living systems within military strategies, optimizing their efficacy while addressing associated grievances or complexities. Additionally, performing detailed simulations and modeling the nuanced interactions of living systems within fleet formations will support ongoing training and operational readiness, preparing personnel for the dynamic complexities of intergalactic warfare.

The landscape of warfare is continuously evolving; the advent of biotech ships heralds a future where the strategies and tactics deployed in combat are as adaptable as the living systems they integrate. By combining the agility of biological processes with the precision of military engineering, the roles of fleet formations will redefine defensive and offensive maneuvers in intergalactic conflict. As we push the boundaries of military capability, it is imperative to consider not only the effectiveness of these tactics but also the ethical frameworks that will shape their responsible implementation in navigating the vastness of space.

11.3. Communication in Organically Enhanced Fleets

In the vast and complex domain of intergalactic warfare, communication in organically enhanced fleets evolves as one of the most crucial aspects that significantly impact strategy, operational success, and overall cohesion among integrated bio-mechanical systems. As we integrate biological components with technological advancements, the way fleets communicate must adapt to this innovative paradigm—promoting efficient collaboration and real-time responses to evolving circumstances.

Central to organic fleet communication is the concept of biological signaling, which allows for a more intuitive interaction between living systems and technology. Biological organisms possess intricate communication pathways, from chemical signals exchanged through pheromones to electromagnetic signals that various species use for navigation and warning. By harnessing the natural signaling mechanisms found in biological organisms, fleets can develop sophisticated communication systems that operate seamlessly within the biological and mechanical frameworks of the battleships.

For instance, genetically engineered organisms aboard biotech vessels could be designed to communicate their physiological states to the ship's command systems via biochemical signals. This communication can relay real-time data on environmental health, stresses, or threats, enabling immediate action based on the living components' responses. Such biological feedback would enhance the usability of these living systems, creating a network where both the ship and its crew can adapt to changing conditions through responsive strategies.

Moreover, an effective communication strategy for organically enhanced fleets must address the integration of traditional communication systems with biological signaling. While organic components may offer rich and responsive channels of information, conventional communication protocols—such as satellite links and electronic data transmission—remain integral for tactical coordination among fleets and with command structures. Establishing interoperability between these two distinct communication modalities requires robust engineering and a clear plan to ensure that all components work cohesively.

One potential approach is to develop hybrid communication systems that synergize biological and electronic networks. For example, live sensors could feed data to command units while also interfacing with electronic systems that process this input. By creating a unified communication platform, fleet commanders can have access to a comprehensive situational awareness picture that incorporates both biological feedback and traditional tactical intelligence—enabling them to make well-informed decisions swiftly.

Training becomes paramount in preparing crews to adeptly navigate this new communication landscape. Operators must develop familiarity with both biological signaling mechanisms and traditional communication tools, ensuring that they can effectively interpret the data received from living systems while coordinating actions with fellow crew members. Simulations and drills that emphasize the interconnectedness of biological and technological communication can cultivate proficiency and confidence among personnel, enhancing their capacity to manage unexpected situations that arise during missions.

Furthermore, psychological elements of communication must be considered as fleets integrate living systems into military operations. Over time, personnel interacting with biologically integrated systems may develop emotional and cognitive connections with these organisms, which can influence their decision-making processes and task execution. Understanding the psychological implications of this symbiotic relationship is critical, as it can impact the overall effectiveness of communication while also fostering a culture of respect and stewardship toward the living components.

However, implementing communication systems within organically enhanced fleets also presents challenges. Balancing the reliability of traditional communication systems with the unpredictable nature of biological signaling can complicate operational coherence. Ensuring that all elements within the fleet maintain a shared understanding and access to pertinent information is essential, calling for continuous improvements to both biological and mechanical communication frameworks.

Ethical considerations surrounding communication in organically enhanced fleets are equally vital. As military forces embrace the use of living systems, establishing guidelines surrounding transparency and responsibility in decision-making is crucial. The autonomy of living systems may necessitate discussions about their place within the command hierarchy and how operators determine when human intervention is appropriate. Fostering an ethical framework that governs communications and interactions with living technologies will not only align military objectives with moral imperatives but also serve to maintain trust among operators and the public.

In summary, communication in organically enhanced fleets is a multifaceted endeavor that requires integrating biological signaling mechanisms with traditional military communication frameworks. The ability to share real-time information among living systems and crew members will enhance situational awareness, operational readiness, and adaptive responses to threats. As we navigate the intricacies of biotechnology in warfare, a commitment to responsible innovation, continuous training, and ethical engagement will empower fleets to operate effectively—ushering in a new era of intergalactic defense that harmonizes life and technology amidst the stars.

11.4. Interfacing with Traditional Armada

In the evolving realm of warfare, interfacing with a traditional armada represents a critical junction in maximizing the operational effectiveness of biotech battleships. As we usher in a new era characterized by the integration of biological systems into military strategies, navigating the complexities of combining living technologies with conventional fleets becomes an essential consideration. This integration not only facilitates tactical innovations but also presents opportunities for enhanced adaptability, collaboration, and effectiveness in intergalactic combat.

One of the primary advantages of incorporating biotech battleships into an existing fleet lies in their potential to augment traditional naval capabilities. The adaptability inherent in biological systems allows these vessels to act synergistically with conventional warships, enhancing situational awareness and responsiveness. For instance, biotech battleships equipped with advanced biological sensors can provide real-time intelligence on enemy movements, terrain assessments, or environmental threats. This intelligence can be shared across the fleet, creating a cohesive operational network that leverages the strengths of both organic and mechanical systems.

Moreover, the integration of biotech ships can enable traditional fleets to evolve in their operational roles. As these vessels can perform diverse functions—ranging from reconnaissance to offensive strikes —the traditional ship's capabilities can be enhanced through cooperation. Operating in close formations allows for seamless transitions between attack and support roles, optimizing the advantages presented by both biological innovation and mechanical reliability. The introduction of living technologies can shift the tactical paradigms of fleet engagements, empowering commanders to capitalize on the unique adaptive qualities of biotech vessels.

Furthermore, the unique features of biotech battleships, such as self-repairing materials and resource recycling, can significantly contribute to logistical efficiency within traditional armadas. By minimizing downtime associated with repairs and reducing reliance on frequent resupply missions, these hybrid vessels can streamline operational capabilities. The efficiencies gained from these biological systems extend beyond cost savings; they also improve fleet readiness, allowing traditional ships to engage in extended missions without compromising effectiveness.

However, integrating biotech battleships with traditional fleets prompts discussions concerning interoperability and command structures. Effective communication between varied systems will be critical for smooth operations. Establishing protocols that enable seamless data sharing and coordination between organic and mechanical components assures that commands are executed efficiently across the fleet. This integrated communication will require innovations that harness both biological signaling methods and traditional electronic protocols, creating hybrid networks where living systems and machines collaborate effectively.

Addressing safety and biosecurity becomes paramount as traditional naval forces incorporate biotech vessels. Ensuring that engineered organisms remain controlled and contained during engagements is crucial to prevent unintended ecological impacts or risks associated with biological behaviors. Mitigating these concerns requires rigorous containment measures and monitoring protocols to ensure that living systems do not compromise operational integrity or contribute to unintended environmental consequences.

From an ethical standpoint, blending biotech battleships with traditional armadas also raises profound considerations. Traditional warfare already operates within established moral frameworks. Still, the integration of biological systems necessitates evaluations regarding responsibilities toward engineered life forms and the wider implications for ecosystems. Military leaders must establish ethical guidelines that govern the respectful treatment of living organisms, reflecting society's values and expectations as humanity navigates this frontier of intergalactic conflict.

Ultimately, successful interfacing of biotech battleships with traditional fleets heralds possibilities for innovation and collaboration in warfare. While embracing the advantages of biological systems, military planners must strategically address the complexities that arise as these technologies reshape mission dynamics and operational capabilities. By fostering open communication channels and inclusive command structures, leveraging the strengths of both traditional and biotech systems will create a formidable naval force ready to tackle the challenges of tomorrow's battles among the stars.

As we explore the potential for integrating biotech battleships within traditional armadas, the possibilities for tactical innovation and operational enhancements begin to unfold—each offering new avenues for redefining warfare and highlighting the importance of collaboration between life and technology. The future of intergalactic conflict may well shape the legacy of our species as stewards of both their creations and the ecosystems that sustain them, prompting us to consider how best to navigate this path together.

11.5. Future Outlook: Defensive and Offensive Strategies

In a universe driven by the relentless pursuit of innovation, the future of warfare lies at the intersection of biotechnology and military strategy. In the ongoing evolution of combat, having both defensive and offensive strategies effectively articulated will be paramount in determining not just the outcomes of battles, but the broader implications of humanity's engagement with life and technology across the stars. As we extend our reach into interstellar realms, it becomes essential to consider how these strategies can be molded by the capabilities endowed through biotechnological advancements.

Defensive strategies, rooted in the inherent adaptability of living systems, may redefine traditional concepts of fortitude. The integration of self-healing materials and systems utilized within biotech battleships signifies a shift from static defenses to dynamic networks capable of autonomously gauging threats and responding in real-time. Living armor that can adjust its properties based on exposure to damage represents the next frontier of military defense. This not only fortifies the structure but also reduces the need for extensive repairs, thereby improving sustainability during extended engagements. Furthermore, employing bioengineered organisms that can produce defensive chemicals in response to attacks—similar to how certain plants defend against herbivores—will create an environment where countermeasures are embedded directly within the ship's operational protocols.

Additionally, the capabilities of bio-sensing systems will allow biotech battleships to perceive potential threats well before conventional detection methods can identify them. By leveraging genetically altered organisms capable of detecting specific environmental signals many of which might be imperceptible to human operators, these vessels can institute evasive maneuvers or deploy countermeasures even before a threat becomes overtly apparent. This anticipatory approach not only enhances defensive tactics but also allows commanders to make informed decisions and counter actions with minimal delay, fortifying their position in engagements.

On the offensive front, biotechnologically enhanced weaponry introduces profound changes to how military engagement is conceptualized. The ability to create smart munitions that can autonomously track and adapt to targets signifies a transformative leap in precision warfare. By utilizing living organisms to provide real-time feedback and guidance, military strategists can execute more accurately defined strikes with reduced collateral damage—aligning offensive capabilities with both ethical imperatives and operational effectiveness.

The deployment of organisms designed for lethal purposes opens conversations surrounding bioweapons that can target adversaries while leaving surrounding ecosystems unharmed. These living munitions could, for instance, incapacitate enemy systems through specialized biological agents that affect only the intended targets, a stark contrast to the indiscriminate nature of conventional armament. Therefore, integrating biological systems into offensive tactics fabricates new modalities of warfare that endorse precision and minimize the consequences of conflict on broader global ecosystems.

However, deploying these strategies will also require careful consideration of the psychological dimensions associated with employing living systems in warfare. The potential for operators to experience empathy or emotional connections with the biological entities under their command necessitates the development of a new combat ethos, one that balances military objectives with ethical responsibilities toward engineered life forms. Leaders in this space must cultivate awareness and consideration for the intricacies of these relationships, fostering a culture that respects both innovation and the ethical treatment of living systems in warfare.

Navigating the regulatory and ethical frameworks surrounding both defensive and offensive strategies plays a crucial role in informing the future of biotech battleships. As these innovations unfold within the military sphere, public perception, societal values, and legislative oversight will shape how strategies are enacted and received by both military personnel and civilians alike. Leaders must engage in active discussions about responsibility and transparency, ensuring that strategic innovations align with contemporary ethical standards.

In conclusion, the future outlook for both defensive and offensive strategies in interstellar warfare, empowered by biotechnological advancements, hints at a profound transformation of military engagement paradigms. A commitment to cultivating adaptability, precision, and ethical responsibility will define not only the operational success of biotech battleships but also the legacy they bestow upon future generations. As we stand on the cusp of this transformative journey among the stars, a collaborative approach that emphasizes innovation and stewardship will serve as our guiding compass in shaping the future of warfare. Equip oneself with the understanding and foresight necessary to navigate this new frontier, blending biology with technology in pursuit of a more resilient and effective defense.

12. Ethical Implications and Considerations

12.1. The Morality of Biologically Enhanced Warfare

The exploration of the morality of biologically enhanced warfare brings forth an intricate tapestry of ethical, societal, and political considerations that lie at the heart of the integration of biotechnology into military practices. As humanity charts its course into an era defined by bioengineering and living machines, a robust discourse surrounding the moral implications of weaponizing biological organisms must take center stage.

At the core of this moral inquiry is the question of what it means to create life for the purpose of warfare. The historical context of warfare is laden with advancements that prioritized military objectives, often overshadowing the ethical considerations surrounding the impacts of technology on life. Biologically enhanced warfare compels us to confront the notion that engineered organisms, unlike traditional weapons, possess qualities of life—adaptability, resilience, and biological responses. As we advance towards the deployment of these living constructs as tools of war, it becomes essential to assess the implications of our actions on not only human actors but also the organisms we create. We must grapple with the responsibility that accompanies the creation and deployment of life forms that have been engineered specifically for conflict, reflecting upon the potential consequences of wielding such power.

Moreover, the concept of collateral damage in warfare takes on new dimensions when biologically integrated systems are employed. While traditional military operations have often accepted the inevitability of collateral damage as a cost of combat, engaging with living systems raises profound questions about the rights of these entities and the ecological impacts of their utilization. Potential ecological disruptions resulting from engineered organisms escaping into the environment or interacting with natural ecosystems must be considered. By disregarding the rights and welfare of engineered life forms, we risk perpetuating a cycle of harm that not only threatens the ecological balance but also poses moral dilemmas that must be carefully navigated.

The psychological impact of biologically enhanced warfare encompasses the emotional burdens experienced by operators tasked with engaging living systems. The symbiotic relationship between human operators and the living entities they command introduces unique challenges, as empathy and emotional connections may influence decision-making. The ethical implications of using living organisms in combat scenarios call for robust discussions about the responsibilities and moral obligations that accompany the manipulation of life —and how these considerations interplay with military hierarchy and command structures.

The integration of biotechnology into warfare also necessitates cross-disciplinary engagement among scientists, military personnel, ethicists, and policymakers. Disseminating knowledge on the ethical implications of biologically enhanced warfare through education and collaborative dialogue will forge pathways toward responsible innovation. Establishing ethical guidelines and principles to govern this landscape, while simultaneously respecting the complexities of life, will foster an environment that promotes accountability and transparency. The future of warfare where biological organisms are deployed as agents of conflict must be rooted in the principles of stewardship and respect for life, emphasizing the need for adaptable frameworks that address emerging ethical inquiries.

Public perception and acceptance of biologically enhanced warfare also play a critical role in shaping the discourse around its moral applications. As awareness surrounding the implications of biotechnological advancements grows, military organizations must remain vigilant in addressing public concerns, cultivating dialogue that emphasizes transparency, responsibility, and ethical scrutiny. Engaging citizens in discussions about the role of living technologies in national defense fosters an atmosphere of collaboration between military endeavors and societal values.

In conclusion, navigating the morality of biologically enhanced warfare entails deep reflection, rigorous ethical discourse, and critical engagement with the broader implications of employing living systems in combat. As we design the future of warfare with biotechnological advancements, acknowledging the complexities and responsibilities intertwined with our actions is essential. The path ahead demands a commitment to balancing innovation with ethical stewardship, promoting an increasingly integrated understanding of how life and technology converge in the pursuit of security among the stars. This multifaceted conversation serves as an invitation for continuous dialogue, urging us to explore the multifarious ways in which we can responsibly engage with life's potential as we traverse the frontiers of war and peace.

12.2. Ethical Dilemmas in Biotechnology Use

In contemporary discussions surrounding the ethical dilemmas posed by the use of biotechnology, particularly in the realm of military ap plications, we find ourselves confronting profound questions. As the integration of biological systems into the fabric of warfare becomes a reality, the implications ripple through various spheres—moral, ecological, social, and political. This analysis aims to unpack the complexities associated with the ethical dilemmas of biotechnology use in the context of developing biotech battleships and their implications for future interstellar warfare.

At the core of the ethical inquiry is the fundamental question of obligation and responsibility: What rights do the engineered organisms possess, and what moral considerations must guide our interaction with them? Unlike conventional weapons, which are inanimate objects devoid of life, biologically enhanced weaponry and living systems embody characteristics of life. As humanity takes the leap into redesigning living organisms for specific military purposes, it becomes essential to contemplate our moral duty towards these living entities and the broader ecosystems they inhabit. The ethical stewardship of life—whether human, animal, or bioengineered—demands a commitment to respecting their dignity and rights.

The implications of deploying living systems in combat scenarios introduce complex layers of responsibility. With organisms engineered for specific military purposes, the potential for misuse and unintended ecological consequences heightens. Can we ethically justify creating and releasing organisms intended for warfare? What are the ramifications of such actions, not only for the organisms themselves but for the ecosystems into which they may be released? Establishing an ethical framework around the deployment of biotechnological advancements in military settings will be critical. This involves discussions on accountability, the potential of organisms to adapt or mutate, and the long-term impacts on local ecosystems and communities.

A key dimension of the ethical dilemmas arises around public perception and societal acceptance of biotechnologically enhanced warfare. Engaging with living systems as instruments of conflict poses questions about the role of warfare in society and how emerging technologies redefine human relationships with life itself. The public may harbor fears regarding the potential consequences of bioweapons —or question the morality of employing life forms as military tools— prompting protests, opposition, and demands for transparency. Thus, military leaders must foster open dialogues around the ethical implications of biotechnological advancements, ensuring that the broader societal values are considered in strategic decisions.

The complexities of cross-disciplinary collaborations also affect the ethical dialogue surrounding biotechnology in warfare. Scientists, engineers, military strategists, and ethicists must come together to engage in in-depth conversations about the implications of deployment. This collaboration encourages the creation of comprehensive ethical guidelines informed by diverse perspectives. As we navigate this challenging landscape, we need to establish interdisciplinary pathways that facilitate transparent communication and collective responsibility for the well-being of engineered life systems.

Furthermore, examining the historical precedents surrounding the use of emerging technologies in warfare can provide insights into how to approach this ethical conundrum. The legacies of nuclear weapons, chemical warfare, and biological warfare remind us of the profound consequences of technological advancements in military contexts. Historical reflections can guide contemporary practice as we seek to avoid repeating mistakes and aspire to prioritize ethical boundaries.

The establishment of guidelines and principles for ethical biotech development will be paramount as military applications of biotechnology advance. These principles should encompass considerations related to human rights, ecological sustainability, and the moral treatment of living systems. The development of comprehensive frameworks would promote not only responsible innovations but also inspire public trust in military endeavors leveraging living technologies.

In summary, the ethical dilemmas surrounding the use of biotechnology in warfare compel us to reevaluate our responsibilities and obligations as we integrate living systems into military applications. Engaging in thoughtful discussions about the nature of life, ecological impacts, and technological advancement is essential in paving the way for responsible practices that respect the intricate relationships between humans and the living organisms we create. As we navigate this complex landscape, embracing a commitment to ethics, sustainability, and respect for life will significantly shape the legacy we leave for future generations of interstellar explorers and warriors.

12.3. Balancing Innovation with Responsibility

Balancing innovation with responsibility is perhaps one of the most significant challenges faced by humanity as we navigate the complexities of integrating biotechnology into warfare. This delicate balance requires a nuanced understanding of not only the transformative potential of biotechnological advancements in military applications but also the ethical, environmental, and societal implications of wielding such power. As we embrace the integration of living systems into combat scenarios, it becomes essential to consider the responsibilities that accompany these innovations and ensure that our endeavors do not compromise the integrity of life itself.

At the heart of this balance lies the responsibility to ensure that biotechnological innovations are developed and deployed ethically. The advent of bioengineered organisms designed for military purposes evokes questions about the rights of these engineered life forms. As we create and manipulate living systems, we must confront the potential moral dilemmas arising from our actions—such as the implications of deploying organisms in warfare, their treatment, and their ecological impacts. Establishing ethical guidelines and standards to govern the development and application of biotechnology in military contexts will be vital in shaping responsible practices that reflect our commitment to the dignity of all forms of life.

Moreover, the environmental consequences of biotechnological warfare demand urgent attention. Biological systems are intrinsically interconnected, and their disruption through warfare or irresponsibly managed innovations can lead to catastrophic ecological repercussions. The introduction of engineered organisms into ecosystems carries risks; if not managed judiciously, these organisms might outcompete native species or create ecological imbalances. Balancing innovation with responsibility means actively prioritizing ecological stewardship, ensuring that the deployment of biotechnological advancements aligns with principles of sustainability and respect for biodiversity.

Importantly, public perception plays a significant role in shaping the acceptance and integration of biotechnology in military applications. As society grapples with the implications of merging life and technology, fostering open dialogues surrounding these innovations becomes crucial. Engaging with diverse stakeholders—including scientists, ethicists, military officials, and the public—will lead to a more informed understanding of the potential benefits and risks associated with biotechnological warfare. This conversation must emphasize transparency and accountability while addressing public concerns about the responsible use of life in conflict.

In addition, training military personnel to navigate the complexities of working with living systems is central to effectively balancing innovation and responsibility. Operators must be equipped not only with technical knowledge but also with an understanding of ethical considerations inherent to engaging with living organisms. Training programs should emphasize the importance of empathy, stewardship, and respect for life, cultivating a sense of responsibility that empowers personnel to act thoughtfully in the deployment and management of bioengineered systems.

The role of regulatory frameworks, laws, and international agreements becomes integral in maintaining this balance. As advancements in biotechnology challenge existing legal structures, there is a pressing need for robust policies that govern the use of living systems in warfare. Working collaboratively, policymakers must navigate the complexities of international treaties—not only to prohibit irresponsible practices but to establish standards that ensure the ethical treatment of engineered organisms and safeguard ecological integrity.

Ultimately, the quest to balance innovation with responsibility calls for a collective commitment to cultivating a culture of thoughtfulness and foresight in the application of biotechnology in warfare. As we embrace the extraordinary potential offered by living systems—enhancing our military capabilities and expanding the horizons of what is possible—we must also remain vigilant to the ethical and ecological ramifications of our actions. This dual commitment strengthens our position as stewards of both technology and nature, guiding the course of future interstellar warfare toward a path that prioritizes humanity's greater moral obligations to life in all its forms.

In this era of transformative change, it is the responsibility of visionaries, military leaders, scientists, and ethicists alike to converge in cultivating robust discussions that shape a future defined by the responsible use of biotechnology. By nurturing this balance, we not only pave the way for advanced military practices but also ensure that our innovations today lead to a more ethical, sustainable, and respectful engagement with life as we journey into the unknown realms of the cosmos. As we push the boundaries of what is possible, we must concomitantly nurture our ethical commitments—ensuring that our choices align with the betterment of society, life, and the environment, ultimately guiding us into a future enriched by responsibility and innovation.

12.4. Public Perception and Acceptance

In a rapidly evolving universe where the boundaries between biology and technology are continually blurred, humanity stands on the brink of the next revolutionary leap in interstellar warfare. What was once limited by the constraints of steel and electronics is now being reimagined with the intricate complexities of living organisms. As we venture into realms that were once the exclusive domain of science fiction, we are compelled to ask: What will the war machines of the future look like, and how will they alter the cosmos forever? In "Biotech Battleships: Designs of Future Intergalactic War Machines," we embark on a journey through this fascinating frontier, exploring the possibilities and challenges posed by biotechnology in the design of the future's most formidable battle vessels. This book seeks to equip readers with a thorough understanding of the scientific principles, design methodologies, and ethical considerations that underpin the creation of these advanced interspecies technologies. Join me, Sylvia L. Wright, as we demystify the extraordinary and transform the way we envision warfare among the stars.

Public perception and acceptance of biotechnology in warfare represent a significant factor in the successful integration and deployment of such technologies. As military entities explore the potential of biologically enhanced designs, understanding how society perceives these innovations is imperative for shaping policies, guidelines, and practices that align with ethical standards and community expectations.

Historically, public acceptance of military technologies has been influenced by a combination of factors, including media portrayal, catastrophic events, technological advancements, and the evolving moral landscape surrounding warfare. The landscape of biotechnology presents unique challenges and opportunities, as it invites both fascination and trepidation. On one hand, the integration of living systems into military applications may evoke excitement about the possibilities of enhanced capabilities; on the other hand, concerns over the ethical implications of employing life as a tool of war can lead to deep public apprehension.

As biotechnological advancements continue to unfold, transparency in military communications becomes paramount. Engaging the public through outreach initiatives creates platforms for informed discussions about the potential benefits and risks associated with biotech warfare. By proactively addressing concerns, the military can foster a climate of trust and collaboration, emphasizing responsible stewardship of life forms and technological innovations. Though fear may stem from a lack of understanding, clear dialogue helps demystify the technologies and promotes constructive engagement.

Moreover, education plays a critical role in influencing public perception. Implementing educational programs that illuminate the science and ethics behind biotechnological advancements can empower communities to engage in meaningful conversations about military applications. By demystifying the principles of biotechnology and encouraging understanding of the ethical and ecological considerations involved, these programs can pave the way for open discussions regarding the deployment of biotechnologies in warfare.

The impact of biotech innovations on military operations can also serve as a focal point for garnering public support. Highlighting success stories that connect these systems to broader goals—such as resource sustainability, enhanced operational readiness, and reduced collateral damage—can resonate with community values. Demonstrating how responsible development aligns with the interest in ecological stewardship can help swing public sentiment in favor of biotechnological warfare innovations. As conflicts evolve to encompass not just military objectives, but humanitarian goals as well, the narrative surrounding biotechnology must align with the principles of responsibility and care for life.

Regulatory frameworks surrounding biotechnology must also reflect evolving public sentiment. Informed by feedback gathered through public discussions, regulations can be shaped to ensure that ethical standards are inherent to biotechnology development. The issue of biosecurity, concerning the potential risks posed by engineered organisms beyond military engagements, necessitates robust governance. Demonstrating a commitment to environmental sustainability and ethical oversight within military frameworks can thus foster public confidence in the responsible management of living technologies during both peacetime and combat scenarios.

Ultimately, public perception and acceptance of biotechnology in warfare hinge on transparent communication, education, and the establishment of ethical frameworks that unite military aim with societal values. As humanity navigates the complexities of merging biological systems with machines in warfare, continuously fostering these dialogues will be vital to ensure that the advancements reinforced in "Biotech Battleships" resonate positively within the context of public sentiment. The journey into this new frontier emphasizes that the future of warfare not only lies in technological innovation but also in cultivating an ethical commitment to responsibly harnessing life amidst the calls of conflict. As we venture forth together, bridging understanding and responsibility will reinforce the promise of biotechnological advancements as we explore the frontier among the stars.

12.5. Guidelines and Principles for Ethical Biotech Development

In nurturing the role of biotechnology within warfare, it is critical to establish robust guidelines and principles underpinning its ethical development. As we traverse the complexities of integrating biological systems into interstellar battleships, these guidelines serve not just as a framework for innovation but also as a moral compass that informs our responsibilities toward the living systems we engineer. The dual nature of biotechnology prompts us to consider both its extraordinary potential to enhance military capabilities and the profound ethical implications accompanying its application in combat scenarios.

At the forefront of these principles is the concept of respect for life. As we embark on engineering living organisms for military purposes, we must recognize the intrinsic value of the organisms we create. This perspective emphasizes that engineered life forms should be treated with dignity and care, fostering a culture of responsibility within military operations. Establishing ethical guidelines that articulate the rights of these organisms and ensure humane treatment during their design and deployment is paramount. Just as we advocate for human rights in societal contexts, a commitment to the ethical treatment of bioengineered life must resonate throughout military practices.

Furthermore, the guideline of transparency plays a fundamental role in fostering public trust in biotechnological innovations. As militaries investigate the potential of biotechnology in warfare, engaging the public in meaningful dialogues about the implications of these technologies can empower communities to voice their concerns and hopes. Transparency regarding the methods of engineering and deploying living systems—eschewing proprietary secrecy for openness —can foster collaboration between military entities and the public while ensuring that ethical considerations remain at the forefront of strategic discussions.

Additionally, the principle of ecological responsibility is critical to effective ethical biotech development. Understanding the potential ecological consequences of introducing engineered organisms into combat scenarios must guide planning and decision-making processes. Robust ecological assessments should accompany any application of biotechnology, ensuring that the impacts on ecosystems and biodiversity are integral to operational considerations. Establishing fail-safes to prevent ecological disruption supports a commitment to both innovation and environmental stewardship—vital considerations as humanity navigates the complexities of interstellar warfare.

As we mold these ethical guidelines, it is also essential to consider continuous engagement with bioethicists, scientists, policymakers, and military leaders. Interdisciplinary collaboration fosters an inclusive dialogue that strengthens our approach toward navigating the moral dilemmas inherent in biotechnologically enhanced warfare. Regular consultations with diverse stakeholders can cultivate a culture of ethical reflection and adaptability crucial for addressing emerging challenges that arise during the development and deployment of biotech technologies.

Education and training programs that integrate ethical considerations into the development of futuristic warfare will empower military personnel to cultivate a sense of responsibility and awareness regarding their actions. Above technical training, embedding ethics into foundational education ensures that operators are equipped with the tools necessary to navigate ethical dilemmas when managing living systems. Fostering a culture that upholds ethical stewardship will enhance operational effectiveness and promote harmony within broader societal engagements.

Finally, establishing international legal frameworks around the military use of biotechnology becomes essential as our engagement with living systems evolves. Recognizing that the implications of biotechnological warfare extend beyond national borders necessitates collaboration among nations in crafting regulations that govern its use. Establishing international treaties wherein standards for ethical and responsible biotech development in warfare are acknowledged and upheld will bolster accountability and transparency on the global stage.

In conclusion, the establishment of guidelines and principles for ethical biotech development embodies a commitment to responsible innovation in warfare. By emphasizing respect for life, transparency, ecological responsibility, interdisciplinary engagement, education, and international cooperation, we can navigate the ethical landscape alongside the remarkable potential of biotechnology. Thus, the effectiveness of integrating living systems into military strategies will not solely rely on technological advancement but also on our collective dedication to ensuring that these innovations serve as agents of good, forging a future aligned with ethical principles and the enhancement of life itself among the stars.

13. Legal Framework: Navigating Through Regulations

13.1. Existing Regulations on Biotechnical Warfare

Existing regulations regarding biotechnical warfare are an essential component of the broader discussion around the integration of biotechnology into military applications, especially as we venture into the realm of intergalactic warfare. Historically, the advent of bioweapons has raised profound concerns about the potential for misuse, leading to international treaties and regulations aimed at mitigating the risks associated with biological warfare. Understanding these frameworks is crucial as we navigate the complexities of deploying biotech battleships and their accompanying biological systems.

The regulatory landscape surrounding biotechnical warfare is built upon various international agreements, legislations, and ethical guidelines, which have evolved in response to historical precedents of biological weapon use. One of the most significant milestones in this evolution is the Biological Weapons Convention (BWC) established in 1972. This treaty prohibits the development, production, and stockpiling of biological weapons, creating a legal framework that aims to prevent the use of living organisms for hostile purposes. Significantly, the BWC emphasizes the importance of cooperation and transparency among its signatory nations to promote peaceful uses of biological technology while maintaining safeguards against misuse.

Additionally, the 1925 Geneva Protocol prohibits the use of chemical and biological weapons in warfare, emphasizing harm reduction and ethical considerations in the conduct of war. As biotechnology advances and the opportunities for weaponizing living systems become more apparent, these existing frameworks necessitate ongoing evaluation and adaptation to account for new technological realities.

While the current regulations offer a foundational structure for managing biotechnical weapons, the rapid pace of advancements in biotechnology, genetic engineering, and synthetic biology underscores the need for new legislation that explicitly addresses these emerging threats. Innovations such as CRISPR gene-editing technology and bioengineering techniques present unique challenges that existing treaties may not adequately manage. A comprehensive understanding of the implications surrounding these technologies will be vital in shaping policies that can effectively govern their use in military contexts.

The advent of biotech battleships raises complex legal questions around the ethical use of bioengineered organisms in warfare. The implications of deploying living systems as weapons necessitate not only a clear understanding of their legal status but also of the potential consequences for both combatants and civilians. For instance, if a bioengineered organism were to escape control and cause ecological disruption, determining liability and responsibility could become contentious issues, particularly if international norms are not firmly in place.

Another challenge related to existing regulations involves enforcement mechanisms. The decentralized and often clandestine nature of biotechnological research can complicate efforts to monitor compliance with international treaties. Ensuring that nations adhere to established agreements while protecting sensitive research information presents obstacles for regulators seeking to maintain oversight over biotechnological advances. Stronger collaborative initiatives among countries—including transparency mechanisms and regular reporting—are essential for developing systems that foster trust and stability in the international community.

Future directions for legal oversight must focus on adapting existing regulations to address the unique challenges posed by biotechnical warfare. This adaptation will involve engaging with diverse stakeholders, including scientists, policymakers, ethicists, and military leaders, to establish new frameworks that encourage responsible innovation while ensuring public safety. Collaborative efforts will also play a vital role in developing comprehensive guidelines surrounding the responsible use of biologically enhanced technologies in warfare, fostering a culture of accountability and transparency.

In conclusion, while existing regulations on biotechnical warfare provide a critical foundation for addressing the moral and ethical implications of employing living systems in military contexts, the rapidly evolving landscape of biotechnology demands an informed and adaptable approach. As we progress towards a future defined by biotechnological advancements in warfare, it is imperative to foster dialogue and collaboration among stakeholders to strengthen legal frameworks. By doing so, we can navigate the intricacies of biotechnological warfare while ensuring responsibility and respect for life remain at the forefront of our endeavors in intergalactic conflict. The role of policy and regulation, aligned with the ethical commitment to humane treatment of all life forms, will be crucial in determining how we wield the power of biotechnology as we venture deeper into the cosmos.

13.2. International Treaties and Agreements

In the rapidly evolving realm of interstellar warfare, the role of international treaties and agreements surrounding biotechnology stands as a pivotal element in shaping the ethical, legal, and operational frameworks that govern the interaction between humanity and living systems in combat settings. As the boundaries between biology and technology blur, it becomes imperative to navigate the complex landscape of international regulations that seek to mitigate risks while promoting responsible innovation in the military use of biotechnology.

Historically, the development of international treaties regarding biological weapons can be traced back to the early 20th century when the horrors of World War I prompted the first global discussions on the regulation of chemical and biological warfare. The 1925 Geneva Protocol was a landmark treaty that sought to prohibit the use of asphyxiating, poisonous, or other gases and bacteriological methods of warfare. This convention established the foundational principles that would guide the evolution of bioweapons regulation, leading to the more comprehensive Biological Weapons Convention (BWC) of 1972. The BWC prohibits the development, production, and stockpiling of biological and toxin weapons, thereby providing a solid framework protecting against the misuse of living organisms in conflict.

However, the emergence of advanced biotechnological capabilities, such as genetic engineering, synthetic biology, and bioinformatics, has prompted calls for updates to existing regulations. The rapid pace of innovation in these fields outstrips the capacity of current legal frameworks to address potential threats effectively. Therefore, there is an urgent need for new legislation that encompasses a broader array of biotechnological advancements while explicitly addressing the ethical considerations surrounding the use of living systems within military applications.

Inherent in this call for new legislation is the challenge of ensuring effective enforcement mechanisms. The decentralized nature of biotechnological research creates difficulties in monitoring compliance with international treaties. Many biotechnical innovations occur within academic institutions or private sector laboratories, often beyond the purview of military oversight. To address this challenge, nations must commit to collaborative oversight—establishing robust partnerships between governments, research communities, and international organizations to synchronize efforts in monitoring compliance with legal standards. Developing transparent reporting mechanisms that require researchers and military entities to disclose their studies and applications of biotechnology can foster trust and accountability within the global community.

Moreover, the need for international cooperation in the governance of biotechnological warfare highlights the importance of engaging diverse stakeholders throughout the regulatory process. Military leaders, scientists, ethicists, and policymakers must converge to create guidelines that reflect shared values and principles, promoting responsible development while upholding international norms. Engaging experts from various fields in the discussions around biotechnological warfare can ensure that regulations remain flexible and adaptive to future advancements.

As nations explore amendments to current legal frameworks, pertinent ethical principles must be woven into the fabric of treaties governing biotechnological warfare. The moral obligations associated with employing biotechnology in military contexts cannot be overstated, and guidelines must be established to safeguard the rights and welfare of engineered life forms. These frameworks should promote a culture of responsibility that recognizes the potential consequences of utilizing living organisms for combat purposes.

In conclusion, international treaties and agreements regarding biotechnology in warfare represent significant foundations for addressing the moral, legal, and operational complexities associated with the use of living systems in conflict. The current regulatory landscape, while historically significant, must evolve to accommodate the extraordinary advancements in biotechnological capabilities. By fostering international cooperation, developing adaptable legal frameworks, and integrating ethical considerations, we can navigate the intricacies of this emerging field. As we move forward into the uncharted territories of interstellar warfare, these treaties will not only enhance the defensive strategies of military forces but also ensure a commitment to ethical responsibility that honors the principles of life and sustainable practices amid the stars.

13.3. The Need for New Legislation

In a universe where the integration of biotechnology into military applications is becoming increasingly evident, there arises an urgent need for new legislation to govern the complexities of biologically enhanced warfare. The rapid advancements in genetic engineering and synthetic biology usher in possibilities that challenge traditional notions of warfare, presenting both opportunities and ethical dilemmas. This chapter explores the critical aspects surrounding the need for new regulations to address the unique challenges posed by the deployment of biotechnology in military contexts, particularly as we consider the designs of future intergalactic war machines.

Historically, military engagements have been primarily guided by established conventions and treaties that focus on conventional arms control. However, as biotechnology evolves and the prospect of utilizing living systems in combat becomes a reality, we must recognize that existing legal frameworks may not adequately address the implications associated with the creation and deployment of engineered life forms. Current regulations, such as the Biological Weapons Convention (BWC), provide important foundations but are often insufficient to encompass the rapidly developing field of biotechnology and its applications in warfare.

One significant area of focus in shaping new legislation is the ethical considerations surrounding the use of engineered organisms in military applications. As we manipulate life forms for combat purposes, we must grapple with the moral obligations that accompany such actions. Are we breaching ethical boundaries by weaponizing living systems, and what rights do these engineered organisms possess? Addressing these questions requires the establishment of comprehensive ethical guidelines that govern the treatment of living organisms in military contexts. Such frameworks should emphasize respect for life while ensuring accountability on the part of military entities engaged in biotechnological warfare.

Additionally, the complexity of interactions between engineered organisms and their environments poses challenges that necessitate regulatory oversight. Each deployment of living systems introduces uncertainties regarding their ecological impacts, behavior, and interactions with natural ecosystems. New legislation should focus on biosecurity measures that mitigate the risks of unintended ecological consequences. This includes establishing protocols for containment, monitoring, and assessment of the impacts of deployed engineered organisms on local fauna and flora, ensuring that the principles of ecological sustainability are maintained.

As we look toward the future of interstellar warfare and the potential whose features may drastically evolve, we must conduct thorough evaluations of novel biotechnological innovations. Comprehensive risk assessments should inform the development of new legislative frameworks, ensuring that both operational needs and societal values are balanced in the pursuit of military advancements. The collaboration between interdisciplinary stakeholders—scientists, ethicists, military planners, and policymakers—will be essential in shaping these comprehensive and adaptable frameworks.

Moreover, fostering international cooperation will be critical in establishing rigorously enforced legal standards surrounding biotechnological warfare. A global dialogue that encourages consensus among nations can help create common ground regarding the ethical use of living systems in combat, promoting responsible innovation while safeguarding ecological integrity. Such discussions must extend beyond national borders, recognizing that the challenges posed by biotechnological advancements are inherently international in scope.

Another layer to this complexity lies in the public's perception of biotechnology in warfare. Public acceptance hinges on establishing trust through transparency and open communication about the implications of deploying living systems in military contexts. Fostering public discussions that engage communities and inform them about the benefits and risks associated with biotechnological innovations is essential for mitigating fear and apprehension. Clarity and honesty around military objectives tied to biotechnology can bridge gaps in understanding and cultivate greater societal support.

In conclusion, the need for new legislation to govern biologically enhanced warfare is both pressing and multifaceted. As we transition into an era where biotechnology becomes integral to military operations, our legal frameworks must reflect the unique challenges associated with the integration of living systems into combat scenarios. By addressing ethical considerations, establishing robust biosecurity measures, fostering international cooperation, and communicating transparently with the public, we can create a comprehensive landscape of regulations poised to guide the responsible deployment of biotechnological innovations in warfare. As we move toward this new frontier, the legacy of our actions will ultimately shape the future of how humanity navigates the complexities of life, technology, and warfare across the stars.

13.4. Enforcement Mechanisms and Challenges

In the pursuit of innovative warfare technologies, the importance of enforcement mechanisms and the challenges associated with regulating biotech applications are paramount. As military strategies increasingly rely on the integration of biologically enhanced systems into combat scenarios, establishing robust frameworks to oversee the development, deployment, and ethical use of these technologies becomes essential.

One fundamental aspect of enforcement mechanisms is their reliance on existing legal frameworks that govern the use of biological organisms in warfare. International treaties, such as the Biological Weapons Convention (BWC) and the Geneva Protocol, provide foundational guidelines to prevent the proliferation of biological weapons and to promote the responsible use of biotechnology. However, the rapid advancement of biotechnological capabilities often outpaces these pre-existing treaties, creating a pressing need for new legislation that explicitly accounts for the dual-use nature of biotechnology in military contexts.

The challenges associated with enforcement mechanisms predominantly stem from the decentralized and often clandestine nature of biotechnological research and development. Unlike traditional military technologies that can be more easily monitored and regulated, biotechnological innovations often emerge from a diverse array of institutions—including universities, private companies, and research organizations—that may operate independently. This decentralization complicates the ability to track and enforce compliance with legal standards, necessitating a more collaborative approach among various stakeholders, including governments, research institutions, and military organizations.

Implementing effective biosecurity measures is critical to mitigating the risks posed by engineered organisms. Containment protocols, which prevent the unintended release of genetically modified organisms into the environment, must be established across all levels of biotechnological research and deployment. Strict monitoring procedures and regular inspections will help ensure compliance with biosafety standards, thereby minimizing the ecological impacts of using living systems in warfare. Collaborating with international organizations and agencies, such as the World Health Organization (WHO) and the United Nations (UN), can facilitate transparency and accountability in these efforts.

Moreover, the ethical dimensions of deploying biotechnological weapons necessitate careful attention. Military leaders must navigate the moral implications of utilizing living organisms in combat, reflecting on the rights of both engineered and native organisms. Engaging bioethicists in discussions surrounding new legislation can help provide a framework for addressing these concerns, ensuring that the use of biotechnology respects ethical considerations while maximizing operational effectiveness.

Establishing educational programs that promote awareness and understanding of biotechnology among soldiers and military personnel also plays a crucial role in enforcement mechanisms. Training should encompass the moral and ethical implications of using living systems in warfare, enabling operators to engage thoughtfully with biotechnological innovations. A well-informed military workforce equipped with knowledge about the responsibilities associated with biotechnological deployment can enhance compliance with ethical and legal frameworks.

It will be essential to involve public perspectives in shaping enforcement mechanisms related to biotechnological warfare. Perceptions of biotechnological advancements are deeply intertwined with societal values and ethics, necessitating community engagement to foster trust and transparency. Developing open communication channels between military organizations and the public can facilitate a better understanding of the motivations behind biotechnological innovations and the measures in place to govern their use responsibly.

Looking ahead, the future of enforcement mechanisms will demand flexibility and adaptability to accommodate the rapidly changing landscape of biotechnology. As advancements continue to unfold, the interplay between technological innovation and ethical considerations will shape the legal framework governing biotechnological warfare. Encouraging a proactive approach, military leaders must remain attuned to emerging scientific developments to adapt legislation and ensure that enforcement mechanisms remain effective.

In conclusion, the enforcement mechanisms and challenges of biotechnological warfare are multifaceted and complex. Balancing innovation with responsibility will require the establishment of robust legal frameworks, ethical guidelines, biosecurity measures, and educational programs within military organizations. By engaging diverse stakeholders ranging from scientists to the public, we can shape a future where the integration of biotechnology into warfare is conducted ethically and sustainably, ultimately redefining the relationship between life and technology in the cosmos.

13.5. Future Directions for Legal Oversight

In the context of rapidly evolving warfare shaped by the integration of biotechnology, the future of legal oversight emerges as a crucial element that will guide and govern the ethical, operational, and strategic dimensions of using living systems in military applications. As biotechnologically enhanced designs transition from theoretical constructs to practical implementations, establishing a comprehensive legal framework that addresses the unique challenges posed by this convergence of biology and technology will be imperative. This chapter explores potential directions for legal oversight surrounding biotechnological innovations, emphasizing the need for adaptable and forward-thinking regulations to ensure responsible deployment and use in interstellar warfare.

The first step in developing future legal oversight involves reevaluating existing regulations within the context of modern biotechnological advancements. The Biological Weapons Convention (BWC) remains a cornerstone for addressing the potential risks associated with biological weapons, but its framework may not fully encompass the intricacies of deploying engineered life forms in warfare. Expanding the scope of international treaties to include specific provisions that address the ethical use of engineered organisms in military settings will be paramount. This could include establishing guidelines related to the rights of these organisms, considerations regarding biosecurity, and protocols for ecological assessments to prevent unintended consequences resulting from their deployment.

Furthermore, as technological innovations in biotechnology continue to blur the lines between life and weaponry, it becomes essential to engage multidisciplinary perspectives in shaping legal frameworks. Collaborative discussions must encompass not only legal experts and military strategists but also scientists, bioethicists, environmentalists, and public stakeholders. This collaborative approach can ensure that laws governing biotechnology reflect a comprehensive understanding of scientific realities, ethical considerations, and societal values. It fosters a sense of collective responsibility among all parties involved, creating an environment where innovative practices are grounded in ethical stewardship.

Developing flexible and adaptive regulations that can evolve with advancing technology is crucial as well. Legal frameworks must be agile enough to accommodate rapid advancements in biotechnology, mirroring the innovations that will emerge as engineers and scientists continue to push the boundaries of living systems. Regulatory bodies should prioritize real-time assessments and updates to laws, ensuring that legal oversight for biotech warfare remains relevant and effective. This may involve establishing temporary regulatory committees tasked with evaluating new developments, addressing potential concerns, and making recommendations for updates to existing laws.

Public engagement and transparency in legal oversight processes will play critical roles in shaping societal acceptance of biotechnological advancements in warfare. Fostering open dialogues surrounding the implications, benefits, and risks associated with biotechnology encourages informed public discourse, ultimately building trust and acceptance. Legitimizing the role of the military as a responsible steward of biotechnological innovations requires regular communication about ethical considerations, operational practices, and safety measures—reinforcing a commitment to accountability.

Additionally, addressing the complexities intertwined in cybersecurity and data privacy will be vital as biotechnology continues to intersect with digital technologies in warfare. Comprehensive regulations must encompass protections for both biological systems and sensitive information related to their deployment—recognizing that breaches of these systems could have substantial ramifications for both human participants and engineered organisms. Establishing robust cybersecurity standards and incorporating them into legal frameworks concerning biotech warfare will enhance operational security and fortify trust in military operations.

Finally, international cooperation will be essential in navigating the complexities of legal oversight for biotechnology in warfare. As biotechnological advancements transcend national boundaries and pose global challenges, nations must collaborate to establish common legal frameworks to govern the responsible use of biotechnology in military contexts. This cooperation facilitates dialogue among countries, aligning ethical standards and legal approaches while fostering mutual understanding and trust.

In summary, the future directions for legal oversight surrounding biotechnology in warfare necessitate a multifaceted approach that anticipates the challenges and complexities introduced by integrating living systems into combat scenarios. By re-evaluating existing regulations, fostering interdisciplinary collaboration, promoting flexibility in legal frameworks, ensuring transparency and public engagement, addressing cybersecurity issues, and enhancing international cooperation, we can cultivate an infrastructure that facilitates responsible innovation in interstellar warfare. As we advance into this uncharted territory, comprehensive legal oversight will play a decisive role in ensuring that the integration of biotechnology reflects not only technological progress but also a commitment to ethical standards and responsible stewardship of life in all its forms.

14. Cultural Impact: Reimagining Space Conflicts

14.1. Biotech in Science Fiction and Popular Media

Biotech in science fiction and popular media has long served not only as a reflection of societal hopes and fears but also as a compass guiding our understanding of bioengineering's potential in areas like warfare. By analyzing the narratives that surround biotechnology in various forms of media, we can glean insights into the profound implications of these technologies on our vision of future conflicts among the stars. The portrayal of biotechnology has evolved significantly, moving from imaginative speculation to credible projections as advancements in the real world advance.

Historically, science fiction has offered imaginative frameworks for understanding the benefits and risks associated with bioengineering. Early depictions often evoked dystopian scenarios where biological enhancements led to loss of autonomy or ethical dilemmas surrounding the manipulation of life. The fear of "playing God" has pervaded these narratives, prompting contemplation of questions about humanity's role in creating and potentially corrupting life. Works like Mary Shelley's "Frankenstein" exemplify this anxiety, highlighting the consequences of unchecked scientific ambition and the ensuing struggle between creator and creation.

Contemporary science fiction takes these themes further by exploring new dimensions of biotechnology and warfare. Media such as "Altered Carbon" and "Ghost in the Shell" presents cyborgs and biomechanical beings as pivotal figures within their narratives, challenging our perceptions of identity, humanity, and the line between human and machine. These portrayals may resonate with the advancement of biotechnology in real-world military contexts, inviting audiences to confront the ethical implications that arise when living systems and technology are fused.

Cultural narratives within popular media also play a crucial role in shaping the discourse around biotechnology in warfare. Series such as

"Star Trek" embrace the notion of bioengineering as a means of enhancing capabilities, portraying technology as a tool for exploration and peace rather than conflict. This optimistic vision showcases biotechnology's potential for fostering progress and understanding in the cosmos, balancing the fears with aspirations for harmony and betterment among species.

Conversely, portrayals of military applications of biotechnology often reflect concerns about power, control, and the potential for misuse. Series like "The Expanse" present conflicts resulting from bioengineered plagues or bioweapons, emphasizing humanity's precarious relationship with its creations. As the integration of biotechnology into warfare becomes more relevant, media narratives serve as cautionary tales that paint a vivid picture of what could go wrong if responsibility is sidelined in pursuit of military advantage.

The psychological impact of engaging with biotech concepts in media becomes part of a larger cultural understanding of conflict during our transition to an era defined by biotechnological advancements. As societies engage with the implications of living technology, public perception can shift, and fears may turn to acceptance or even advocacy. This evolution prompts reflections on the role of biotechnology in shaping our identity, governance of life through military technology, and our moral responsibilities as creators.

Educational and awareness programs centered around the themes of biotechnology in warfare can also benefit from insight drawn from popular media representations. By utilizing narratives from films, television shows, and literature, educators can engage audiences in meaningful discussions regarding the ethical ramifications of engineered life forms. Such initiatives can serve to inform communities while fostering critical thought about how innovations intersect with military objectives. By harnessing the power of storytelling, we can develop a more nuanced understanding of biotechnology's implications and encourage informed public discourse.

In conclusion, the portrayal of biotechnology in science fiction and popular media serves as both a reflection and a catalyst for societal values and concerns regarding its integration into warfare. These narratives not only illuminate hopes and fears but also play a significant role in framing how we perceive the evolving relationship between humanity and bioengineering. By examining these cultural stories, we can find pathways to responsible innovation and ethical governance of biotechnological advancements as we navigate into the uncertain territories of the future, contemplating both the promise of life and the weight of our choices in the cosmos.

14.2. Imagining the Other: Cyborgs and Biomechanical Beings

Imagining the future of warfare transcends just the nuts and bolts of technology; it challenges our fundamental understanding of what constitutes a combatant, a weapon, and even life itself. Within this transformation lies the realm of cyborgs and biomechanical beings —entities that blend organic matter with machines, raising profound questions about identity, agency, and ethical implications in a conflict scenario.

As biotechnological innovations advance, the concept of cyborgs —beings that unite flesh and machine—challenges the traditional dichotomy of human versus technology. These constructs are not merely machines outfitted with biological parts; they embody a new paradigm in which the boundaries between human capabilities and technological enhancements blur. In the context of warfare, cyborgs offer profound advantages: enhanced strength, improved reflexes, and augmented cognitive processes, all of which can dramatically shift the landscape of battle.

The incorporation of biomechanical beings into military applications redefines the nature of combat. Imagine soldiers equipped with biotechnologically enhanced exoskeletons that amplify their physical abilities, allowing them to perform extraordinary feats while minimizing fatigue. This synergy between man and machine creates hybrid warriors capable of surpassing human limitations, suggesting that the definition of what it means to be a soldier is interwoven with advancements in biotechnology and engineering.

However, the rise of cyborgs and biomechanical beings prompts an array of ethical dilemmas. Questions about identity, autonomy, and the implications of augmenting human capabilities necessitate rigorous discourse. If human operators are integrated with machines, what does it mean for their agency? To what extent do enhancements alter their duties, responsibilities, or decision-making processes in combat? These queries challenge military leaders and ethicists to confront the profound implications of merging living beings with technology —a contemplation that demands careful attention to not only their operational efficiency but also their moral status.

Moreover, the psychological dimensions associated with engaging with cyborgs and biomechanical beings raise additional concerns. As soldiers engage with enhanced soldiers or combat units, the relationship between human operators and their technologically augmented counterparts may lead to emotional complexities. The development of bonds with cyborgs—whether based on admiration, fear, or identification—can influence dynamics within the military hierarchy. Having to manage not just their technological assets but also their psychological wellness will demand new training models that incorporate emotional resilience as a key component of operational effectiveness.

In addressing these new challenges, strategies must be put in place to ensure responsible implementation of cyborgs and biomechanical beings in warfare. It is imperative to establish ethical guidelines that govern the integration of living systems with technology, advocating for respect towards the sentiments and rights of those involved in military operations. By embedding ethics into the design and deployment processes, military entities can maintain accountability while cultivating a respectful relationship with augmented beings.

Furthermore, public discourse regarding cyborgs and biomechanical beings plays a significant role in shaping policies and societal acceptance of these innovations. As societies grapple with the implications of merging biology and technology, fostering open discussions concerning military applications can bridge the gap between fear and understanding. Engaging the public will empower communities to voice concerns and ideas, fostering a collaborative environment that promotes responsible development.

Ultimately, the future of warfare as imagined through the lens of cyborgs and biomechanical beings signifies an unprecedented evolution in our understanding of combat, identity, and ethics. As humanity continues to explore the intersection of life and technology, these advancements invite us to reflect on our moral obligations to both individuals and the world they inhabit. Through deliberation, interdisciplinary collaboration, and responsible stewardship, we can navigate the emerging landscape of warfare, ensuring that the innovations we embrace are rooted in values that respect and honor life across the cosmos. As we stand on the threshold of this new paradigm, the journey ahead presents both extraordinary opportunities and formidable questions that will ultimately define the nature of humanity's engagement with its own creations.

14.3. Cultural Narratives Shaping Future Warfare

Cultural narratives play a pivotal role in shaping the future of warfare, particularly as biotechnology increasingly integrates with military strategies. As we explore the complex tapestry of these narratives, it becomes clear that they reflect and influence societal values, fears, and aspirations. By examining how biotechnology is portrayed in various forms of media—education, literature, art, and popular culture —we can better understand how these narratives not only inform public perception but also craft the ethical, moral, and operational landscapes of future combat scenarios.

One of the primary narratives surrounding biotechnology in warfare is rooted in the thrills and terrors of manipulating life itself. Literature and film have long depicted biotechnology as a double-edged sword, capable of great advancements and perilous consequences. For instance, works like H.G. Wells' "The Island of Doctor Moreau" and Mary Shelley's "Frankenstein" encapsulate the fear associated with playing God—the ethical dilemma of creating and controlling life. These narratives send cautionary messages about the potential hubris of scientists delving into biotechnological innovations without checks and balances. As society witnesses real-world advancements in genetic engineering and synthetic biology, these cautionary tales resonate profoundly, prompting discourse about the responsibilities that accompany such power.

Conversely, popular media often extols the heroic possibilities of biotechnology, framing it as a means to achieve extraordinary feats. Movies like "Gattaca" and television series such as "Altered Carbon" celebrate the notion of transcending human limitations through biotechnological enhancements, offering narratives that explore both the potential for human evolution and the challenges posed by an ethics of enhancement. This optimistic perspective cultivates hope for the future, suggesting that innovations in biotechnology could lead to improved quality of life and even create super-soldiers for intergalactic warfare. Such narratives encourage public excitement around military applications of biotechnology, fostering societal support for research and collaboration.

The juxtaposition of these narratives influences how both military and civilian entities approach the development of biotechnological warfare. As public sentiment shifts toward optimism or caution, military leaders must navigate these cultural currents to engage effectively with society. Acknowledging the fears associated with biotechnological advancement while simultaneously leveraging public aspirations for innovation presents a complex challenge.

Educational institutions also contribute to shaping cultural narratives around biotechnology and warfare. By integrating biotechnology education within curricula, educators can guide future generations in understanding both the promises and pitfalls of these advancements. Addressing the ethical implications of bioengineering can promote informed discussions and critical thinking, encouraging students to grapple with the responsibilities that come with innovation. Through science fairs, workshops, and seminars dedicated to biotechnology's role in societal progress, educational programs can stimulate interest and awareness, fostering a balanced understanding of the implications for warfare.

Furthermore, the narratives fostered by cultural expression are intrinsically tied to public policy. Social movements advocating for environmental ethics, animal rights, and responsible innovation challenge the militarization of biotechnology, demanding that societies prioritize sustainability in tandem with technological advancements. The desire for accountability extends to military applications of biotechnology, where movements calling for ethical standards and regulatory oversight gain traction. As public perception evolves, these social dynamics influence policy decisions surrounding the research, development, and deployment of biotechnological weapons.

In examining the implications of these cultural narratives, it is essential to recognize the potential for the scientific community to engage actively with them. Scientists and researchers must foster dialogues about the real-world applications of biotechnology, demonstrating how these innovations can align with broader societal goals. By translating complex biological concepts into relatable narratives, they can bridge the gaps between technical understanding and public sentiment—encouraging collaboration and informed debate.

In summary, cultural narratives surrounding biotechnology in warfare hold profound implications for how society perceives and engages with biotechnological advancements. By embracing both cautionary tales and hopeful visions of the future, we can cultivate a discourse that aligns technological innovation with ethical responsibility. As military leaders, scientists, and policymakers navigate this complex landscape, acknowledging and addressing the cultural narratives that shape public perception will be essential for forging a future that respects both the potential of biotechnology and the ethical implications entailed in its use as a tool of warfare. The narratives we construct today will ultimately influence the world we create tomorrow, governing both the direction of our innovations and our responsibilities as stewards of life among the stars.

14.4. Impact on Human Psyche and Understanding of Conflict

In understanding the impact of biotechnology on the human psyche and our comprehension of conflict, we encounter a complex interplay between innovation and perception amidst the backdrop of warfare. As we usher in a new era characterized by the integration of living systems into military practices, the psychological ramifications of bioengineering not only affect the operators of biotech battleships but also extend to society's broader perceptions of conflict, ethics, and the very essence of life itself.

The deployment of biotechnologically enhanced warfare raises fundamental questions about the nature of combatants, weapons, and even the moral fabric of society. Historically, humans have developed weapons that are extensions of their physical capabilities; however, as living systems become integral to warfare strategies, this relationship blurs the lines between human and machine. This shift challenges our identity as warriors and raises existential questions: What does it mean to engage in conflict when the tools of that conflict are living organisms? Such inquiries can provoke anxiety, ambivalence, and moral reflection among operators positioned at the intersection between humanity and machine.

For operators directly engaging with biotechnologically enhanced systems, the psychological burden of wielding living technology introduces a myriad of emotional complexities. There exists the potential for attachment to the very systems with which they work, prompting feelings of empathy or responsibility for the organisms involved. This emotional relationship can influence decision-making processes during combat situations, possibly leading to conflicts between military objectives and the welfare of the living systems they command. Operators may find themselves grappling with the weight of their actions, torn between efficiency in warfare and a sense of stewardship toward engineered life.

Additionally, the unpredictability of biological systems can evoke stress and anxiety among military personnel. Knowing that biological components may not function as anticipated introduces an element of uncertainty that is distinct from traditional technologies that have established reliability. This stress may necessitate enhanced mental health support systems within military structures, aimed at preparing operators for the pressures associated with managing living technologies. Comprehensive training that incorporates psychological preparedness, resilience development, and emotional intelligence will be critical in fostering a healthy operational culture where personnel can effectively navigate the complexities of this new technology landscape.

The impact of biotechnology on the public's understanding of conflict extends beyond military personnel to encompass broader societal perceptions. As nations increasingly integrate biotechnological warfare into their arsenals, public distrust or fear surrounding the application of living systems becomes a critical factor influencing policy and military practice. Cultural narratives and representations in popular media often highlight the moral implications of using living organisms as weapons, raising concern about the potential consequences of engineering life for conflict. This discourse not only shapes perceptions of biotechnology in warfare but also influences global cooperation and response to biotechnological advancements.

Public sentiment around biotechnology may oscillate between fascination and trepidation, prompting military leaders to engage in transparent dialogues with communities about the implications of biotechnological warfare. By fostering understanding of the potential benefits while addressing ethical concerns, military organizations can cultivate trust and support for responsible innovations in defense strategies. Ultimately, as societies grapple with the dilemmas presented by biotechnological advancements, it becomes imperative to include diverse stakeholder voices in discussions concerning deployment ethics, regulatory oversight, and long-term societal impacts.

The moral complexities surrounding the employment of biotechnology in conflict resonate deeply within the psyche of humanity. Engaging with living systems as tools of warfare invites examinations of human identity, ethical responsibilities, and the implications for civilization as it embraces unprecedented advancements. These reflections compel us to confront our roles as stewards of both technology and life, mapping a path forward that prioritizes ethical considerations alongside innovative possibilities.

In summary, the impact of biotechnology on the human psyche significantly reconfigures our understanding of conflict and warfare. As we integrate living systems into military practices, we must recognize and address the emotional, ethical, and societal dimensions that accompany these advancements. By fostering dialogue, understanding, and responsible stewardship amid the rapidly evolving landscape of biotechnological warfare, we can ensure that our engagement with these innovations respects both life and our moral imperatives, shaping a future where humanity's technological endeavors enrich our understanding of the cosmos and our shared responsibilities therein.

14.5. Educational and Awareness Programs

In a rapidly evolving universe, the synergy of education and awareness programs proves essential in shaping the future trajectories of biotechnology in military applications. As humanity integrates living systems into warfare strategies, understanding the implications of these advancements becomes crucial. Educational initiatives serve not only to equip military personnel with the necessary knowledge but also to engage the public in meaningful dialogue regarding the ethical, ecological, and societal considerations surrounding the use of biotechnology in combat scenarios.

To effectively foster understanding and promote awareness, educational programs must adopt an interdisciplinary approach that emphasizes the interconnectedness of biology, engineering, ethics, and military strategies. These initiatives should aim to create a foundation for future operators of biotech battleships, ensuring that soldiers and military leaders possess a thorough understanding of the biological components they will interact with. Training programs should emphasize foundational knowledge in biology, including principles related to genetics, ecology, and metabolic processes. Familiarity with biological systems will empower military personnel to make informed decisions while managing complex systems that incorporate organic functions alongside mechanical capabilities.

Awareness campaigns directed toward the general public will help demystify biotechnology and its applications in warfare. By providing transparent information regarding the benefits, risks, and ethical considerations associated with biotechnological advancements, these programs will cultivate a more informed populace. Engaging communities in open discussions fosters trust and addresses concerns surrounding the misuse of biotechnology, reflecting a commitment to responsible stewardship of living systems. Initiatives could include workshops, public forums, and interactive exhibits that highlight the potential benefits while also acknowledging the moral dimensions of bioengineering in combat.

Furthermore, collaboration with academic institutions can enhance educational and awareness efforts. Partnering with universities and researchers allows for the development of specialized curricula that incorporate cutting-edge research in biotechnology. By creating programs where soldiers receive training alongside scientists, a culture of interdisciplinary cooperation can emerge. This collaborative approach will promote a deeper understanding of the complexities associated with integrating biologically enhanced systems into military operations and pave the way for responsible innovation.

Corporate partnerships within the biotech industry can also play a role in these educational initiatives. Collaborating with private entities can provide military organizations with access to advanced technologies, funding for research projects, and insights into trends and developments within the biotech landscape. By engaging corporate stakeholders in conversations about responsible practices, military leaders can cultivate partnerships that ensure mutual understanding of the ethical implications of biotechnology in warfare.

The establishment of certification programs to recognize and validate the competencies of military personnel in handling biotechnological systems can further reinforce the importance of education in this field. By creating recognized qualifications that signify expertise in both operational and ethical considerations, the military can gauge personnel readiness and promote a culture of accountability. These certifications can pave the way for career development, ensuring that military operators are recognized for their specialized skills in managing the complexities of biotechnology in warfare.

In conclusion, education and awareness programs are essential components for navigating the complexities associated with integrating biotechnology into military operations. By fostering interdisciplinary learning, engaging the public and stakeholders, and promoting responsible stewardship, these initiatives will shape the perceptions, understanding, and competencies of both military personnel and civilians towards the use of living systems in warfare. As we stand on the threshold of a new era characterized by biotechnology, our commitment to education as a foundation for ethical and operational success will inevitably play a crucial role in forging a responsible path forward among the stars. The convergence of knowledge, ethics, and innovation will set the stage for a future where biotechnology enhances not just military effectiveness but also our understanding of life and our responsibilities to it.

15. Economic Aspects: Production and Funding

15.1. Investment in Biotechnological Research

Investment in biotechnological research represents a crucial pillar in the quest to harness the full potential of living systems for military applications, particularly in the context of developing biotech battleships for intergalactic warfare. The commitment to biotechnological advancements not only promises to enhance operational effectiveness but also shapes the very framework of how humanity engages with the cosmos. This intricate relationship between investment, innovation, and military strategy necessitates a holistic understanding of the economic, ethical, and societal implications that accompany such advancements.

A primary driver of investment in biotechnological research is the recognition of the potential return on investment in military capabilities. As nations seek to maintain a competitive edge in defense technologies, funding research initiatives targeting bioengineering, genetic modification, and synthetic biology has become increasingly strategic. The military applications of biotechnology—ranging from enhanced life support systems to adaptive weaponry—are viewed as instrumental in extending operational reach while reducing logistical burdens associated with traditional systems. By capitalizing on living organisms' inherent adaptability and resilience, military planners can envision a future where battleships are not merely machines but symbiotic entities capable of thriving in hostile environments.

Investment in biotechnological research also aligns with broader goals of sustainability and ecological stewardship. As humanity traverses toward extended missions in space, the integration of biological systems presents opportunities for closed-loop life support and resource recycling. This sustainable approach not only enhances military operational longevity but also responds to public concerns regarding environmental impacts associated with warfare, reinforcing the idea that military research and ecological responsibility can coexist. The societal value of investing in biotechnology lies in its promise to advance both defense capabilities and ethical, environmentally conscious practices—aligning military objectives with the greater good.

The role of collaborations between public and private sectors cannot be overstated in advancing biotechnological research. Partnerships among government agencies, research institutions, and private biotech firms enable the pooling of resources, expertise, and cutting-edge technology—facilitating innovation that might not be achievable within isolated silos. Public funding can support ambitious research initiatives, while private investment can speed up commercialization and practical applications. By fostering strong collaborative frameworks, nations can ensure that military biotechnology projects benefit from diverse inputs, leading to enhanced outcomes for both the defense sector and society.

Economic models for sustainable bio-warfare markets are also vital in shaping investment strategies surrounding biotechnological advancements. Developing regulations and frameworks that account for the potential ecological risks of deploying genetically engineered organisms will create a sustainable marketplace that promotes responsible innovation. Establishing economic pathways that prioritize ethical considerations ensures that military investments align with societal values, thereby strengthening public support and trust in biotechnological advancements for warfare.

The role of venture capital in advancing warfare technology plays a pivotal part in fostering innovation within the biotechnology sector. As investments from venture firms target promising startups engaged in biotechnological research, this influx of funding can significantly accelerate the development of groundbreaking technologies. Whether focusing on genetic editing techniques, bioreactor designs, or pathogen sensing systems, venture-backed initiatives can drive innovations that reshape our approach to combat.

Tracking global market trends and future projections is crucial for maintaining a proactive investment strategy. As the military landscape continues to evolve, understanding shifts in biotechnological research—both domestically and internationally—can inform decisions related to funding and project priorities. Analyzing geopolitical developments, emerging technologies, and societal expectations allows military organizations to align their investments with anticipated market opportunities, maximizing the potential for successful applications of biotechnology in defense.

In summary, investment in biotechnological research is paramount to realizing the potential of biotech battleships and the broader landscape of intergalactic warfare. By understanding the complexities surrounding economic models, public and private partnerships, and sustainability, military leaders can effectively harness the power of biotechnology to enhance operational effectiveness while addressing societal concerns regarding ecological responsibility. The strategic investment in biotechnological advancements not only secures a competitive advantage in military applications but also cultivates a path toward a future where innovation harmonizes with ethical considerations—ultimately redefining the relationship between humanity and the cosmos.

15.2. Collaborations between Public and Private Sectors

In examining the collaborations between public and private sectors in the context of developing biotechnology applications for warfare, it becomes crucial to recognize the profound impact that partnerships have on innovation, funding, and the application of ethical standards. As biotech battleships emerge as a cornerstone in intergalactic military strategy, the interplay between government initiatives and private sector expertise will significantly shape the trajectory of these advanced technologies.

Historically, military-driven research and development have relied on public funding and governmental support to establish foundational biotechnological advancements. When the government articulates its need for innovations—be it for enhancing soldier capabilities through bioengineering or creating self-sustaining life support for extended missions—research institutions and biotech companies can respond to these demands. Government initiatives often set the stage for advancing foundational research, encouraging public interest and investment in the exploration of potential military applications for biotechnology.

Public-private partnerships are particularly beneficial for fostering innovation in this area. Collaborations that unite the strengths of academic research institutions with the flexibility and agility of private companies can yield impressive results. For example, a government-facilitated research grant could empower a biotech firm to explore innovative applications of gene editing technology. This synergy accelerates the pace of discovery, as private industry often possesses the capacity to expedite the commercialization and implementation of new technologies. By investing in joint ventures that prioritize the research and application of biological innovations, public entities can ensure that breakthroughs translate into tangible military capabilities.

The landscape of biotechnology also benefits from shared expertise across sectors. Government projects, often tied to military objectives, present subject matter experts the opportunity to collaborate with private sector innovators who bring diverse skills, insights, and agility to the table. For instance, a fusion of academic expertise in genetic modification paired with private sector experience in manufacturing and scaling products can yield effective solutions to challenges faced during the development of biotech battleships. This fusion of knowledge allows for richer ideas and perspectives to flourish, driving forward the field of biotechnology in the military context.

However, these collaborations cannot be without concerns surrounding ethical implications and regulatory accountability. Given the potential impacts of biotechnological innovations, ensuring a collaborative framework that prioritizes responsible practices is essential.

Public engagement in discussions of biotechnology's implications is required to maintain transparency, trust, and social acceptance regarding military advancements. As biotechnology ventures deeper into the sphere of warfare, establishing an ethical framework that all parties adhere to should not only align the objectives of military efficiency with broader societal values but also promote ethical drug approvals, environmental assessments, and the treatment of engineered life forms.

Funding sources also play a critical role in advancing biotechnological research. Public sectors often allocate substantial budgets to fund military-oriented projects, yet private sector investment can supplement these funds and fuel innovation. Engaging with venture capital firms specializing in biotech can provide the influx of resources necessary for startups and established companies to explore ambitious projects. This financial backing can mitigate the risk associated with pioneering applications that might otherwise be too uncertain for traditional military procurement routes. As public interest in ethical militancy grows, so does the opportunity for funding innovative solutions that address the dual demands of security and responsibility through biotechnology.

As we analyze the future of collaborations between public and private sectors in the realm of biotechnology within military contexts, it is clear that these partnerships are key to innovation and development for biotech battleships. Collaboration must evolve continually to address societal concerns, ethical considerations, and the dynamic landscape of biotechnology; reliable and effective channels of cooperation will ensure that the advancements made provide sustainable and ethical solutions to intergalactic warfare. By establishing frameworks that prioritize transparency, responsible stewardship of living systems, and accountability among stakeholders, the fusion of public initiatives with private innovation can pave the way toward a future where biotechnology enhances military operations while upholding humanity's moral obligations to life.

15.3. Economic Models for Sustainable Bio-Warfare Markets

In a rapidly evolving universe where the boundaries between biology and technology are continually blurred, biotechnology's role in warfare emerges as a double-edged sword. The potential benefits of harnessing living systems for military applications are accompanied by profound ethical implications and complexities. As policymakers, military leaders, scientists, and society at large seek to navigate this new territory, the development of economic models for sustainable bio-warfare markets becomes imperative. This exploration does not only address the practical deployment of biotechnological innovations for military purposes but also actively engages the ethical considerations and societal impacts tied to such advancements.

Economically, the transition toward integrating biotechnological systems within military frameworks creates unique market dynamics that necessitate consideration of funding, research, and resource allocation. Sustainable economic models can provide a structured approach to harnessing biotechnology for military applications while ensuring long-term viability and a commitment to ethical standards. These models can draw inspiration from existing regulatory frameworks in the biotechnology industry while addressing specific aspects related to biowarfare.

One core principle of these economic models centers around investment in biotechnological research, particularly in areas that focus on developing biologically integrated systems conducive to military operations. By fostering public-private partnerships that pool investment resources, rigorous research can be supported to explore the full potential of bioengineering in combat scenarios. These collaborations can promote innovation through advancements in genetics, synthetic biology, and ecological sustainability, ultimately ensuring that the military has access to cutting-edge technologies capable of enhancing operational effectiveness.

As military operations continue to expand beyond Earth into the cosmos, funding mechanisms that prioritize ethical considerations will be critical. For example, governments can develop grants and incentives for organizations that prioritize environmentally responsible practices in the development of biotechnological innovations for warfare. By tying economic support to adherence to ethical standards and sustainability goals, these models create a framework that rewards responsible innovation while discouraging projects that disregard ecological balance.

The economic implications of biotechnology also extend to examining global market trends and projections. As military forces all over the world seek to remain technologically advanced, the competition drives rapid innovations across biotechnological sectors. Understanding these shifts allows policymakers to make informed decisions regarding investments, collaborations, and research priorities. The landscape of biotechnological warfare is characterized by an increasingly interconnected market wherein advancements in one nation can influence the strategic choices of another, prompting countries to reconsider their own capacities and commitments in this rapidly evolving arena.

Cost-benefit analysis will also play a significant role in evaluating the efficacy and practicalities of deploying biotechnology in military contexts. By carefully assessing operational outcomes within various biowarfare applications—factoring in specific financial commitments alongside anticipated military advantages—military planners can establish a clearer interpretation of how biotechnology aligns with their strategic objectives. This evaluation process can guide resource allocation, helping military organizations prioritize which technologies bear the most significant potential for innovation and effectiveness in combat.

Furthermore, public perception and acceptance play a crucial role in shaping sustainable economic models for biotechnology in warfare. As societal attitudes evolve, understanding how to engage the public in discussions surrounding biotechnological advancements will influence funding, collaboration, and regulations. Initiatives aimed at fostering transparency and dialogue can contribute to building public trust. Effective marketing and communication strategies that high-light responsible innovations and ethical commitments can help align societal values with military applications of biotechnology, creating a supportive environment for investment and advancement.

In summary, the development of economic models for sustainable bio-warfare markets encompasses multifaceted challenges and considerations that extend beyond military effectiveness. By prioritizing ethical standards, fostering public-private partnerships, and critically evaluating investment opportunities in biotechnological research, military leaders can navigate the complexities of integrating living systems into their strategies. As we embrace the potential for these advancements in biotechnology, it is imperative to remain committed to responsible practices, ensuring that our innovations reflect both operational success and our ethical responsibilities towards life and the environment. Balancing these dimensions will be vital as we redefine what it means to engage in warfare among the stars.

15.4. The Role of Ventures in Advancing Warfare Technology

In the context of increasingly sophisticated warfare, the role of ventures in advancing warfare technology plays a pivotal part in shaping the future landscape of military capabilities. The integration of biotechnology into military applications, particularly through ventures focused on innovative research and development, has the potential to revolutionize how conflicts are engaged and managed. This section explores the dynamics that drive advancements in biotech warfare technology, elucidating the impacts, challenges, and prospects for the future.

The current landscape of biotechnology boasts substantial investments from both public and private sectors, each recognizing the strategic importance of biotechnological innovations in military applications. Private ventures have emerged as key players in this realm, often driving research that is cutting-edge and responsive to the evolving needs of military forces. By leveraging agile project management and rapid prototyping, these ventures can invest in exploratory projects that may not be feasible through traditional military procurement methods, leading to breakthroughs in areas such as bioengineered weaponry, living armor, and sustainable life support mechanisms.

In this innovative landscape, biotech startups and established companies alike can collaborate with military organizations to advance battlefield technology. By establishing partnerships, these ventures provide the necessary agility to navigate the fast-paced realities of warfare technology development. Collaborative research agreements enable military entities to access insights from cutting-edge biotechnological developments, while startups benefit from military expertise and funding. This symbiotic relationship fosters a positive feedback loop— advancements in one sector fuel progress in the other, thus propelling both military and biomedical innovations forward.

However, the challenges inherent in advancing warfare technology through biotechnological innovation cannot be understated. As military forces embrace living systems, the ethical and ecological implications become increasingly significant. The potential for misuse or unintended consequences must be carefully managed. Herein lies the responsibility of ventures engaged in biotechnology research— to pursue advancements while adhering to ethical frameworks that prioritize the well-being of created organisms and the ecological implications of their deployment.

Moreover, ensuring the longevity and stability of living organisms deployed in warfare presents unique logistical challenges. Ventures in biotech must grapple with the unpredictability of biological systems, where factors such as health, viability, and external environmental conditions can profoundly impact operational outcomes. Collaborations between ventures focusing on biotechnology and military strategists become essential in developing contingency plans and adaptive strategies that account for these uncertainties in combat situations.

The excitement surrounding the potential of biotechnology is matched by public curiosity and concern. As biotechnology plays a more prominent role in military applications, fostering public discourse becomes necessary to ensure transparency and address societal fears surrounding bioweapons and engineered organisms. This dialogue not only builds trust between military organizations and the public but also creates platforms for discussing the ethical implications of military biotechnology, further informing regulations that govern its use.

Looking toward the future, the trajectory of biotechnology in warfare promises not only advancements in living technologies but also the emergence of entirely new methodologies for engagement and combat. As ventures continue to innovate, we may witness the evolution of biotechnological applications that enhance not just military effectiveness but also humanitarian goals, seamlessly merging the dual priorities of security and ethical stewardship.

In conclusion, the role of ventures in advancing warfare technology is critical to shaping the landscape of biotechnological innovations. By fostering collaborative, ethical, and adaptive approaches to research and development, these ventures can drive forward the integration of biotechnology in military applications. As society grapples with the implications of such advancements, the interplay between innovation and responsibility will determine the legacy of biotechnological warfare in the cosmos. Through proactive engagement in dialog, ethical considerations, and innovation, we can ensure that the journey into this new reality reflects humanity's commitment to life, technology, and the responsible pursuit of advancement in the vast expanse of interstellar warfare.

15.5. Global Market Trends and Future Projections

In a rapidly evolving universe where the boundaries between biology and technology are continually blurred, humanity stands on the brink of the next revolutionary leap in interstellar warfare. What was once limited by the constraints of steel and electronics is now being reimagined with the intricate complexities of living organisms.

As we venture into realms that were once the exclusive domain of science fiction, we are compelled to ask: What will the war machines of the future look like, and how will they alter the cosmos forever? In "Biotech Battleships: Designs of Future Intergalactic War Machines," we embark on a journey through this fascinating frontier, exploring the possibilities and challenges posed by biotechnology in the design of the future's most formidable battle vessels. This book seeks to equip readers with a thorough understanding of the scientific principles, design methodologies, and ethical considerations that underpin the creation of these advanced interspecies technologies. Join me, Sylvia L. Wright, as we demystify the extraordinary and transform the way we envision warfare among the stars.

Global market trends and future projections regarding biotechnology and its application in military settings indicate a significant transformation of both global defense strategies and societal perceptions of warfare. As nations race to advance their capabilities, investment in biotechnological innovations will increasingly become pivotal in shaping the capabilities of military forces worldwide. The following sections will explore the factors driving these trends, considerations surrounding ethical use, and projected advancements that promise to redefine intergalactic conflict.

At the forefront of these developments is the increasing investment in biotechnology by both public and private sectors. Military budgets are adapting to prioritize research and development to explore biotechnological innovations, reflecting an understanding that living systems can provide unique advantages over traditional technologies. This trend aligns with broader societal movements concerned with sustainability, as nations strive not only for military efficacy but also for ecological responsibility amidst growing awareness of climate challenges.

Furthermore, as advancements in fields such as genetic engineering, synthetic biology, and bioinformatics progress, we anticipate emerging trends in military strategy that emphasize adaptability and dual-use technologies. The ability to rapidly respond to evolving threats—

whether they be human foes or environmental challenges—will guide the design of future biotechnological systems. Warfare involving biotechnological innovations will emphasize not only combat efficiency but also resource management, self-sustainability, and ethical adherence to the principles of responsible stewardship of engineered organisms.

Global market trends indicate a collaborative environment where military, industrial, and academic entities will converge to innovate and develop biotechnological applications. This synergy between sectors encourages the exploration of new technologies that augment traditional military capabilities—resulting in hybrid systems that leverage the strengths of both biological and mechanical components. The development of bioengineered materials for vessel construction, organic-based weapon systems, and self-sustaining life-support mechanisms signals a profound shift in military procurement and operational philosophies.

Looking toward the future, we can predict significant paradigm shifts in global defense strategies. As biotechnological innovations take a more prominent role in military operations, the strategies surrounding deploying these systems will evolve. Countries will likely prioritize ethical frameworks that govern the responsible use and treatment of living entities in combat, ensuring compliance with international laws and a commitment to minimizing harm. Anticipating the consequences of biotechnological advancements will drive governments to establish strict regulatory measures to ensure that these technologies are harnessed for peace rather than destruction.

In terms of technological advancements, the emergence of novel bioengineering techniques could redefine existing combat paradigms. For example, the development of smart munitions capable of adapting in-flight via biological feedback could enhance precision targeting and reduce collateral damage. The synergistic use of machine learning alongside living systems will form a cornerstone of intelligent military strategies, promoting adaptive responses to combat scenarios.

As we delve deeper into future projections, tracking how these global trends might influence long-term tactics and operations becomes essential. We might observe shifts from conventional warfare tactics toward more complex strategies that emphasize psychological impacts, surprise engagements, and adaptability. These tactics will be informed by the capabilities of biotechnology and how living systems can respond dynamically to threats, leading to an evolution in engagement methods that challenges traditional conceptions of martial conflict.

Ultimately, the global market trends for biotechnology in warfare signal an impending transformation that marries innovation with ethical responsibility. As humanity forges ahead into this new frontier, a steadfast commitment to ethical considerations, sustainable practices, and responsible technological deployment will shape a future where the promises of biotechnology empower us to navigate the ever-changing landscape of intergalactic conflict. Through these developments, we stand to reimagine not only the nature of warfare but also our profound responsibilities as stewards of both life and technology in the cosmos.

16. The Future of Warfare: Emerging Trends and Predictions

16.1. Predictive Models for Biotech Advancements

In the realm of advancing interstellar warfare technologies, the significance of predictive models for biotech advancements remains integral to shaping the future of military operations. As society integrates biological systems into combat strategies, a clear understanding of potential developments and their implications is crucial. Predictive models serve as essential tools that allow military planners, scientists, and strategists to visualize how emerging biotechnologies might unfold within both the frameworks of warfare and broader societal contexts.

At its core, predictive modeling involves using mathematical frameworks, simulations, and data analysis to estimate future outcomes based on current and historical data. In the context of biotechnology, these models can help identify key trends, relationships, and potential impacts of synthetic organisms and technologies on military operations and human interactions with living systems. By mapping out various scenarios, predictive models can aid military leaders in strategic decision-making processes regarding the integration of biotechnological advancements into warfare.

One of the primary applications of predictive models is assessing the viability of new biotechnologies in military operations. By simulating the performance of bioengineered organisms under a variety of stressors, including environmental challenges and combat conditions, these models allow for informed assessments of how organisms might behave in real-world scenarios. This predictive approach facilitates the identification of potential weaknesses in engineered systems, allowing designers to make evidence-based modifications and optimizations ahead of deployment.

Moreover, predictive models can inform logistical planning surrounding biotechnological applications. For instance, understanding the resource requirements—such as nutrient inputs and environmental controls—for the sustained functioning of bioengineered life support systems can shape long-term operational strategies. These logistics not only encompass the supplies needed for sustaining the organisms but also entail predictions regarding crew maintenance needs, rotations, and the sustainability of operations during prolonged missions in space.

Additionally, predictive modeling can serve a dual purpose in evaluating the ethical implications of utilizing living organisms in warfare. By analyzing the potential ecological impacts of deploying engineered life forms—be it through environmental shifts or interactions with natural ecosystems—military leaders can proactively address concerns surrounding biosecurity and ecological balance. Through scenario-based modeling, ethical responses to unforeseen consequences can be prepared in advance, facilitating rigorous discussions surrounding responsible stewardship of engineered organisms in military contexts.

As the field of biotechnology evolves, emerging trends can be captured through predictive models, allowing planners to keep pace with developments while anticipating future challenges. The advancements in synthetic biology, CRISPR technologies, and bioinformatics will yield innovations capable of reshaping combat paradigms. Predictive models can aid in determining which technologies are likely to emerge as critical tools for military applications, shaping the direction of research and investment in these areas.

Furthermore, as military organizations grapple with public perception surrounding biotechnological warfare, predictive modeling can also inform communications strategies. Understanding how different demographic groups and societal stakeholders perceive biotechnological advancements can allow military leaders to craft narratives that resonate with public sentiment. This predictive analysis can help balance concerns about deployment with the benefits that biotechnological innovations bring to national security objectives.

As we contemplate the long-term implications of predictive models for biotech advancements within military applications, interdepartmental collaboration becomes vital. The convergence of insights from scientists, ethicists, military strategists, and social scientists can facilitate enriched dialogue and shared understanding of how biotechnology might impact warfare's future. Ongoing refinement of predictive models based on empirical data collected from real-world deployments will enhance our ability to adapt to future challenges while ensuring that ethical concerns remain central to discourse regarding biotechnological innovations.

In summary, predictive models for biotech advancements play a fundamental role in advancing our understanding of the integration of biological systems into military operations. These models allow us to anticipate potential developments, optimize designs, evaluate ethical implications, and navigate the complexities of public perception. As we navigate this brave new frontier defined by the integration of biology and technology, the utilization of predictive models will empower military organizations to make informed decisions that align operational effectiveness with ethical responsibilities while positioning society to embrace the future of warfare responsibly. By fostering a culture of collaboration and transparency, we can hold true to our commitments as stewards of life and innovators in the cosmos.

16.2. New Trends in Intergalactic Warfare

In recent years, a significant transformation in the discourse surrounding intergalactic warfare has emerged, notably marked by the intersection of biotechnology and military applications. As nations work toward establishing robust and adaptable military capabilities, the emergent trends in intergalactic warfare showcase not only innovative technologies but also evolving strategies that integrate biological systems with mechanical frameworks. This transition from traditional combat paradigms to biotechnologically infused methodologies presents profound implications for how we perceive and execute war.

Central to this evolution is the recognition of biotechnology as a multifaceted tool that can enhance both offensive and defensive operations. With the advent of living technologies, military planners are beginning to appreciate not only the physical capabilities afforded by bioengineered systems but also the psychological and environmental dimensions that accompany such deployments. The potential for adaptability, self-sustainability, and autonomous functions positions biotech battleships as formidable entities capable of contending with contemporary and future warfare scenarios in ways unheard of in previous generations.

The incorporation of biotechnology into military strategies will yield significant advancements in maneuverability and efficiency on the battlefield. Future trends indicate a shift toward weapon systems equipped with smart biological components that utilize real-time data to optimize performance under demanding conditions. These living systems can adapt to the environmental shifts and tactical demands encountered in space, allowing them to execute complex maneuvers that traditional weapons systems may struggle to achieve.

Moreover, the implications for supply chain logistics and resource management cannot be overlooked. By implementing closed-loop life support systems, biotech battleships will reduce dependency on traditional resupply missions, a critical consideration in prolonged engagements across interstellar distances. Resource recycling and ecological balance become paramount functions that ensure combat units can operate independently without relying on terrestrial resources. This self-sufficiency aligns with the broader societal interest in sustainability and responsible stewardship amid the backdrop of military operations.

As we look ahead, long-term projections for battle tactics will invariably shift alongside technological advancements. The fusion of biological and mechanical capabilities will lead to new strategies that prioritize flexibility and resilience. The engagements of the future may increasingly involve scenarios where adaptability becomes the cornerstone of military effectiveness, challenging conventional approaches that favor static formations and rigid strategies.

The evolving narrative of intergalactic warfare will compel military leaders to re-examine traditional combat doctrines in light of new technologies. Scalar tactics, incorporating both biotech and conventional systems, will emerge as essential maneuvers—not only in response to enemy actions but also to leverage the unique capabilities of biotech battleships. The battlefield promises to evolve into a dynamic arena where intelligence, adaptability, and ethical engagement coexist, challenging our understanding of conflict and warfare as we journey into the vast unknown.

However, embracing organisms as instruments of warfare inevitably fosters ethical dilemmas that impact the global discourse surrounding biotechnological advancements in conflict. With the potential for unintended ecological consequences, the militarization of biotechnology must be navigated with ethical vigilance. The narratives that emerge surrounding these innovations will shape public perceptions, necessitating robust dialogues that confront societal values and responsibilities towards engineered life.

Potential paradigm shifts in global defense highlight the necessity for international treaties and regulations to govern the military application of biotechnology. As nations advance their capabilities, collaborative frameworks must be established to address the ethical implications of deploying living systems in warfare. By situating these discussions within the context of shared responsibility for ecological and societal integrity, we can craft a future in which the integration of biotechnology into warfare embodies not only tactical prowess but also moral accountability.

In summation, the emerging trends in intergalactic warfare reveal a promising yet complex landscape where biotechnology takes center stage. As we envision the future of combat, the interplay of living systems and technology challenges the very essence of our approach to warfare. Engaging with the potential that biotechnologically enhanced military innovations hold must be counterbalanced with a commitment to ethical stewardship, responsible innovation, and environmental consciousness. The convergence of biology and technology shapes the path ahead, illuminating a future where humanity must align its military aspirations with ethical imperatives—a journey as exhilarating and treacherous as the stars themselves.

16.3. Emergence of New Technologies augmenting Biotech

The emergence of new technologies augmenting biotech signifies a pivotal moment in the evolution of warfare, as military applications begin to seamlessly integrate living systems with advanced mechanics. The rapid advancement in fields such as genetic engineering, synthetic biology, and biocomputation is reshaping not just our understanding of combat, but also the operational capabilities of military forces. As we look ahead, a multitude of new technologies will interweave with biotechnological innovations, influencing everything from weaponry to life support systems in interstellar battleships.

At the forefront of these advancements is the development of biocompatible materials—substances engineered to work harmoniously with living organisms. These materials promise to revolutionize the structural components of biotech battleships, enhancing combat resilience and durability. For instance, the creation of living armor composed of bioengineered cellulose or proteins can provide a lightweight yet robust defense mechanism that can dynamically respond to threats. Living armor has the ability to regenerate after damage, mimicking biological processes observed in nature. This innovation not only reduces maintenance requirements but also optimizes the operational metrics of vessels engaged in protracted campaigns.

Furthermore, new technologies enable enhanced bio-sensing capabilities, allowing biotech battleships to gather and process vast amounts of data from their surroundings. Engineered organisms capable of sensing environmental changes can be employed within the ship to detect chemical or biological threats long before traditional sensor systems are activated. Such proactive bio-sensing mechanisms would empower commanders to make strategic decisions based on accurate and timely data inputs, significantly enhancing the effectiveness of military operations.

The convergence of artificial intelligence (AI) and biotechnology cannot be overstated. AI algorithms are increasingly being employed alongside biological systems to drive automation and optimization in combat strategies. These algorithms can process real-time data from living systems and adjust operational parameters accordingly. Imagine an AI system working alongside bioengineered organisms to autonomously coordinate resource allocation throughout the ship, optimizing energy use based on fluctuating mission demands. The potential application of AI in tandem with living systems holds immense promise for creating adaptive, responsive combat platforms that can thrive in unpredictable environments.

Moreover, breakthroughs in bioengineering will enable the design of smart munitions equipped with living agents. These munitions could utilize biologic guidance systems that enhance targeting precision while employing living organisms tailored to incapacitate or neutralize enemy defenses. For example, genetically modified organisms used in conjunction with missile systems could create secondary effects, deploying agents that undermine enemy technologies through biological means. This new methodology could reshape engagement protocols, prioritizing adaptive strategies and minimizing collateral damage.

The application of biotechnology also extends to life support systems critical for crew sustainability, particularly in long-duration missions. Developments in closed-loop life support systems that use engineered organisms for recycling air, water, and waste will become essential. The ability of these systems to replenish resources while reducing logistical dependencies will enable extended operability in spaces far removed from terrestrial supply chains.

Education and public engagement will be crucial in navigating the ethical considerations that arise from these advancements. As biotechnological innovations take center stage in warfare, it is imperative to foster ongoing dialogues surrounding their implications. By promoting awareness and understanding of how innovations intertwine with ethical principles, we can cultivate a culture that embraces responsibility and accountability in their development and usage. Engaging communities through outreach initiatives will help bridge gaps in understanding and ensure that societal values are reflected in the trajectory of military applications of biotechnology.

In conclusion, the emergence of new technologies augmenting biotech heralds a transformative era that redefines future warfare. The integration of living systems with advanced military applications enhances operational capabilities, promotes sustainability, and raises critical ethical questions that must be navigated thoughtfully. As biotechnology continues to evolve, the intersection with innovative technologies will unlock new avenues for strategic advantages in intergalactic conflict. By framing this journey within the context of responsible stewardship, ethical engagement, and open dialogue, we can ensure that these advancements serve not only military objectives but also reflect our broader societal values as custodians of life in the cosmos.

16.4. Long-Term Projections for Battle Tactics

In a future steeped in the integration of biotechnology within military endeavors, analyzing long-term projections for battle tactics reveals profound shifts in the operational landscape of intergalactic warfare. War strategies that once revolved around infantry tactics and static machinery are evolving toward dynamic, bio-integrated methodologies that leverage the unique capabilities of living systems. As we embrace these advancements, it is crucial to consider the implications for how battles will be fought in this new era.

As biotechnology continues to permeate military design and strategy, one of the first significant projections is the shift towards adaptive tactics that emphasize flexibility. Unlike traditional warfare, which often relies on the predictability of rigid formations and predefined plans, the integration of biotech battleships encourages a more fluid strategy where units can respond in real-time to evolving threats and environmental conditions. Living organisms, with their capacity for autonomous adaptation, allow for more strategic maneuvers that can quickly shift based on battlefield intelligence. This emphasis on adaptability not only enhances survival rates but also optimizes operational efficacy, enabling forces to outmaneuver opponents by dynamically adjusting tactics on-the-fly.

In conjunction with the emphasis on adaptability, the increasing use of predictive analytics powered by AI will play an instrumental role in shaping tactics. By processing vast amounts of data gleaned from bioengineered sensors and historical combat scenarios, AI can inform commanders about potential outcomes and recommend tactical adjustments. These insights will allow military leaders to anticipate enemy movements and behaviors—transforming engagement protocols to prioritize proactive rather than reactive responses. The role of predictive analytics signifies a substantial shift from traditional battlefield decision-making centered on human intuition, evolving into a more data-driven paradigm where biological systems serve as a source of actionable intelligence.

Moreover, long-term projections for battle tactics suggest a greater emphasis on asymmetric warfare, where biotech battleships can engage adversaries in unconventional manners. Armed with biotechnologically enhanced weaponry designed to incapacitate or undermine enemy capabilities, these vessels can employ tactics that disrupt traditional military formations. For example, deploying smart munitions equipped with living agents capable of counteracting specific types of enemy defenses could shift the balance in favor of attacking forces. This strategy reflects a movement away from standardized engagements towards personalized tactics that highlight the unique biological capabilities of integrated systems.

Operating in collaborative formations will also become a hallmark of future battle tactics. Bio-integrated fleets that communicate through biological channels can create a cohesive operational network, enhancing the effectiveness of collective tactics. The synergy that emerges from combining intelligent biological systems with strategically positioned military craft fosters interdependence that promotes rapid responses to emerging threats. These collaborative dynamics will challenge conventional hierarchical structures within military operations, encouraging decentralized decision-making as units interact organically and draw upon their collective capabilities to pursue shared objectives.

Nonetheless, the execution of these advanced tactics requires a critical examination of ethical implications surrounding biotechnologically enhanced warfare. As the military utilizes living organisms as instruments of conflict, the moral ramifications—concerning both human operators and the engineered systems—demand regular reflection. Establishing guidelines that underscore the responsibilities of employing living technologies must remain central to discussions surrounding future combat.

As we anticipate these long-term projections for battle tactics, ongoing education and training for military personnel will be essential. Engaging operators in understanding the design and operating principles of living systems will foster a culture of accountability and preparedness as they navigate the multidimensional complexities of combat scenarios involving biotechnology.

In conclusion, the projection of long-term tactics within the realm of biotechnology in warfare reveals an exciting yet uncertain future, filled with possibilities for operational transformation. As we reimagine combat strategies centered around adaptability, intelligence-driven decisions, and collaborative formations, we must remain attuned to the ethical considerations inherent in wielding living technologies. The path forward demands innovative thinking and responsible stewardship as societies and militaries alike engage with the extraordinary potential that biotechnology offers in reshaping the landscape of interstellar conflict. Together, we stand on the brink of a new frontier

—one that challenges us to rethink how we understand warfare, life, and our collective responsibilities as we traverse the cosmos.

16.5. Potential Paradigm Shifts in Global Defense

In the context of global defense, potential paradigm shifts signify a remarkable evolution in military strategies and technologies, particularly as newly integrated biotechnological advances take center stage. The fusion of living systems with combat capabilities represents a transformative approach to warfare that could redefine conflict dynamics and operational efficiency. As we delve into this transformative potential, several key factors emerge that point toward significant changes in defense paradigms.

One crucial shift is the move toward adaptive and resilient military systems. As biotech battleships increasingly utilize living organisms to enhance their capabilities, they can respond dynamically to various threats and environmental conditions. Unlike traditional weaponry, which relies heavily on fixed mechanisms, bioengineered systems offer inherent flexibility, enabling them to self-repair and react in real-time. This adaptability not only enhances the survivability of troops and systems but also fundamentally alters how military engagements are planned and executed.

Moreover, the reliance on biotechnological advancements compels a rethinking of logistics and resource management in conflict scenarios. With self-sustaining ecosystems that can recycle resources such as air and water, biotech battleships can operate independently for extended periods, reducing supply chain vulnerabilities that have traditionally plagued military operations. This shift promises to enhance operational readiness and strategic autonomy, allowing forces to engage in longer missions without the constant need for resupply.

Additionally, the integration of artificial intelligence (AI) into the command and control of biotech battleships facilitates real-time situational awareness and decision-making. As AI systems support the analysis of data sourced from living sensors and environmental inputs, commanders gain an unprecedented level of insight that empowers them to make proactive and informed tactical choices. The interplay between biological responsiveness and machine intelligence translates to a military strategy that aligns with the demands of modern warfare where speed and precision are paramount.

Ethical considerations will also drive paradigm shifts in global defense. As biotechnological innovations become increasingly integrated into military constructs, the responsibilities associated with deploying living systems raise complex moral questions. Ensuring that the use of biotechnology aligns with societal values and acknowledging the rights of engineered organisms will challenge military entities to engage in philosophical and ethical considerations about their strategies. Crafting robust and transparent ethical guidelines will be essential as nations adopt biotechnological means for defending against adversaries.

Furthermore, public perception of biotechnology in warfare can influence the trajectory of defense strategies. As societal understanding of the implications of living technologies grows, military organizations must prioritize engagement to address concerns and misinformation. Establishing constructive dialogues with communities, stakeholders, and the general public can help build trust, garner support, and reinforce the narrative of biotechnological innovations as tools of peace and security, rather than instruments of destruction.

Ultimately, these potential paradigm shifts underscore a broader transformation in military doctrine that emphasizes sustainability, collaboration, and ethical engagement. The future of global defense will hinge on how effectively military leaders and policymakers can integrate these advancements into cohesive strategies that align with both operational efficacy and societal values. As we anticipate these changes, the interplay between biology and technology presents both extraordinary opportunities and formidable challenges—inviting us to rethink the nature of military engagement and our responsibilities as stewards of both technological innovation and life. In this new era, the military may evolve from a traditional role of conflict into a more expansive mission, fostering security and stability through responsible biotechnological advancements in warfare.

17. Case Studies: Existing Biotech Innovations

17.1. Summary of Current Biotechnology Applications

In the realm of contemporary warfare, biotechnology has emerged as a revolutionary frontier that redefines traditional military paradigms. As we explore the current applications of biotechnology, we uncover a landscape where science, innovation, and responsibility converge, shaping the design and functionality of future interstellar war machines, particularly biotech battleships. These advanced vessels are being developed with the potential to integrate living systems into their operational framework, offering adaptive, resilient, and sustainable solutions to the challenges of combat in the cosmos.

The applications of biotechnology in modern warfare span numerous domains, each offering unique advantages that extend beyond conventional capabilities. One of the most significant areas of biotechnology application is in the enhancement of resource management through biological life support systems. By leveraging engineered organisms, these systems can recycle air and water, generate essential nutrients, and convert waste into usable resources, thereby ensuring the sustainability of operations over long missions in hostile environments. This capability fundamentally alters how military strategies are approached, emphasizing self-sufficiency and reducing the reliance on external supply lines.

Moreover, the military is increasingly integrating bioengineering in the development of weaponry. The creation of biologically enhanced munitions capable of autonomously adjusting their targeting based on environmental stimuli represents a paradigm shift in offensive capabilities. These smart munitions can incorporate living organisms that provide real-time feedback, enabling them to modify their trajectories toward enemy assets dynamically. This adaptability offers significant tactical advantages, allowing for greater precision and a reduced risk of civilian casualties—a pressing concern in modern warfare.

Biotechnology also enhances the defensive capabilities of military forces through the utilization of living armor and self-healing materials. Research into bioengineered materials that mimic the regenerative properties of specific organisms leads to innovations in armor that can respond to damage and repair itself in real-time. This integration not only extends the lifespan of military vessels under fire but also reduces maintenance demands, allowing crews to focus on operational readiness rather than repair tasks.

The landscape of biotechnology also encompasses the realm of bio-sensing technologies, which can revolutionize intelligence-gathering operations. Military planners are exploring the potential of engineered microorganisms that can detect chemical or biological agents in the environment, circumnavigating traditional limitations faced by electronic sensors. This innovation enhances situational awareness, enabling commanders to make swift, informed decisions based on accurate data regarding threats lurking in the environment.

In the following sections, we will look at notable developments in biotech warfare, discussing key players and their contributions to the field's advancement. As various organizations collaborate to explore the potential of biotechnological innovations, lessons learned from prior endeavors will guide future research and operational strategies. These findings will prove crucial as military entities seek to harness the full potential of biotechnology while navigating the ethical, ecological, and societal implications intrinsic to their use in warfare.

Throughout the examination of current applications, it becomes evident that the pursuit of biotechnology in warfare is accompanied by the dual-edge nature of innovation and responsibility. Understanding these dynamics and their impact on future interstellar conflicts will be pivotal as we embrace the possibilities and acknowledge the complexities of merging living systems with military objectives. Ultimately, the ongoing exploration of biotechnology serves as a testament to our capacity to innovate while remaining vigilant stewards of both technology and life in the cosmos.

17.2. Notable Developments in Biotech Warfare

In a universe characterized by the rapid fusion of technology and biology, biotechnology's role in warfare has become multifaceted and highly complex. The advent of biotech warfare not only redefines traditional military strategies but also raises critical questions regarding ethics, ecological sustainability, and societal impacts. Notable developments in this field provide valuable insights into the trajectory of future interstellar conflicts, the key players fueling advancements, the challenges encountered, and the innovative breakthroughs continually reshaping our understanding of warfare.

Recent progress in the field has been remarkable, with innovations in bioengineering that speak to a new era of military technology. Researchers and military strategists are actively exploring the potential of living systems to enhance combat capabilities through self-repairing materials, adaptive weaponry, and sustainable life-support systems. These innovations extend beyond mere enhancements of existing technologies; they represent a paradigm shift in how we perceive the integration of life and warfare.

Key players in this venture include a mix of governmental agencies, private biotechnology firms, and academic research institutions. Each of these entities contributes uniquely to the exploration of biotechnology's capabilities, either by developing new technologies, pushing ethical boundaries, or providing the necessary research frameworks for military applications. Collaborations among these parties facilitate rapid advancements, leveraging diverse expertise that speed up the translation of scientific innovations into actionable military strategies.

However, this integration into military contexts has not been without formidable challenges. Pioneering efforts in biotech warfare face scrutiny over ethical dilemmas, regulatory oversight, and public perception. These challenges must be addressed to ensure responsible practices that reflect societal values and maintain public trust. Lessons learned from early endeavors highlight the need for extensive testing, evaluation, and public engagement in shaping how biotechnology is perceived and accepted within military frameworks.

Moreover, the future of biotech warfare is rife with potential innovations on the horizon, promising advances that could redefine how we engage in combat. As we navigate these corridors of possibility, ethical stewardship, transparency, and sustainability must remain at the forefront of discussions about how biotechnology will shape the narratives of war.

Ultimately, the journey toward building and integrating biotech battleships, from blueprint to reality, encapsulates the efforts to create the next generation of military vessels that combine living systems with mechanical design. This undertaking is a delicate balance that requires robust design processes, rigorous testing, and careful scaling of production to transform conceptual designs into operational realities. The steps involved in realizing such ambitious projects will inform future directions as we look to empower future generations—military leaders, researchers, and citizens alike—to engage thoughtfully in discussions surrounding the implications of biotechnologically enhanced warfare.

As we draw our conclusions, we recognize that the economic aspects of biowarfare technologies, alongside public perceptions and controversies, will heavily influence the path forward. It is incumbent upon all stakeholders to foster a culture of innovation that aligns with ethical considerations, societal values, and a commitment to responsible stewardship of life. In embracing the challenges posed by biotechnological warfare, we pave the way for a new era in interstellar conflict, one that harmonizes technological achievement with the profound responsibilities that accompany our creations in a universe filled with endless possibilities.

In this ever-evolving landscape of warfare characterized by biotechnology, the journey emphasizes not just the extraordinary potential captured within our innovations, but also the enduring quest to uphold our moral compass and purpose as we navigate amidst the cosmos.

17.3. Key Players and Their Contributions

Key Players and Their Contributions in the field of biotech warfare represent an essential facet of understanding the rapid advancements reshaping military applications of biological systems. As we venture into a future characterized by integrated living technologies, collaborations across diversity become paramount in determining the trajectory of biotechnological advancements. This section will explore the significant individuals, organizations, and institutions leading the charge in this transformative realm, highlighting their contributions and the unique expertise they bring to the development of biotech battleships and innovative military strategies.

One of the foremost key players in this space has been governmental defense agencies. Entities such as the Defense Advanced Research Projects Agency (DARPA) in the United States have become pivotal in funding and fostering research in biotechnology for warfare. DARPA has initiated numerous projects aimed at exploring bioengineering's potential, from developing self-healing materials to understanding the implications of bioinformatics in decision-making processes. Their emphasis on high-risk, high-reward research has catalyzed breakthroughs that bridge the gap between biology and military engineering, illustrating how public investment can facilitate transformative innovation.

In parallel, private biotechnology firms have emerged as crucial contributors to the field. Organizations such as Amgen, Genentech, and smaller startups focused on specific biotech applications have begun to engage in partnerships with military entities. These businesses possess the agility and resources to invest in cutting-edge research, rapidly bringing innovations to market. By collaborating with military planners, private firms can tailor research initiatives to align with the operational objectives of biotechnological warfare, ensuring that developments directly address the unique challenges associated with combat.

Academic institutions are also vital players shaping the landscape of biotech warfare. Universities worldwide engage in groundbreaking research, contributing to our understanding of biological systems and their potential military applications. Interdisciplinary collaborations between departments, ranging from biology to engineering and ethics, yield insights that inform military strategies and technologies. Noteworthy initiatives such as the MIT Media Lab's work on bioengineering and the Stanford University Bio-X program focus on bridging technological and biological realms, nurturing creativity, and generating innovations that drive forward military applications of biotechnology.

Furthermore, key figures within the field of bioethics have gained prominence as the integration of biotechnology into warfare raises complex moral dilemmas. Experts such as Dr. Jennifer Doudna and Dr. George Church, both pioneers in gene-editing techniques, have highlighted the ethical implications of modifying living organisms for military purposes. Their contributions underscore the importance of framing responsible and ethical discussions surrounding biotechnological advancements—ensuring that ethical considerations are as integral to military strategies as technical capabilities.

International organizations such as the World Health Organization (WHO) and the United Nations (UN) also play critical roles in shaping policy discussions around biotech warfare. By fostering dialogues on the ethical use of biotechnology, these organizations remind us of the potential consequences inherent in deploying living systems as tools in conflict. They advocate for international cooperation, aiming to establish frameworks that govern the use of biotechnology in warfare, protect human rights, and guard against harm to ecosystems and civilian populations.

In addition to these established players, grassroots movements advocating for responsible biotechnological advancements have emerged as essential participants in the dialogue surrounding military applications. Organizations focused on bioethics, ecological sustainability, and human rights, such as the Center for Genetics and Society, actively engage communities in discussions around the implications of biotechnology in warfare. These advocates highlight the need for ethical standards and regulations that align with societal values and the protection of life.

The contributions of these diverse key players in the field of biotech warfare converge to create a multi-layered landscape marked by innovation, ethical considerations, and strategic implications. By acknowledging and understanding the unique expertise and perspectives that each contributes, we pave the way for responsible development and deployment of biotechnological advancements within military contexts.

In summary, the advancements in the field of biotechnology are ushered forward by a dynamic interplay among governmental entities, private firms, academic institutions, bioethics experts, international organizations, and grassroots movements. Their collaborative efforts illustrate that the future of warfare rests not only on the technical capabilities of biotech battleships but also on the ethical, social, and cultural frameworks that guide their development and use. As we navigate the intricacies of this new frontier, leveraging the collective knowledge and contributions of these key players will be instrumental in shaping a responsible and effective future for intergalactic warfare.

17.4. Lessons Learned and Challenges Faced

In a rapidly evolving universe, the utilization of biotechnology in warfare has emerged as both an opportunity and a challenge, inviting a comprehensive reflection on the lessons learned and the hurdles faced throughout the integration process. As the military integrates living systems into combat strategies, the underlying complexities manifest on multiple fronts—technological, ethical, ecological, and societal. Each experience informs future decision-making as military leaders strive not only for operational excellence but also for responsible stewardship of life itself.

One of the most significant lessons gleaned from the past involves the necessity of interdisciplinary collaboration. As various stakeholders with different expertise—military personnel, biologists, ethicists, and engineers—come together, the richness of perspectives facilitates well-rounded approaches to innovation. Early projects often suffered from siloed efforts and a lack of clear communication, leading to inefficiencies and ethical oversights. Experiences have underscored the value of establishing collaborative frameworks that promote ongoing dialogue and shared responsibility, paving the way for more informed and effective designs.

Moreover, the charge to navigate the ethical dimensions of biotechnological warfare has yielded crucial insights. As military researchers engage with living systems, they are compelled to consider the treatment of engineered organisms, the ecological consequences of their deployment, and the ramifications of wielding life as a tool of war. This growing moral consciousness highlights the importance of developing robust ethical guidelines that undergo continuous evaluation, ensuring that military efforts reflect broader societal values and respect for all forms of life.

The environmental challenges posed by integrating biological organisms into warfare reveal another key lesson. The introduction of living systems into military contexts necessitates proactive assessments of ecological impacts, emphasizing the importance of biosecurity and environmental stewardship. The consequences of uncontrolled proliferation or disruption of ecosystems will significantly influence the operational viability of biotechnological innovations. From past experiences, military organizations have recognized the imperative to incorporate ecological assessments at the forefront of planning and deployment endeavors, ensuring that biotechnological warfare aligns with responsible practices.

However, navigating opposition and controversy has proven to be both a formidable challenge and an ongoing journey. The dual-edge nature of biotechnological advancements ignites debates surrounding public safety, ethical considerations, and the role of life in warfare. Protests, civil movements, and spirited public discourse challenge military leaders to confront fears and uncertainties surrounding biotechnology's role in combat. The lessons learned from these engagements underscore the importance of transparency and proactive communication strategies to foster community understanding and address public concerns regarding biotechnological innovations.

Additionally, lessons learned regarding the unpredictable nature of living systems further inform strategic development. The challenges posed by the variability and adaptability of engineered organisms highlight the necessity for extensive testing and validation protocols that identify potential points of failure. Experiences have shown that the operational domains of living systems can diverge significantly from traditional mechanical systems, prompting military planners to remain vigilant in monitoring and assessing biological responses to combat conditions.

Moreover, building a deeper understanding of the psychological and cultural dimensions surrounding biotechnology in warfare emphasizes that personal and societal views profoundly influence perceptions. Operators interacting with living technologies must be prepared for the emotional and moral complexities of using biological systems as tools of conflict. The evolving relationship between human operators and biological entities encourages reflection on the broader implications of our technological choices—prompting conversations about identity, agency, and ethical responsibility.

As we look ahead, the promise of future innovations on the horizon continues to inspire enthusiasm within the military community and beyond. New advancements in bioengineering, such as the development of living materials and smart weaponry, hold formidable potential for transforming the landscape of war. Continuous engagement with emerging technologies may yield breakthroughs that enhance strategic advantages while minimizing the ecological impact of conflict.

In summary, the journey toward integrating biotechnology into warfare embodies a synthesis of lessons learned and challenges faced. By fostering interdisciplinary collaboration, prioritizing ethical stewardship, and addressing public concerns, military leaders can effectively shape the future potential of biotech battleships while adhering to values that respect life and the environment. As we tread this uncharted territory, the commitment to responsible innovation, transparency, and continuous dialogue will define how humanity navigates the complexities of life and technology in the pursuit of peace and security among the stars.

17.5. Future Innovations on the Horizon

In a rapidly evolving universe where the boundaries between biology and technology are continually blurred, the future of warfare emerges as a dynamic and transformative landscape. As we delve into 'Future Innovations on the Horizon', a comprehensive understanding of upcoming trends and developments in biotech battleships reveals not only extraordinary potential but also complex challenges that must be navigated.

The integration of biotechnology into military applications signifies a paradigm shift, wherein living systems and organisms play critical roles in enhancing the capabilities of war machines. One notable area poised for innovation is the development of advanced bioagents designed for tactical advantages. These bioagents can be engineered to amplify combat effectiveness by utilizing unique properties that allow them to adapt to various combat conditions. For instance, living projectiles might be equipped with smart, responsive biological components that can detect environmental changes or enemy movements in real-time, enabling them to modify their trajectory or effectiveness dynamically.

Furthermore, the emergence of biocomputing technologies has opened new doors for the integration of living systems with advanced computational frameworks. By harnessing the power of metabolic processes—where biological functions are utilized for data processing and analysis—military strategies can utilize a new breed of intelligent systems. These innovations promise to increase the operational efficiency of biotech battleships while allowing for seamless communication between biological entities and their mechanical counterparts.

Moreover, as our understanding of synthetic biology continues to advance, the potential for creating entirely new forms of living organisms tailored for specific military tasks becomes a reality. The ability to engineer organisms that produce essential compounds on-demand or respond to specific stimuli has implications for both offensive and defensive strategies. For instance, bioengineered organisms could be developed to serve as living shields or chemical countermeasures, ready to act autonomously to neutralize threats or enhance the ship's defensive capabilities.

Sustainability remains a critical focal point of innovation for biotech battleships. As interstellar missions extend over longer durations, creating life support systems that rely on closed-loop biological processes is vital for ensuring the crew's survival. The engineering of self-sustaining ecosystems onboard these vessels can reduce dependency on external supplies and minimize logistical challenges. Advancements in resource recycling and regenerative capabilities will pave the way for a more sustainable approach to military operations in the cosmos, addressing both operational efficiency and environmental responsibility.

The exploration of future innovations in the context of biotechnology also invites a reckoning with ethical considerations. As military forces grapple with deploying advanced living systems, the implications of using engineered life forms in combat raise complex moral questions. Establishing robust guidelines governing their treatment, usage, and implications for ecological balance will be paramount in fostering a responsible approach to biotechnological innovations in warfare.

As these innovations unfold, the perception of biotechnology in warfare will become increasingly central to shaping public sentiment and policy. Ample opportunities exist to engage communities in dialogue about biotechnological advancements, addressing fears and aspirations while fostering a culture of transparency. As understanding develops, societies can ensure that innovations reflect shared values and uphold ethical standards.

In summary, 'Future Innovations on the Horizon' illustrate the remarkable potential of biotechnology to revolutionize warfare while also presenting profound challenges that must be navigated through careful consideration, ethical engagement, and collaborative innovation. As we embrace the hidden complexities shaped by integrating living systems into military applications, we can redefine the future of warfare in a universe filled with undiscovered possibilities. The path toward responsibly leveraging these advancements will rely on a collective commitment to navigate ethical landscapes, enhance operational capabilities, and shape a future where life and technology harmoniously coexist in the pursuit of peace and security among the stars.

18. Opposition and Controversy: The Dual Edge of Biotech

18.1. The Detractors of Biotechnical Innovation

In the burgeoning landscape of biotechnological warfare, the conversation surrounding the detractors of biotechnical innovation is a vital narrative that demands attention. While advancements in biotechnology promise revolutionary changes to military capabilities, they also evoke significant skepticism and concerns from various stakeholders. Critics of biotechnological innovation often raise valid points that reflect broader societal apprehensions about the potential consequences of integrating living systems into military applications. Understanding these dissenting perspectives is crucial for navigating the complexities surrounding the deployment of biotechnology in warfare and for fostering a culture of responsible innovation.

One of the primary concerns expressed by detractors is the ethical implications of employing living organisms in warfare. The prospect of creating organisms specifically designed for conflict raises moral questions that challenge our understanding of life and responsibility. Opponents often argue that intentionally engineering organisms for destruction undermines intrinsic values associated with life and can lead to a slippery slope where the lines between humane conduct in war and the exploitative use of life are blurred. The creation and potential loss of engineered life forms in combat scenarios create an ethical dilemma about the value assigned to life—whether biological or mechanistic.

Moreover, critics often highlight the unpredictability that comes with using living systems in military operations. Unlike traditional mechanical systems, which operate based on predictable principles, biological organisms can be subject to variability and unforeseen consequences. The fear that engineered organisms could malfunction, adapt unexpectedly, or even escape control has led to apprehension regarding the operational risks associated with bioengineered warfare. Such unpredictabilities call into question the overall reliability of biotech applications in high-stakes combat scenarios.

Detractors also emphasize the potential ecological ramifications surrounding the deployment of biotechnological innovations. The integration of genetically modified organisms into warfare raises concerns regarding their impact on natural ecosystems and biodiversity. Historically, the disruption of ecological balances due to anthropogenic actions has led to devastating consequences. Critics argue that introducing engineered life forms into the environment, especially during wartime, may result in unintended consequences that can propagate throughout natural systems. The long-term implications of using biotechnological constructs in warfare demand thorough risk assessments and ecological studies, which critics assert may not be adequately addressed by current military protocols.

Public perception plays a pivotal role in shaping the discourse around biotechnology in warfare. The fear surrounding bioweapons coupled with a lack of public understanding of biotechnological advancements can contribute to resistance against these innovations. Detractors leverage these sentiments by framing biotechnology as a threat to public safety, drawing attention to the potential for misuse and the need for stringent regulations. Concerns about biosecurity, including the idea that bioweapons could fall into the wrong hands, exacerbate the anxiety surrounding the militarization of living systems.

Public protests and movements opposing the militarization of biotechnology often emerge as powerful expressions of dissent. Activism surrounding these issues seeks to challenge not just specific innovations but the broader ethical stance taken by governments and military organizations toward biotechnology. Activists advocate for transparency, accountability, and ecological stewardship in military advancements through grassroots movements, highlighting the need to engage diverse voices in dialogues about the future of warfare.

Detractors also contend that there is a need for careful discernment between security requirements and the implications for personal privacy, particularly as surveillance technologies become intertwined with biotechnological applications. The utilization of bioenhanced systems should prompt discussions about the ethical implications of deploying such technologies for surveillance and control, sparking debates around autonomy and the right to privacy amidst the demands of national security.

Addressing propaganda against biotechnology is another significant challenge in securing acceptance for biotechnological innovations in warfare. Misinformation and exaggerated narratives surrounding the use of living technologies can foster public fear or distrust. Military organizations must be proactive in countering these narratives through clear communication strategies, transparency in research processes, and forthright discussions about ethical considerations surrounding the application of biotechnology.

Navigating the multifaceted nature of controversy surrounding biotechnological innovations requires military leaders to adopt an agile and responsive approach rooted in ethical responsibility. Acknowledging and engaging with dissenting perspectives can foster constructive dialogues that enhance public trust and understanding of biotechnological advancements. By creating forums for open discussion involving critics, scientists, and policymakers, we can reinforce a culture of dialogue that emphasizes responsibility while pursuing the revolutionary potential of biotechnology.

The integration of biotechnological innovations in warfare is as daunting as it is exhilarating, presenting both opportunities for unprecedented advancements and challenges that reflect societal values and ethical obligations. As we contemplate the future of warfare characterized by biotechnology, it is imperative to engage thoughtfully with the detractors of biotechnical innovation—understanding their concerns while charting a course toward responsible advancement that honors both the promise of life and humanity's profound responsibilities in our endeavors among the stars. Through this journey, we can not only harness the extraordinary capabilities offered by biotechnology but also embrace a narrative that reflects careful stewardship and our collective aspirations for a more ethical and capable future in warfare.

18.2. Public Protests and Movements

In the vast and complex landscape of public protests and movements surrounding biotechnology in warfare, the impact of societal perception on the trajectory of these innovations cannot be underestimated. As advancements in biotechnological applications for military use become increasingly prominent, grassroots opposition movements, ethical debates, and public dissatisfaction serve as powerful counter-narratives to the prevailing discourse of progress. Understanding the dynamics of these protests sheds light on the multifaceted relationship between technology, society, and ethics, and emphasizes the need for military and governmental entities to engage with the public thoughtfully and transparently.

At the heart of many protests against the militarization of biotechnology lies a growing awareness of the potential consequences of deploying living systems as instruments of war. Public movements often emerge from fears regarding the unpredictability of engineered organisms, concerns over ecological impacts, and ethical dilemmas associated with manipulating life for military objectives. Activists voice apprehensions that bioweapons could escape control, create ecological imbalances, or inflict unintended harm on civilians, thus framing the conversation around biotechnology as a moral rather than purely technological issue. This sentiment reflects the broader societal concerns related to the implications of biological manipulation and the potential for unforeseen consequences in both human health and environmental sustainability.

Historical context plays a pivotal role in shaping public sentiment regarding biotechnological warfare. Previous instances of misuse of biological agents in warfare—drawn from World War I, the Cold War, and oppressive regimes experimenting with biological warfare—resonate in the collective memory of societies. These historical precedents foster an atmosphere of skepticism regarding the military's motives and the perceived risks of deploying living technologies. This skepticism is further compounded by stories and depictions of bioweapons in popular media, where biotechnology is often portrayed as synonymous with hubris and catastrophic failure. Such narratives can undermine public trust and increase scrutiny of military research initiatives that leverage biotechnological advancements.

In response to these concerns, grassroots movements often advocate for transparency, democracy, and ethical engagement with biotechnology. Public protests take the form of demonstrations, petitions, and community discussions aimed at challenging existing military practices. Advocacy groups, scientists, and ethical organizations join forces to amplify these concerns, calling for regulatory oversight, public accountability, and comprehensive ethical guidelines for the development and deployment of biotechnological innovations. By creating awareness around these issues, movements strive to hold governments and military entities accountable for their actions and decisions regarding biotechnology, emphasizing the profound interplay between policy and societal values.

The importance of public engagement in the discourse surrounding biotechnology and warfare cannot be overstated. Establishing platforms for dialogue, where different voices can express concerns, hopes, and aspirations, fosters a collaborative environment that can bridge gaps in understanding. The military and governmental entities must take proactive steps to address public apprehensions by communicating the intended benefits and potential risks associated with biotechnological advancements. Transparent discussions about ethical considerations, research methodologies, and the ecological impacts of using living systems in warfare can foster trust and cooperation among key stakeholders.

Moreover, efforts to educate the public about biotechnology's potential benefits—in tandem with awareness of its risks—can mitigate the polarization that often accompanies innovation in warfare. Initiatives aimed at promoting the understanding of the scientific principles underpinning biotechnology can help demystify the technology and counteract fears stemming from misinformation and propaganda. Engaging communities in the conversation allows for a more nuanced understanding of the complexities involved in deploying living systems while ensuring that societal values remain a cornerstone of military practices.

As we look toward the future, the interplay between protests, movements, and biotechnology will continue to shape the narrative surrounding the militarization of living systems. By addressing public concerns through thoughtful engagement, the military can promote responsible innovation that aligns with ethical stewardship while navigating the complexities of intergalactic warfare. The narrative surrounding biotechnology in warfare will be a product of both its technological advancements and the societal imperatives that define how society approaches its integration into military practices. Only by cultivating a culture of dialogue, transparency, and accountability can the lessons learned from public protests effectively inform future decisions and strategies grounded in both progress and ethical responsibility.

In conclusion, the landscape of public protests and movements surrounding biotechnology in warfare reflects the complexities and challenges of integrating living systems into military applications. Engaging with societal concerns, fostering understanding, and promoting responsible innovation are integral to navigating this landscape. By addressing public apprehensions and prioritizing ethical considerations, military and governmental entities can create an environment conducive to collaboration and trust, ultimately ensuring that advancements in biotechnology serve as mechanisms for progress and enhancement across the cosmic frontier.

18.3. Balancing Security and Privacy Concerns

In the realm of biotechnological advancements in warfare, 'Balancing Security and Privacy Concerns' becomes an increasingly complex and crucial topic. The integration of biotechnology into military applications, particularly with the development of biotech battleships, necessitates a nuanced approach that carefully considers both the imperative for national security and the rights and privacy of individuals. As biotechnological innovations continue to evolve, this dual focus presents challenges and opportunities that must be navigated with care.

The primary concern regarding security is centered around the implications of utilizing living organisms within military constructs. While bioengineered systems promise enhanced adaptability and operational efficiency, they also introduce risks associated with unpredictability. The notion of engineered life forms acting autonomously raises important questions: How can militaries ensure that these living systems do not pose collateral risks to civilian populations or environments? What measures will be implemented to contain or neutralize organisms if they malfunction or escape? Furthermore, the potential for adversaries to exploit technology for unauthorized purposes heightens the necessity for stringent security measures. Safeguarding the integrity of biotech systems while maintaining robust biosecurity protocols will be paramount in preventing unintended consequences.

As militaries navigate the complexities of employing biotechnology in warfare, they must also contend with public concerns regarding privacy. The deployment of biologically enhanced systems raises questions about how data generated by living technologies will be collected, stored, and utilized. For instance, if bioengineered sensors are integrated into military operations to monitor environmental threats or human behavior, how will the military protect individual privacy rights? The potential for surveillance through biological means evokes apprehension among citizens who fear invasive monitoring. Trust in the military's ability to manage sensitive information and responsibly utilize living systems is critical if public acceptance of biotechnological advancements is to be secured.

Addressing privacy concerns in the context of bioengineering also involves establishing clear and transparent policies surrounding data collection and usage. It is imperative that military organizations commit to ethical frameworks that prioritize the rights of individuals while still preserving national security. Developing guidelines that govern how data from living systems is utilized—ensuring that information regarding civilians is protected and that any surveillance endeavors are undertaken with ethical scrutiny—will be essential in maintaining public trust and cooperation.

Moreover, effective communication strategies play a pivotal role in addressing security and privacy concerns. Engaging with the public through outreach initiatives, community discussions, and academic collaborations can facilitate understanding about the implications of biotechnology in warfare. By providing transparent information regarding the measures taken to protect individual rights while ensuring national security, military entities can foster public engagement and mitigate fears surrounding biotechnological deployment.

The potential for anti-biotech propaganda further complicates the landscape of balancing security and privacy. Public fears often amplified by media narratives can lead to resistance against deploying biotechnologies in military contexts. Addressing these fears requires proactive engagement strategies that clarify misconceptions and emphasize the intended benefits of responsibly integrating living systems into warfare. Educational programs that develop critical thinking skills and scientific literacy can empower communities to engage in informed discussions, moving beyond fear-based reactions to a more balanced perspective on biotechnology in combat scenarios.

Finally, interdisciplinary collaboration among scientists, ethicists, military leaders, and legal experts will be vital in navigating the complexities of balancing security and privacy in biotechnological warfare. Creating forums for dialogue encourages the exchange of perspectives, allowing stakeholders to formulate policies that effectively address potential risks while upholding ethical standards and individual rights. Ongoing assessments and adaptations of existing regulations and frameworks will be necessary to keep pace with advancements in biotechnology and ensure responsible integration into military strategies.

In conclusion, balancing security and privacy concerns within the framework of biotechnological warfare is an ongoing challenge that demands attention and thoughtful engagement. As we embrace the advancements offered by living technologies in combat scenarios, we must keep our commitments to ethical responsibility, transparency, and public engagement at the forefront of discussions. By fostering a culture of dialogue, employing clear communication strategies, and promoting interdisciplinary collaboration, we can ensure that the integration of biotechnology into warfare reflects not only operational success but also a profound respect for human rights and life. As we navigate the starry realms of conflict among the cosmos, this balance between security and ethics will shape our legacy as both innovators and stewards of life.

18.4. Addressing Anti-biotech Propaganda

Addressing anti-biotech propaganda is a critical endeavor as societies navigate the complexities of integrating biotechnology into military applications. As the integration of living systems into warfare becomes more prominent, misinformation and skepticism surrounding these technologies can create significant obstacles to their acceptance and potential deployment. It is essential to cultivate a comprehensive strategy that counters propaganda while fostering public understanding and engagement with the promising innovations that biotechnology offers.

One of the primary sources of anti-biotech sentiment stems from fear and misunderstanding. Many individuals harbor concerns regarding the ethical implications of manipulating life forms for military objectives, fearing that such technologies may lead to unforeseen consequences or be used irresponsibly. Propaganda often emphasizes worst-case scenarios—depictions of uncontrollable bioweapons or ecological disasters—perpetuating anxiety and distrust. Counteracting these narratives requires a proactive approach centered on engagement, education, and transparency.

Educational initiatives represent a fundamental step in combating anti-biotech propaganda. Developing programs that demystify biotechnology by presenting clear, factual information can empower the public to engage critically with the topic. Initiatives that outline the scientific principles underlying biotechnology, its applications, and ethical considerations can foster informed discussions and alleviate fears. Schools, universities, and community organizations can play significant roles in disseminating knowledge, with informal learning opportunities, workshops, and public forums that encourage conversation and articulate the potential benefits and risks of biotechnological advancements in warfare.

Moreover, collaboration between military leaders, scientists, and communication experts can establish messaging strategies that resonate with public concerns while simultaneously promoting the responsible use of biotechnology. By addressing ethical implications directly and emphasizing the safeguards implemented within military organizations, leaders can build trust with the public and alleviate fears associated with biotechnological applications. Strategic communication that illustrates the potential for biotechnology to enhance combat effectiveness while prioritizing ecological sustainability and ethical stewardship serves to counter sensationalized narratives.

Transparency in research and military practices is crucial to addressing skepticism. By openly sharing research findings, operational protocols, and the ethical frameworks guiding the development and deployment of biotechnological systems, military organizations can demystify the processes involved and strengthen public trust. Information dissemination that includes details about biosecurity measures, containment strategies, and ongoing assessments will help reassure communities about safety and responsible practices.

Engaging with communities through interactive platforms can also enhance understanding and mitigate anti-biotech sentiment. Public forums, town hall meetings, and online discussions can provide opportunities for communities to ask questions, voice concerns, and engage directly with experts in biotechnology. Bringing together diverse perspectives encourages open dialogue, allowing for collective insights and a deeper understanding of the implications of biotechnology in warfare.

The role of popular media and societal narratives is also paramount in countering anti-biotech propaganda. Media producers, writers, and artists hold the power to shape perceptions and influence public opinion surrounding biotechnology. Collaborating with these stakeholders to create accurate, nuanced portrayals of biotechnology can counterbalance sensationalist narratives that have historically dominated popular culture. Education-focused documentaries, literature, and storytelling that emphasize the promise of biotechnological innovations in military settings encourage positive engagement with these developments.

In conclusion, addressing anti-biotech propaganda is a multifaceted approach that requires cultural sensitivity, public engagement, and transparent communication. By fostering educational initiatives, developing strategic communication methods, and engaging with diverse communities, we can counter disinformation and cultivate a supportive discourse surrounding biotechnological advancements. A commitment to addressing concerns and providing clear, factual information will ultimately enhance public perception of biotechnology, allowing society to embrace its potential benefits while responsibly preparing for the evolution of warfare that integrates living systems. As we venture into this new frontier, the ability to navigate and counter anti-biotech narratives will significantly influence our collective future amidst the stars.

18.5. Navigating the Fine Line of Controversy

In an era of unprecedented technological advancements, the path to effective intergalactic warfare increasingly involves navigating the fine line of controversy that accompanies biotechnology's role in military applications. As military forces look to integrate living systems into combat strategies, the discussions surrounding the ethical implications, ecological responsibilities, and societal perceptions of these innovations take center stage. Understanding how to traverse this complex landscape will be essential for realizing the full potential of biotech battleships while addressing the diverse concerns that arise.

The controversy surrounding biotechnology in warfare stems from the inherent duality of innovation and fear. On one hand, the integration of living systems into military designs holds the promise of enhancing operational effectiveness through adaptability, self-sustainability, and resilience. Techniques such as using bioengineered organisms for self-repairing materials, optimizing resource production, and intelligent data communication enable military advances that traditional technologies simply cannot match. Yet, on the other hand, the specter of misuse, ecological disruption, and moral dilemmas associated with manipulating life can evoke deep-seated unease among the public and within scientific communities.

To navigate this fine line, it is crucial to establish robust ethical guidelines that guide the development and deployment of biotechnology in military contexts. This involves engaging with interdisciplinary stakeholders—including scientists, ethicists, military professionals, and the public—to foster discussions surrounding the ethical treatment of engineered organisms and to define the responsibilities that come with wielding such technologies. Transparent engagement with communities can demystify advancements and foster understanding of the ethical considerations that underpin biotechnological innovations.

Additionally, addressing concerns related to environmental impacts and biosecurity is vital to reducing controversy. Establishing thorough risk assessments and ecological evaluations surrounding the deployment of engineered organisms in warfare will provide insights into potential consequences and accountability mechanisms. Proactively developing certifications and monitoring procedures that ensure ecological safety will build credibility and trust in the responsible use of biotechnology in military operations.

Furthermore, public perception plays a significant role in shaping the discourse surrounding biotech in warfare. As discussions emerge around the essence of life, the implications of bioweapons, and the responsibilities tied to engineered organisms, military leaders must participate in dialogues that articulate the benefits of these advancements while acknowledging ethical limitations. Building public trust requires open communication and a willingness to engage with critics, providing reassurance that military organizations are committed to responsible stewardship of living systems.

As we deepen our understanding of biotechnological innovations, initiatives aimed at educating military personnel regarding the ethical, ecological, and technical dimensions of biotechnology will be crucial. Providing comprehensive training that emphasizes awareness of the intricate relationships between humans and living systems will enable operators to navigate the complexities of these technologies prudently. Engaging soldiers in discussions about their responsibilities when managing living organisms in warfare cultivates a culture of ethical awareness that can permeate military practices.

Moreover, the influences of popular media cannot be underestimated as they shape public perceptions of biotechnology in warfare. The portrayal of biological systems in literature, film, and art can evoke both fascination and fear, driving societal sentiment surrounding these advancements. As military organizations engage with the public, they should actively provide insight into the technologies being developed, utilizing mediums to educate and inform while countering anxiety-inducing narratives surrounding bioweapons.

In conclusion, navigating the fine line of controversy in regard to biotechnology in warfare is essential for the successful integration of living systems into combat scenarios. By establishing ethical frameworks, promoting transparency, addressing ecological concerns, and fostering public discourse, military leaders can shape the dialogue surrounding biotechnological advancements. As we move forward in realizing the extraordinary potential of biotech battleships, the collective commitment to ethical and responsible practices must guide our steps, ensuring that the integration of living systems reflects not only operational effectiveness but also our enduring responsibilities as stewards of life in the cosmos. The journey ahead beckons us to embrace innovation while treading thoughtfully on the delicate terrain of ethics, ensuring that humanity's venture into the unknown respects both technological progress and the vivid complexity of life itself.

19. Building a Biotech Battleship: From Blueprint to Reality

19.1. Steps in the Design Process

In the design process of biotech battleships, various steps lead to the realization of these advanced war machines, illustrating a careful blend of biological innovation, engineering expertise, and military strategy. Each step in the process encompasses meticulous planning and collaboration among diverse stakeholders, ensuring that these vessels are prepared for the complexities of interstellar warfare.

The journey begins with conceptualization, where military strategists and researchers outline the fundamental objectives of the biotech battleship. This phase involves defining the ship's mission capabilities, operational environments, and the integration of biological systems that will enhance its functionality. Input from biologists, engineers, and military experts fosters a multidimensional understanding of how living systems can be incorporated into the design to achieve the desired performance.

Next comes the detailed design phase, where blueprints and specifications of the battleship are created. Engineers collaborate with biotechnologists to determine the optimal materials, structures, and systems required to integrate biological components effectively. The selection of biologically compatible materials that can incorporate living organisms poses unique challenges about durability, flexibility, and sustainability. Additionally, the engineers work on establishing environmental controls to create an optimal habitat for the onboard biological systems, ensuring their health and performance during the ship's operational life.

Following the design phase, prototyping becomes a pivotal step. During this phase, engineers construct scaled-down models of the battleship to evaluate aesthetic and functional aspects. Testing these prototypes in controlled environments provides insights into how the biological systems and mechanical components interact under various conditions, revealing any potential issues that need to be addressed before full-scale production. This iterative testing process can result in significant modifications to both the design and operational protocols of the battleship.

As development progresses, scaling up production soon becomes critical. Transitioning from prototype to full-scale manufacturing involves various challenges, particularly in maintaining the integrity of the biological systems during production. Addressing logistical issues, production timelines, and resource availability is a crucial component of this phase. Collaboration with biotechnological firms that specialize in large-scale biological cultivation and processing can provide effective solutions to maintain the resilience and health of the living systems onboard.

Quality assurance in biotech manufacturing is another indispensable step. Ensuring that both biological and mechanical components meet established standards is vital to the operational integrity of the battleship. Rigorous testing protocols must be established to assess the performance, safety, and reliability of both components. Continuous monitoring of the biological functions will ensure that the organisms integrated within the ship remain viable and effective.

A compelling case study can center around a specific biotech battleship project that exemplifies the challenges and triumphs faced in bringing such an ambitious design to life. This journey could detail the initial concept design, collaborative efforts among interdisciplinary teams, insights gleaned from testing prototypes, hurdles encountered during scaling up production, and lessons learned throughout the quality assurance phase. By recounting the specific challenges faced in incorporating living systems into combat-ready vessels, this case study can provide valuable learning opportunities for future endeavors in biotech warfare.

In summary, building a biotech battleship from blueprint to reality requires an intricate interplay of design, testing, production, and quality assurance. The successful execution of each phase demands effective collaboration among engineers, biologists, and military strategists, culminating in the development of resilient and capable war machines prepared to navigate the complexities of interstellar conflict. As we venture into this exciting frontier, the journey of creating biotech battleships will serve as a testament to human ingenuity, innovation, and our capacity to explore the confluence of life and technology among the stars.

19.2. Testing and Prototyping

In the evolving landscape of intergalactic warfare, the process of testing and prototyping biotechnologically integrated battleships is crucial in ensuring their effectiveness, reliability, and safety in combat scenarios. This phase represents a pivotal step where theoretical designs are rigorously evaluated, refined, and validated to ensure they meet strategic military objectives while addressing the inherent complexities of integrating living systems with mechanical structures.

The testing phase begins with the establishment of a comprehensive testing framework that outlines the key performance indicators and objectives for the biotech battleship. These indicators should encompass various operational metrics, including engine performance, resource sustainability, biological system responses, and overall combat readiness. Collaborating with military strategists, engineers, and biologists, stakeholders delineate clear protocols and metrics to evaluate each component's functionality within the ship's integrated systems.

One significant aspect of testing is the simulation of combat scenarios that the battleship may encounter during actual operations. Utilizing advanced modeling techniques and virtual simulations allows for a safe, controlled environment in which to assess how both biological and mechanical systems interact under stress and pressure. For instance, virtual environments can simulate the effects of radiation exposure, gravitational variances, and enemy action, providing insights into the robustness and resilience of bioengineered systems.

Moreover, the development of physical prototypes becomes essential in this phase. These scaled-down or full-sized models allow for hands-on testing of integrated components. Bioreactors for life support systems, bio-sensors for intelligence, and self-repairing materials can be evaluated to determine their effectiveness in real-world conditions. Testing prototypes under various operational scenarios provides valuable data that informs the design iterations, ultimately leading to more resilient and competent biotech battleships.

One of the most critical challenges faced during prototyping is maintaining the health and stability of biological systems in simulated combat conditions. Living organisms can exhibit unpredictable behaviors when subjected to stressors, which must be monitored closely to ensure they perform consistently with expectations. The necessity for ongoing assessments of biological viability may require regular interventions and adjustments to environmental controls, emphasizing the need for interdepartmental collaboration between engineers and biologists.

Following the testing phase, scaling up production emerges as a pivotal consideration in transforming prototypes into operational vessels. Navigating the challenges associated with mass-producing biotechnological components necessitates robust logistics and resource management. Engineering teams must ensure that the biological systems remain healthy during production while maintaining the integrity of the mechanical systems. This complexity underscores the importance of developing bioreactors and cultivation environments that can efficiently produce the living organisms needed for the battleships while ensuring that they thrive under manufacturing conditions.

Quality assurance becomes indispensable in the production of biotech battleships. Establishing protocols that assess both biological and mechanical components ensures that the finished vessels meet stringent performance criteria. Testing methodologies should encompass both laboratory evaluations and field trials, providing comprehensive data on how the battleship functions under planned operational conditions. Regular assessments allow for early detection of issues and foster a culture of continuous improvement—a principle that is especially crucial when working with complex biological systems.

An illustrative case study encapsulating the journey of developing a biotech battleship can serve as an effective demonstration of the challenges encountered and lessons learned throughout the design and testing processes. This case study could involve a detailed analysis of a specific prototype, beginning with its original design concepts, moving through phases of testing and iteration, highlighting the obstacles faced, and culminating in the successful deployment of a fully operational vessel.

In summary, the testing and prototyping phase is crucial in transforming biotech battleship concepts into operational realities. Understanding the intricacies of integrating biological systems with mechanical frameworks enlightens the journey from theory to practice, emphasizing the collaborative efforts of engineers, biologists, and military strategists. The lessons learned throughout these phases provide insights that will shape future endeavors in biotechnology and warfare, paving the way for resilient, adaptable, and innovative war machines that are prepared for the challenges of intergalactic conflict. As we navigate this frontier, the journey of design, testing, and production underscores humanity's capacity for blending creativity and responsibility in shaping the future of warfare among the stars.

19.3. Scaling up Production: Challenges and Solutions

Scaling up production in the context of biotechnology presents unique challenges and opportunities in the development of future biotech battleships. As the military pivots toward leveraging living systems in combat scenarios, understanding the hurdles associated with mass-producing bioengineered components becomes paramount. This undertaking not only necessitates strategic planning but also grapples with ethical considerations and resource management to create resilient, adaptable, and effective war machines capable of navigating the demands of interstellar conflict.

One of the most significant challenges in scaling up production lies in maintaining the health and viability of living organisms throughout the manufacturing process. Biological systems, by their very nature, are subject to a range of environmental stressors that can impact growth rates, metabolic functions, and overall performance. This variability raises concerns about the consistency of production, as any fluctuations in the conditions necessary for sustaining healthy organisms can lead to diminished quality or compromised functionality in the final product. Ensuring that bioreactors and cultivation environments maintain optimal conditions for growth—such as temperature, pH, and nutrient availability—becomes critical in the scaling process.

Logistical complexities are inherent in scaling up production as well. The infrastructure required to support mass production of bioengineered materials must accommodate the specialized needs of living systems, often challenging traditional manufacturing paradigms. Synchronizing the cultivation of biological components with mechanical construction schedules necessitates meticulous coordination along the supply chain. This challenge necessitates robust project management frameworks that integrate biological and mechanical production timelines, ensuring that operational readiness is maintained across all facets of vehicle development.

Another critical aspect of scaling production is the need for interdisciplinary collaboration among biologists, engineers, and supply chain experts. Addressing the intricacies associated with biointegrated designs requires effective communication channels between these groups to ensure seamless information flow and resource management. Establishing cross-functional teams capable of addressing the challenges of scaling biotech production fosters a culture of innovation where diverse skill sets combine to manifest breakthrough solutions.

Quality assurance emerges as a crucial component in the scaling up process. While traditional manufacturing methods typically employ standardized quality control protocols, the unique nature of biotech production demands customized approaches to ensure that both biological viability and mechanical performance meet stringent military specifications. Developing robust testing frameworks that assess living systems before they are integrated into military applications is essential for maintaining operational integrity. Rigorous evaluations, including both laboratory testing and simulations under combat scenarios, help identify potential weaknesses or deficiencies before full-scale deployment, thereby optimizing performance.

To illustrate the complexities involved in scaling production, a case study of a specific biotech battleship can provide concrete insights. This study could detail the journey of a unique vessel—highlighting the initial design concepts, the partnerships established for sourcing biological materials, the logistical challenges faced in mass-producing organisms, and the iterative processes employed to maintain quality and functionality. By dissecting this journey, key lessons can be extracted that inform future projects and enhance our capacity to integrate biotechnology into military engineering.

Moreover, addressing ethical implications associated with scaling biotech production requires deliberate consideration. The potential for bioengineered organisms to operate autonomously in combat raises questions surrounding their welfare, rights, and implications for ecological balance. Civil society, in tandem with military leadership, must engage in dialogues that recognize these concerns while seeking pathways for responsible deployment. Establishing guidelines that ensure the ethical treatment and management of biological systems will be crucial as military forces move forward with biotechnological advancements.

In conclusion, scaling up production for biotech battleships entails a multifaceted approach that addresses the challenges of maintaining organism viability, logistical complexities, interdisciplinary collaboration, quality assurance, and ethical considerations. Navigating these hurdles will be essential in realizing the full potential of biotechnological advancements in warfare. As we strive to create resilient, capable, and sustainable military vessels, the lessons learned throughout this journey will guide future initiatives and shape the evolving relationship between life and technology in our quest to navigate the cosmos. Emphasizing responsible innovation, collaboration, and transparency will ensure that our progress reflects both military imperatives and profound respect for life as we move toward an interstellar future.

19.4. Quality Assurance in Biotech Manufacturing

Navigating the intricate challenges of modern warfare requires a transformative approach that integrates advanced technologies with ethical considerations and sustainability. The chapter on Quality Assurance in Biotech Manufacturing emphasizes the importance of rigorous standards in the development of biotechnologically integrated military systems. As biotech battleships come to the forefront of military innovation, ensuring the reliability and effectiveness of both biological and mechanical components is paramount.

In the realm of biotech manufacturing, quality assurance serves not only as a validation process but also as a framework for continual improvement. Every stage— from the initial design phase to scaling up production—must adhere to stringent quality control measures. These measures encompass biological health assessments to ensure that engineered organisms fulfill their intended roles effectively and consistently. For instance, regular monitoring of growth rates, metabolic pathways, and responses to environmental conditions can provide insights into the viability of living systems and their operational readiness.

Moreover, understanding the intersection between biotechnology and traditional manufacturing principles offers a unique perspective on how these sectors can collaborate to enhance quality assurance processes. For example, bioproduction facilities can adopt best practices from traditional manufacturing to ensure consistent output while maintaining the delicate balance required for managing living organisms. Comparatively, the transparency of biological processes may lead to novel insights in traditional manufacturing, fostering a dynamic exchange of ideas that strengthens quality protocols on both fronts.

In evaluating these production systems, testing protocols must be established that align with both biological performance metrics and mechanical capabilities. This could involve a series of checks and validations that simulate real-world conditions. Utilizing advanced modeling and simulations allows for assessments of how these integrated systems might respond to various stressors in combat situations, ensuring that any design flaws or shortcomings are identified early in the process.

Furthermore, the importance of interdisciplinary collaboration between engineers, biologists, and military strategists cannot be overstated. Creating cross-functional teams dedicated to quality assurance fosters a culture of continuous learning and innovation. By maintaining an open dialogue among experts from various fields, organizations can address potential challenges proactively and cultivate an environment where rigorous standards are genuinely embraced.

Quality assurance protocols also extend beyond manufacturing processes; they encompass ongoing evaluations throughout the operational life cycle of biotech battleships. Continuous monitoring of both mechanical systems and biological functions allows for real-time adjustments that optimize performance. This adaptability not only enhances operational readiness but aligns with broader goals of sustainability and effective resource management—key considerations as military forces engage in long-duration missions across the stars.

In summary, Quality Assurance in Biotech Manufacturing represents a critical component that underpins the success of biotechnologically advanced military systems. As we bridge the gap between living technologies and traditional manufacturing practices, the establishment of rigorous quality protocols becomes integral to ensuring reliable and effective warfare applications. By fostering collaboration among disciplines, implementing stringent testing measures, and maintaining a commitment to continuous improvement, the foundation for a new era in warfare characterized by biotech innovation will be solidified. As we prepare to explore the next frontier of warfare, the principles of quality assurance will be instrumental in guiding our steps toward responsible and effective applications of biotechnology in military endeavors.

The case study of a specific biotech battleship's journey further elucidates the detailed processes involved in realizing these advanced designs. This narrative examining the initial concept, design iterations, challenges encountered during testing and production, and the validation of biotechnological innovations offers invaluable insights for future programs. By chronicling the journey, we can extract lessons learned that inform and refine the strategies employed in subsequent projects, ensuring that we remain vigilant and creative in our commitment to advancing biotechnological innovations for warfare.

As we conclude this exploration of the strategies and technologies driving the future of interstellar warfare, it's clear that the path forward requires a concerted effort to balance innovation with responsibility. By emphasizing quality assurance, fostering interdisciplinary collaboration, and understanding the ethical implications of our advancements, we can seize the extraordinary opportunities presented by biotechnology to reshape our engagement with life, warfare, and the universe at large. As we step into this new frontier, our commitment to responsible stewardship of technological advancements will ensure that the legacy we forge honors both our aspirations and our responsibilities amid the cosmos.

19.5. Case Study: A Biotech Battleship's Journey

In a rapidly evolving universe where the boundaries between biology and technology are continually blurred, humanity stands on the brink of the next revolutionary leap in interstellar warfare. The journey toward deploying biotechnologically enhanced battleships indicates not only a transformation in military capabilities but also the need to navigate complex ethical, ecological, and societal implications. In this case study, we delve into the intricacies of a biotech battleship's journey, emphasizing the various stages of its design, development, and operational integration.

The conceptualization of a biotech battleship often begins at the intersection of military strategy and biological innovation. Military planners and researchers outline objectives that not only identify core capabilities, such as combat support, reconnaissance, and sustained life support but also pinpoint how living systems can be effectively integrated to enhance operational strengths. For example, a potential battleship design might emphasize self-healing capabilities through bioengineered materials and systems that recycle resources—creating a vessel capable of sustaining prolonged engagements in hostile environments.

Once the concept is established, the design phase unfolds. Engineers work alongside biologists to produce blueprints that detail not merely the mechanical frameworks but also how living systems will be incorporated. This multidisciplinary collaboration addresses crucial questions regarding material selection, environmental controls for biological health, and the integration of various forms of biological intelligence into the battleship's operational framework. Through this collaborative design process, principles from both biological sciences and engineering coalesce, paving the way for innovative solutions that enhance the battleship's capabilities.

The transition from design to prototyping reveals both opportunities and challenges. The development of scaled-down models, or prototypes, is essential for evaluating the interactions between living systems and mechanical constructs. Prototyping allows engineers and scientists to test the vitals: does the self-repairing material function as intended? Are the biological systems effectively generating the resources required for life support? These evaluations provide essential data that guides iterative refinements, ensuring that the battleship embodies its intended operational effectiveness.

As prototypes are developed and tested, scaling up production emerges as a critical threshold. The challenge lies not only in maintaining the health of the biological systems throughout the manufacturing process but also in coordinating logistics for resource allocation. Establishing partnerships with biotechnology firms capable of large-scale production becomes vital—creating channels for sourcing organisms needed for the battleship while ensuring they remain viable under mass production conditions. Achieving this harmony between biological and mechanical systems requires thorough planning, structured protocols, and continuous communication among relevant stakeholders.

Throughout the journey, quality assurance emerges as a central pillar to ensure both biological and mechanical systems meet stringent military standards. The emphasis on testing protocols ensures that every aspect of the biotech battleship functions reliably under combat conditions. Rigorous evaluation may involve simulated combat scenarios and environmental stress tests to discern weaknesses and areas for improvement. This quality assurance framework not only optimizes performance but also reflects a commitment to responsible stewardship of the living organisms integrated into the fighting force.

Ethical reflections enrich this journey, ensuring that the integration of biotechnology in military contexts remains aligned with broader social values. Addressing the implications of using living systems in warfare compels military leaders to engage in ongoing dialogues about their legal and moral responsibilities. Establishing ethical guidelines that govern the treatment and deployment of engineered organisms fosters a culture of accountability that acknowledges the profound intertwining of life and technology in contemporary conflicts.

In summary, the case study of a biotech battleship's journey illustrates a complex yet navigable path from conceptualization to operational deployment. By emphasizing multidisciplinary collaboration, rigorous testing, and ethical practices, stakeholders can cultivate a culture of innovation that not only enhances military capabilities but reflects a deep commitment to safeguarding life and the environment. As we stand on this new frontier, the lessons learned from the journey of creating biotechnologically integrated battleships will inform future endeavors, shaping a responsible and respectful approach to warfare in the cosmos.

Concluding the exploration of design intricacies, the final reflections focus on the visionaries and vigilants of future warfare. Recognizing the importance of fostering education and engagement rooted in ethical responsibility will empower future generations to take ownership of biotechnological advancements, ensuring that both technology and humanity evolve together harmoniously. As we embrace the promise of innovation, we also acknowledge our responsibilities, walking the delicate tightrope between progress and preservation in our exploration of the universe's boundless possibilities. The journey ahead is not just one of technological achievement; it is a quest to redefine how we coexist with life, wielding the extraordinary capabilities offered by biotechnology to create a future that honors our values and responsibilities in the cosmos.

20. Concluding Thoughts: Visionaries and Vigilants of Future Warfare

20.1. The Next Steps for Research and Development

In the ongoing exploration of biotechnology's transformative potential within military applications, the next steps for research and development are pivotal in ensuring that these advancements align with both operational objectives and ethical considerations. The integration of living systems into the design of future battleships requires not only technical innovation but also a commitment to responsible stewardship and societal values. The following considerations encapsulate vital pathways for fostering research and development in this emerging field.

First and foremost, fostering interdisciplinary collaboration will be crucial in driving forward research advancements in biotechnology. It is essential to build partnerships that unite biologists, engineers, ethicists, and military strategists. Such collaborations enhance the depth of understanding regarding both biological systems and technical demands, leading to innovative solutions grounded in empirical research and ethical responsibility. Establishing research consortia among academic institutions, private firms, and military organizations will facilitate the exchange of insights and best practices, resulting in accelerated development timelines for biotechnological innovations.

Additionally, prioritizing investment in biotechnology research will pave the way for advancements that redefine military capabilities. Directing funds toward projects that explore novel applications of bioengineering, such as self-healing materials, bio-sensors, and autonomous organisms, will establish a solid foundation for the future of military biotechnology. Governments and defense agencies should consider grants and funding initiatives that support research efforts, especially those that align with sustainability and the responsible use of living systems, thereby promoting innovative technologies that enhance operational efficiency.

In the realm of ethical considerations, the establishment of robust ethical guidelines, drawn from comprehensive dialogues among stakeholders, will be crucial. Research on the implications of deploying engineered organisms should be deliberate and systematic, embedding ethical scrutiny into every phase of development. Engaging bioethicists in collaborative discussions ensures that ethical frameworks are responsive to emerging challenges and directed towards fostering a culture of accountability within military organizations.

Furthermore, outreach initiatives aimed at educating military personnel about the increasing interplay of biology and warfare will be paramount. Training programs that emphasize the biological, technical, and ethical dimensions of biotechnology will empower operators to engage thoughtfully with these innovations. As the next generation of military leaders emerges, the integration of responsible innovation and ethical stewardship into their education will prepare them to navigate the complexities of biotechnological warfare.

Equally important is the role of visionary leaders in advancing the discourse surrounding military biotechnology. Leaders who prioritize ethical considerations and situational awareness are crucial in shaping a military culture that values transparency, responsibility, and care for life. Their advocacy for responsible innovation will resonate throughout organizations, fostering collaboration among disciplines and galvanizing support for biotechnological advancements grounded in ethical principles.

As we contemplate the future trajectories of research and development amid these advancements, the paths to responsible and innovative warfare become clearer. Pursuing a balanced approach that harmonizes military objectives with ecological and ethical considerations will yield a framework where humanity takes responsibility for both technological advancement and environmental stewardship. This commitment acknowledges the delicate interplay between life and technology, ultimately advancing a legacy of peaceful coexistence amid the stars.

In conclusion, the vision for the future of warfare, especially concerning biotechnology's role within it, rests on thoughtful reflection, collaboration, and commitment. The path forward demands engagement from all stakeholders, a focus on ethical stewardship, and the empowerment of future generations through education. As we boldly venture into the uncharted territories of interstellar conflict, let us be guided by a profound respect for life—a legacy that shapes not only how we perceive warfare but also how we navigate our shared responsibilities as custodians of innovation and stewards of a living universe.

20.2. Empowering Future Generations: Education and Engagement

In an era defined by rapid advancements in both biotechnology and military strategy, empowering future generations through education and engagement emerges as a foundational element in shaping the trajectory of warfare. This endeavor is not merely about imparting knowledge; it involves instilling a sense of responsibility, ethical discernment, and a commitment to sustainable practices among the leaders of tomorrow. As we explore educational pathways and engagement strategies that will ensure responsible innovation in the realm of biotech, it becomes evident that a multifaceted approach is necessary to navigate the complexities presented by living technologies within military contexts.

Central to empowering future generations is the integration of biotechnology education into military training programs. Future military leaders must acquire a thorough understanding of biological systems, genetic engineering, and the ethical considerations surrounding biotechnological innovations. Curricula should encompass not only technical knowledge but also foster critical thinking skills that enable personnel to grapple with the moral complexities of utilizing living systems in warfare. By equipping military operators with a blend of technical acumen and ethical awareness, we ensure that they are prepared to make informed decisions in the face of evolving challenges.

The importance of interdisciplinary education cannot be emphasized enough; colleges and universities must cultivate programs that bridge the gap between biology, engineering, ethics, and military strategy. Initiatives that foster collaborative research projects involving students from diverse backgrounds provide valuable learning opportunities that reflect real-world complexities. For instance, joint workshops between military institutions and research universities can facilitate the exploration of biotechnological solutions, encouraging future leaders to embrace holistic perspectives on innovation.

Public engagement is another critical aspect of empowering future generations. As biotechnology assumes a more prominent role in defense strategies, fostering open dialogues with communities about its implications will play a crucial role in shaping public perception and acceptance. Educational outreach programs can demystify the complexities of biotechnology, clarify misconceptions, and highlight the ethical considerations surrounding its use. In doing so, we can create informed communities that feel invested in the evolving narrative around these technologies, transforming potential critics into active collaborators in discussions about responsible innovation.

Visionary leaders will be instrumental in steering these efforts and addressing the public's concerns regarding biotechnology in warfare. Such individuals must advocate for ethical stewardship and align military objectives with societal values, ensuring that the deployment of biotechnological advancements reflects a commitment to accountability. By fostering an environment where the ethical implications of military biotechnology are prioritized, leaders create pathways for ethical decision-making and build public trust in military endeavors equipped with living systems.

Furthermore, integrating ethics into military education will cultivate a culture of responsibility among future leaders. Emphasizing the ethical dimensions of using bioengineered organisms in warfare prepares military personnel to navigate the moral ambiguities associated with wielding living technologies. This commitment to ethical engagement fosters a sense of stewardship over the life forms they command, instilling an understanding of the responsibilities that accompany the creation and deployment of living systems.

Engaging with various stakeholders—bioethicists, civilian organizations, scientists, and policymakers—will serve to enrich the discourse surrounding biotechnological warfare. Dynamic collaboration among these diverse groups encourages the development of comprehensive guidelines and standards that inform best practices for integrating biotechnology into military operations. Establishing open forums for discussion and knowledge sharing can lead to greater consensus around ethical frameworks and operational considerations.

In conclusion, empowering future generations through education and engagement represents a crucial pathway toward responsible innovation in biotechnology within military contexts. By integrating interdisciplinary education, fostering public engagement, establishing ethical frameworks, and encouraging visionary leadership, we can ensure that the next generation of military leaders is equipped to navigate the complexities surrounding the deployment of living systems in warfare. As we stand on the precipice of a new frontier defined by biotechnological advancements, our commitment to these principles will shape a future where innovation coexists harmoniously with ethical considerations, ensuring that the legacy we forge honors the complexities of life as we journey among the stars.

20.3. The Role of Visionary Leaders in Advancing Biotech

In an era defined by the rapid integration of biotechnology into military operations, the role of visionary leaders becomes increasingly critical in advancing and guiding the ethical application of these innovations. As societies navigate the complexities associated with biotechnologically enhanced warfare, leaders are tasked not only with realizing strategic military objectives but also with fostering a culture of responsibility, sustainability, and ethical stewardship. This chapter explores the essential attributes of visionary leadership in the context of advancing biotechnology and its implications for future warfare.

Visionary leaders possess the ability to recognize and articulate the broader implications of integrating biotechnology into military contexts. They are not solely focused on the immediate operational benefits; instead, they understand the long-term ramifications of utilizing living systems in combat scenarios. This foresight equips them to advocate for ethical considerations that must accompany military advancements, ensuring that the deployment of biotechnological innovations aligns with societal values and environmental sustainability.

Effective communication is a cornerstone of visionary leadership. As military organizations engage with stakeholders, including military personnel, policymakers, scientists, and the public, leaders must facilitate open dialogues that address concerns surrounding biotechnology in warfare. By conveying accurate information about the benefits and risks of biotechnological advancements, leaders can build public trust and propagate a culture of collaboration. Transparency regarding ethical guidelines and operational protocols can mitigate fears and foster a cooperative environment where the implications of biotechnological warfare are thoroughly understood.

Moreover, visionary leaders champion interdisciplinary collaboration within their organizations. They encourage partnerships among scientists, engineers, ethicists, and military strategists, promoting dialogues that transcend traditional disciplinary boundaries. This integration of diverse expertise leads to innovative solutions and a deeper understanding of the complexities associated with integrating biotechnology into military operations. By fostering a culture of collaboration, leaders create environments where creativity flourishes, ultimately enhancing the military's capacity to adapt to new challenges.

The ability to embrace uncertainty is another defining trait of visionary leaders in advancing biotechnology. As they navigate the unpredictable nature of living systems, leaders can develop a culture of adaptability that encourages personnel to learn and innovate amid challenges. Recognizing that setbacks may occur provides space for teams to refine their approaches and develop enhanced practices over time. This resilience is particularly important in the context of warfare, where the dynamics of conflict can shift rapidly, necessitating agile responses and effective decision-making.

Furthermore, visionary leaders must commit to ethical stewardship and responsible governance of biotechnological advancements. As biotechnology blurs the lines between life and technology, establishing ethical frameworks becomes imperative. Leaders must advocate for policies and regulations that prioritize the treatment of living systems with respect and dignity, ensuring that the deployment of engineered organisms is accompanied by a sense of moral responsibility. This commitment not only enhances operational effectiveness but also aligns military practices with broader societal expectations and values.

To advance the conversation surrounding biotechnology in warfare, visionary leaders should also prioritize education and awareness initiatives. By investing in training programs that emphasize the ethical, ecological, and operational dimensions of biotechnological innovations, they can prepare military personnel to navigate the complexities of integrating living systems into combat. Enabling operators to engage thoughtfully with biotechnological advancements fosters a culture of accountability and respect that enhances their operational competence while upholding ethical responsibilities.

In guiding the future direction of warfare characterized by biotechnology, visionary leaders stand at the forefront, ensuring that the legacies of military advancements reflect humanity's aspirations and moral obligations. By embracing innovation while remaining vigilant to ethical considerations, leaders can shape a future that harmonizes technological progress with the complexity of life. As we endeavor into an era defined by biotechnology's transformative potential, the contributions of visionary leaders will steer societies toward a responsible and sustainable military landscape.

In summary, the role of visionary leaders in advancing biotechnology is profoundly impactful. By advocating for ethical considerations, fostering interdisciplinary collaboration, embracing uncertainty, and promoting education and awareness, these leaders can effectively navigate the complexities surrounding biotechnological innovations in warfare. Their commitment to responsible stewardship will shape the legacy of these advancements, ensuring that as we venture into the unknown realms of combat, our choices and innovations reflect our values and responsibilities as custodians of life in the cosmos. Through their guidance, the future of warfare can evolve into a narrative of conflict characterized not only by technological prowess but also by ethical integrity and respect for all living systems.

20.4. Paths to Responsible and Innovative Warfare

In the rapidly evolving context of intergalactic warfare, the paths to responsible and innovative warfare represent a crucial framework that military leaders, researchers, and policymakers must navigate as they integrate biotechnology into combat strategies. The emergence of biotech battleships—vessels that merge living systems with mechanical capabilities—redefines not only the nature of warfare but also the ethical considerations surrounding the deployment of biotechnological innovations. Understanding these paths is essential for ensuring that the military application of biotechnology aligns with societal values, ecological sustainability, and responsible stewardship of life.

At the heart of these paths lies the commitment to ethical innovation. Engaging with biotechnology in military contexts compels leaders to establish clear ethical guidelines that govern the treatment, use, and implications of engineered organisms. This involves directly addressing the rights of living systems while promoting respect for their integrity as organisms with inherent value. Establishing these principles ensures that military objectives are pursued alongside moral responsibilities, fostering a culture of accountability that reflects broader societal commitments.

The cultivation of interdisciplinary collaboration is another critical avenue on the path to responsible warfare. By uniting experts from diverse fields—biology, engineering, ethics, and military strategy—innovators can create holistic approaches that consider the complexities of integrating living technologies into combat. Collaborative frameworks facilitate knowledge exchange and promote innovative solutions, ensuring that advancements in biotechnological warfare are informed by a comprehensive understanding of their operational and ethical implications.

Investing in education and public engagement further enhances pathways to responsible and innovative warfare. Training programs for military personnel that emphasize the ethical dimensions of biotechnology will equip operators with the skills needed to navigate the complexities associated with living systems. Moreover, fostering public awareness through community dialogues, educational outreach, and transparent communication can demystify biotechnological advancements, promoting understanding while addressing fears and concerns. Engaging the public will foster a supportive environment for responsible innovations in warfare.

As we consider the evolving landscape of biotechnology within military contexts, we must also recognize the vital role of adaptability and responsiveness. The unpredictability inherent in biological systems necessitates that military strategies be agile enough to accommodate unexpected behaviors or challenges related to living technologies. Developing protocols for real-time adjustments and contingency planning ensures that military leaders can respond effectively, navigating the complexities that arise from integrating living organisms into tactical constructions.

Moreover, as new technologies emerge that harness biotechnology for military applications, it is crucial to maintain a forward-thinking approach that embraces responsible innovation. Understanding the ecological implications of deploying living systems in combat requires robust assessments that inform decision-making processes. Ensuring that military practices align with principles of sustainability and ecological balance reflects a commitment to protecting both the environment and the living technologies utilized in warfare.

Ultimately, the legacy of integrating biotechnology into military operations will hinge upon our capacity to learn from the past while shaping a responsible future. The paths to responsible and innovative warfare invite reflection on our actions, our commitments to ethical stewardship, and our responsibilities as stewards of both technological advancement and life itself.

In conclusion, the pathways toward responsible and innovative warfare in the realm of biotechnology demand the commitment of military leaders, researchers, and society as a whole. By embracing ethical standards, fostering collaboration, investing in education, and remaining adaptable, we can weave a narrative for the future of intergalactic warfare that reflects both our technological aspirations and our humanitarian responsibilities. The journey into this brave new world challenges us to redefine our relationship with living systems, ensuring that as we propel ourselves among the stars, we do so with integrity and a profound respect for the complexities of life.

The legacy and lessons learned from our integration of biotechnology into warfare will resonate far beyond the battlefield. They will shape the understanding of our role as stewards of innovation, prompting future societies to reflect on how they engage with technology, ethics, and life itself. As we embark on this exciting frontier, our commitment to responsible innovation and ethical stewardship will pave the way for a future that embraces the extraordinary potential of biotechnology while honoring the moral imperatives that guide us all. Together, we can ensure that our legacy among the stars reflects our most profound aspirations and commitments to life in its myriad forms.

20.5. Legacy and Lessons for Future Societies

In the context of biotechnology and warfare, the legacy and lessons learned are shaping a future marked by profound ethical considerations, innovative advancements, and societal implications. As humanity ventures deeper into the integration of living systems within military applications, the impact of these developments extends far beyond immediate tactical advantages to influence global views on technology, life, and the moral responsibilities of innovation.

The legacy of biotechnology's role in warfare will reflect not only technological prowess but also the values by which societies choose to wield such innovations. Historical precedents illustrate that the path from scientific discovery to practical application is often convoluted, and the repercussions can reverberate through communities and ecosystems alike. The key to a positive legacy lies in a commitment to responsible development—where ethical guidelines are established, ecological sustainability is prioritized, and the rights of engineered organisms are acknowledged and respected.

A fundamental lesson from the implementation of biotechnology in warfare is the importance of interdisciplinary collaboration. The successful integration of biological systems into military frameworks demands input from fields as diverse as biology, engineering, ethics, and military strategy. As demonstrated in recent developments, collaborative efforts that harness the insights and expertise of interdisciplinary teams enhance creative solutions and promote holistic approaches to complex challenges. The interconnectedness of knowledge fosters a culture of innovation, ensuring that all factors—technical, ethical, and ecological—are considered in decision-making processes.

Moreover, the evolving landscape of biotechnology necessitates continual public engagement to navigate the dynamics of societal acceptance, fear, and trust. Education becomes critical in communicating the implications and potential benefits of biotechnological advancements in warfare. Engaging stakeholders—ranging from military personnel to civilian communities—facilitates transparent dialogues regarding the responsibilities and ethical dimensions of using living systems in combat. By fostering trust and understanding, societies can promote collaboration that aligns military advancements with communal values.

An essential part of this legacy involves addressing the ethical implications surrounding the creation and deployment of bioengineered organisms. Future societies must grapple with moral questions about their role in shaping life and the responsibilities that accompany such authority. The emergence of regulations and international treaties addressing biotechnological warfare reflects the acknowledgment that how societies engage with life fundamentally shapes their legacy. Establishing ethical frameworks that guide the treatment and usage of living systems in military contexts will help ensure that the military's actions are grounded in moral clarity, aligning objectives with principles of stewardship.

The lessons learned through practical applications of biotechnology in warfare should extend into other domains of society. Innovations in sustainable resource management, the development of resilience in communities decimated by conflict, and the appreciation for the diversity of life are but a few areas that can benefit from the insights gained through biotechnological advancements in military practices. As humanity grapples with the challenges of interstellar travel and potential encounters with alien ecosystems, the focus on maintaining ecological integrity demands a broader commitment that applies the lessons gleaned from biotech warfare to other areas of human endeavor.

In conclusion, the legacy and lessons derived from the integration of biotechnology into warfare will echo through future societies, shaping not only military practices but also our collective understanding of life, technology, and ethical responsibility. As we stand on the threshold of a new era marked by biotechnological advancements, the importance of cultivating interdisciplinary collaboration, engaging with the public transparently, and establishing robust ethical frameworks cannot be overstated. Together, these commitments will guide humanity toward a future that embraces innovation while honoring the profound responsibilities we bear as stewards of both technology and life—a legacy that will define not only our capabilities in conflict but also our aspirations among the stars.